THE

ALTAR AT HOME:

PRAYERS

FOR

THE FAMILY AND THE CLOSET.

BY

CLERGYMEN IN AND NEAR BOSTON.

EIGHTH EDITION.

BOSTON:
AMERICAN UNITARIAN ASSOCIATION,
21 Bromfield Street.
1857.

Stereotyped by
HOBART & ROBBINS,
BOSTON.

PREFACE.

WHATEVER diversity of opinion may exist as to the preference between written and unwritten prayers in the public worship of the Church, ancient and extensive usage has assigned a great value to prepared forms of devotion for the Family and the Closet. Even those who can readily express their thanksgivings and requests in their own words oftentimes gratefully resort to this help. Amid the cares, fatigues and varying moods, of daily life, the well-chosen and hallowed words of a *Manual of Prayer* assist in composing their spirit, and suggest many topics of devout reflection, which might not otherwise have been presented to their minds.

But there are others who still more deeply feel the need of a like assistance. They may distrust their ability to express what they feel, and imagine that the use of a form will seem more appropriate to their condition, and believe that its introduction may bring with it the blessing of domestic and private worship where it might not else be enjoyed. How tenderly and kindly did One, who knew what is in man, respond to the request, "Lord, teach us to pray, as John also taught his disciples"! Into how many households has a repetition of the form of prayer which Jesus gave, and the use of other forms expressed for a like purpose, brought a sense of shelter and protection, of pardon and peace!

It is in no disparagement to good manuals of devotion now in use that another is offered to the public. The following work will perhaps be found to reflect more accurately the religious spirit of the present day. Prepared at a time when controversy is suspended, when there is less tendency to extremes through a mere reäction against error, when the aspect of the Gospel which has most deeply interested the heart is that which regards it as a divine spiritual force for the conversion and regeneration of man, this book will be found, it is believed, to recognize more fully the truths which are the springs of the spiritual life, and to breathe more fervently some of the deepest longings of the soul. As a reflection of the spirit now inspiring many hearts, it derives special interest from the manner in which it was made.

The Association, desiring to undertake such works as shall best promote the spiritual growth of our churches, sent a circular to several clergymen, soliciting forms of prayer for use in domestic and private worship. The following morning and evening prayers were written by twenty-five ministers, whose services are among those most highly esteemed in this community. This work, therefore, is not the composition of an individual, nor is it the exhortation only of one person to a devout life. Let it be received as the earnest desire of many, the reader's own minister, it may be, uniting his voice with others, that our families may be families that call on the name of the Lord. In the remembrance of the mercies that crown our daily lot, in the great needs that press on all human souls, their voices are with us, leading us to the Giver of all good, and to the Rock that is higher than we.

The manuscripts of these prayers were sent to the editor without designation of any one subject as the leading thought of each. It became his duty to adapt to each an appropriate passage of Scripture, and to arrange them all so as to secure a variety and natural order of subjects. This was done in order to present a wide choice of topics, some one of which may be suited to the worshipper's frame of mind at the time. In this way may be avoided a feeling of insincerity arising from using a prayer merely because it is marked for the day, while it may have no adaptation to our present feelings. From the necessity of the case, however, the fitness of the prayer to the scripture, or of the scripture to the prayer, could not be very close, as the editor did not feel at liberty freely to interpolate the manuscripts. Perhaps sufficient adaptation may be found to make the subject indicated the true key-note of the devotional exercise.

The wide range of topics in the morning and evening prayers prevented the necessity of enlarging the book under the head of Occasional Prayers, as the subjects of the former adapt each one of them for occasions. For the use of the Closet a few selections are made, chiefly from Jeremy Taylor, whose rich diction is well known to all readers of devotional works. The ancient Collects of the church are added, with appropriate titles, to be used when very short forms are desired; and for this purpose may be read after suitable passages of Scripture prefixed to the prayers. For alternate reading in the family, a few Litanies are added, which are taken from the Service-Book of the Church of the Disciples.

It will be observed that this book is lettered as the first of *The Devotional Library.* Other books in this library will follow, as fast as the Book-Fund of the Association justifies the prosecution of the plan, and other libraries are projected, such as *The Biblical Library*, *The Theological Library*, *The Christian Youth's Library.*

To thousands of families, scattered far and wide, but one in the faith and hopes of our Lord Jesus Christ, this little volume is now offered. May it find a place on our tables, and near our hearts. May it be a mother's gift to her son leaving parental watchfulness to encounter the temptations of the world; may it go with the traveller, reminding him that, if he dwells in the uttermost parts of the earth, God is there, and His hand shall guide him. In our hours of gladness may it furnish a voice to show forth our praise; in our times of sorrow may it invite us to Him who is our only sure refuge and helper. In the circle of endeared domestic ties may it set up an altar of worship; and in the chamber of sorrow, and on the bed of sickness and death, may it direct to that peace which the world cannot take away!

H. A. M.

CONTENTS.

Morning Prayers.

Evening Prayers.

Occasional Prayers.

OCCASIONAL PRAYERS FOR A FAMILY.

OCCASIONAL PRAYERS FOR THE CLOSET.

COLLECTS.

LITANIES.

Morning Prayers.

MORNING PRAYERS.

I.

God our Keeper.

I will lift up my eyes to the hills, from whence cometh my help.

My help cometh from the Lord, who made heaven and earth.

He will not suffer thy foot to be moved: he that keepeth thee will not slumber.

Behold, he that keepeth Israel shall neither slumber nor sleep

The Lord is thy keeper: the Lord is thy shade upon thy right hand.

The sun shall not smite thee by day, nor the moon by night.

The Lord will preserve thee from all evil: he will preserve thy soul.

The Lord will preserve thy going out and thy coming in from this time forth and even forever.

O, THOU, who compassest our path and our lying down, and art acquainted with all our ways, with the light of another morning we would lift our hearts to thee, in grateful acknowledgment of that goodness which is Israel's keeper, and which never slumbers nor sleeps. We know that we are not worthy even to take thy name upon our lips. But thy tender mercies are over all thy works; and to the hills from whence cometh our help we would lift up our eyes.

Wilt thou accept our thanks, our heavenly Father, for thy protecting care of us the past night, and for the countless mercies of which this new day reminds us; and make us more grateful, more sensible of our dependence upon thee for the light and support of our lives. May no vain self-confidence cause us to imagine that we do not need the counsels thou hast given to direct us, or that we can safely encounter life's trials and temptations without that strength from above which thou hast graciously promised to all who seek it.

Thou art our keeper, and thou alone canst preserve our going out and our coming in. May we never doubt thy readiness to hear, to forgive, and to guide us. May no dark cloud hide thy fatherly goodness from our hearts, and no present happiness lead away our thoughts from thee, from whom cometh every good and perfect gift. May our faith in thee be strengthened by every new trial. May every day give practical evidence of our desire to please thee. May no power of evil prevail over our good purposes. May the path of duty be made plain to us. And in the thought of thy approval may we find satisfactory compensation for any present pain or loss. May the memory of thee and of thy word cheer and animate us, save us from impatience and presumption, from unkind words and wrong thoughts, and from every deed we should have occasion to regret as a disobedience of thy holy laws.

Enable us, we pray thee, to discharge faithfully the duties of our different spheres and positions, social, domestic and individual, remembering that each must give account of himself to thee. May those whom we love be sharers with us in every needed aid and blessing of thy providence and grace. May thy kingdom come, thy will be done on earth as it is in heaven, and unto thee ascend from all hearts and lives everlasting praise, in the faith and love of Jesus Christ thy Son. Amen.

II.

The Sure Refuge.

In God is my salvation and my glory: the rock of my strength, and my refuge, is in God.

Trust in him at all times; ye people, pour out your heart before him: God is a refuge for us.

Surely men of low degree are vanity, and men of high degree are a lie: to be laid in the balance, they are altogether lighter than vanity.

Trust not in oppression, and become not vain in robbery: if riches increase, set not your heart upon them.

God hath spoken once; twice have I heard this; that power belongeth to God.

Also to thee, O Lord, belongeth mercy: for thou renderest to every man according to his work.

OUR HEAVENLY FATHER, reverently and gratefully we acknowledge thy goodness and care during another night. In the defenceless hours of sleep thou hast preserved us. And now that thou hast waked us to the light of this new day refreshed and strengthened, we would pour out our hearts before thee, and acknowledge thee to be our salvation, our glory, the rock of our strength and our refuge. We thank thee for all the good gifts of thy love so constantly bestowed upon us. They are new every morning, and fresh every evening. May they inspire us with an abiding gratitude, that shall be shown by the homage of the heart and life to truth and goodness.

Help us to receive this new day as a fresh gift of thy love, opening new opportunities for thy service, and for the discipline of our souls. Prepare our hearts for a proper use of each hour as it comes. Fill our souls with the spirit of thy Son, that we may find our meat and drink in doing thy will. In all the social and domestic relations of life may the gentle and loving temper of our Master rule in our hearts. May the sweet ties of family and kindred be sanctified by the spirit and faith of the Gospel. May we love one another with pure hearts fervently;

forbearing one another, forgiving one another, assisting one another in overcoming all evil, and in exercising always a Christian spirit.

In our intercourse with the world may we show that we have been with Jesus, and learned of him. May we be upright in our dealings; scrupulously honest in all our transactions; truthful in our words; generous and charitable in our deeds.

Inspire us with a cheerful trust in thy providence. Quicken our benevolent affections. Give us a spirit to sympathize with the troubled; to help the needy; to restore the wanderer; to strengthen the weak; to encourage the desponding; and to do good as we have opportunity towards all men. O, may we keep our hearts open to the teaching of thy Spirit, that we may steadily oppose all that is sinful and wrong, and labor on in faith and prayer for the right, the pure, and the good. Never may we trust in oppression, or build our hope upon the uncertain riches of the world. May we feel that life is given us for a high and sacred purpose, and be enabled through thy grace so to use it that each day, as it brings us nearer to the spirit world, will bring us nearer to thee in the spirit and temper of our minds.

Thus may the discipline of this day work together with all good influences for the regeneration of our souls, and fit us for that time when thou shalt render to every man according to his work. We ask it, through our Lord Jesus Christ. Amen.

III.

Thanks and Supplication.

I will love thee, O Lord, my strength.

The Lord is my rock, and my fortress, and my deliverer, my God, my strength, in whom I will trust; my buckler, and the horn of my salvation, and my high tower.

Hearken to the voice of my cry, my King, and my God! for to thee will I pray.

My voice shalt thou hear in the morning, O Lord; in the morning will I direct my prayer to thee, and will look up.

For thou art not a God that hath pleasure in wickedness; neither shall evil dwell with thee.

The foolish shall not stand in thy sight: thou hatest all workers of iniquity.

OUR FATHER who art in heaven. The Father of light, the Giver of every good and perfect gift, on whom we are dependent for life and health, and for all the means of prolonging and enjoying them. We thank thee for thy kind and protecting care of us during the silent and defenceless hours of the last night; that we have laid ourselves down and have slept; that we have been preserved from every danger, and from every alarm, and been brought to see the light, to partake of the blessings, and to perform the duties, of another day. It is because thou, Lord, hast sustained us. It is because thy compassions fail not. They are new every morning; they are fresh every evening, and every moment of our lives; and great is thy faithfulness. In the morning we would direct our prayer to thee. We will love thee, O Lord, our rock, our deliverer, our strength, in whom we will trust.

We thank thee for the bounty of a common providence, which supplies our daily returning wants; for the privilege of consulting the oracles of truth, that we may there learn thy will and our duty, the things which thou requirest of us, and the blessedness thou hast reserved for the pure in heart, the faithful and obedient, in the family above. We thank thee that we are once more permitted to gather round the family altar, and to unite in offering thee our morning sacrifice of prayer and praise.

Behold us in tender compassion. Pity our frailties, and forgive all our sins. With the light of the morning wilt thou lift upon us the light of thy countenance. With the beams of the natural sun may the Sun of righteousness arise upon our souls, with healing in his wings. Wilt thou, who didst command the light to shine out of darkness, shine in our hearts, and give us the light of the knowledge of the glory of God in the face of Jesus Christ. May we place ourselves at his feet, and learn of him who was meek and lowly in heart. May the same mind be in us which was also in him. And may his spirit, taking full possession of our hearts, mould us to a nearer resemblance of his moral perfections, a closer imitation of his pure and perfect example, until Christ be formed in us, and we are changed into the same image from glory to glory.

Be with us through the day on which we have entered. Aid us in the discharge of its duties. Keep us from all evil. Help us to remember that thou art not a God that hath pleasure in wickedness, and that evil shall not dwell with thee. Continue to us the blessings of thy parental providence; and bring us to the close of this day laden with renewed experience of thy never-failing kindness and mercy.

May our absent relatives and friends, wherever they may be, share with us in the bounty and protection of thy omnipresent love, and become heirs together with us of the grace of life.

We look to thee for a blessing upon the inhabitants of this town, and all our towns. May every family be a nursery of virtue and piety, and every house and every heart be consecrated to religion and to God. May all know thee the only true God, and Jesus Christ whom thou hast sent, and whom to know aright is life eternal.

Smile, we beseech thee, upon all the efforts that are made, and the means employed, and the instruments that are raised up, to correct the errors, to purge away the corruptions and wrongs of mankind, and to spread the pure light of Christian knowledge, Christian truth, Christian liberty, and Christian peace, throughout the world; that thy kingdom may come, and thy will be done on earth as it is in heaven.

And unto thee, the infinite Father, through Jesus Christ, thy beloved Son and our Saviour, would we ascribe all the glory. Amen.

IV.

Grateful Confidence.

O come, let us sing unto the Lord; let us make a joyful noise to the God of our salvation.

Let us come before his presence with thanksgiving, and make a joyful noise unto him with psalms.

For the Lord is a great God, and a great King above all gods.

In his hand are the deep places of the earth: the strength of the hills is his also.

The sea is his, and he made it: and his hands formed the dry land.

O come, let us worship and bow down: let us kneel before the Lord our Maker.

For he is our God; and we are the people of his pasture, and the sheep of his hand.

O God, whose light again shines upon us, we desire to unite with thy whole family in heaven and on earth to offer up to thee, the eternal Fountain of light, our morning adoration, and pay our tribute of gratitude and praise to thee, our Preserver. We would come into thy presence with thanksgiving, and bow before thee, the Lord our Maker, grateful for the new-born light of this day. O shine into our hearts with the light of truth, and disperse the shades of error, and prejudice, and sin. Inspire us with the hopes and comforts of true religion, and implant within us thy likeness, the image of our Creator, in righteousness and true holiness. Give us clear and consoling views of thy providence which so mercifully regards us, the people of thy pasture, and sheep of thy hand. Warm our hearts with love to thee; with the love of goodness, of purity, and of all thy moral perfections; that by these our faith and trust in thee may be increased and strengthened; and that we may rejoice that all the different dispensations of our lives are in thy hand, the hand of our heavenly Father.

Encourage us in the faithful discharge of our duties. Guide us by thy counsel; support us in our journey by thy strength; hold us up by thy promises. Animate us with the patience and perseverance of our blessed Lord and Master, who, for the joy that was set before him, endured the cross, despised the shame, and is set down at the right hand of the throne of God. In his name we offer our prayers, and in his words conclude them. Our Father, who art in heaven, hallowed be thy name; thy kingdom come; thy will be done on earth as it is in heaven. Give us this day our daily bread; and forgive us our trespasses as we forgive those who trespass against us; and lead us not into temptation; but deliver us from evil. For thine is the kingdom, and the power, and the glory, for ever and ever. Amen.

V.

Praise and Trust.

I will praise thee with my whole heart: before the gods will I sing praise to thee.

I will worship toward thy holy temple, and praise thy name for thy loving-kindness and for thy truth: for thou hast magnified thy word above all thy name.

In the day when I cried thou didst answer me, and strengthen me with strength in my soul.

All the kings of the earth shall praise thee, O Lord, when they hear the words of thy mouth.

Verily, they shall sing in the ways of the Lord: for great is the glory of the Lord.

Though the Lord is high, yet hath he respect to the lowly: but the proud he knoweth afar off.

Though I walk in the midst of trouble, thou wilt revive me; thou wilt stretch forth thy hand against the wrath of my enemies, and thy right hand will save me.

The Lord will perfect that which concerneth me: thy mercy, O Lord, endureth forever; forsake not the works of thine own hands.

PRAISE be unto thee, O God our Father, that we are again around our family altar. Who but thee was our protector during the night; and what but thy love has opened our eyes on the morning of another day? Thou hast enrobed thyself in glory and majesty amid this wondrous universe. We rejoice that thou hast made us capable of seeing thee in every event and scene of life; of recognizing thee in every change; of hearing thy voice in thy providence, and in our own consciences; and of feeling thy loving-kindness towards us in the minutest blessings of our daily lot. More than all we rejoice that we may see a still brighter manifestation of thyself in thy dearly-beloved Son, whom in the fulness of time thou didst send to seek and to save the lost, and through whom we may look to thee for forgiveness of our sins, and life everlasting.

Before we go forth this day in the fresh strength of mind and body which thou hast infused into us by sleep, we would consecrate ourselves anew, by the prayer of faith, for life's daily duties, enjoyments, and trials. Help us to fulfil our course this day acceptably to thee. May we rightly understand and faithfully discharge the responsibility which belongs to our several domestic relations; work within us by thy Holy Spirit, both to will and to do of thine own good pleasure. May we be affectionate one to another. May we bear each other's burdens, and so fulfil the law of Christ. May we govern our tempers, restrain our angry passions, be sober-minded and temperate, humble and self-denying. May we speak the truth and live in peace. May our hearts ever be turned towards thee, that they may be ever open to receive thy gracious aid.

Lord and Giver of life, of our purest joys, of our richest comforts, of our immortal hopes, to thee we owe ourselves, and all that we possess. And while thou art the all-bountiful source of all the good in which we rejoice before thee, thou hast turned aside the evil which for our sins we have so justly deserved. Give us that true repentance which needeth not to be repented of, that we may amend our lives according to thy holy Word.

Help us this day to receive its enjoyments with gratitude and use them with moderation. May we not labor only for the meat that perisheth, but rather for that which endureth unto everlasting life. May we set our affection on things above, and not on things on the earth. May we seek first and chiefly the kingdom of God and his righteousness, striving to lay up for ourselves treasures in heaven, which shall endure forever. May we meet the trials which thou shalt appoint unto us in a Christ-like temper; and improve them as the discipline of a Father's hand, believing that though we walk in the midst of trouble, thou wilt stretch forth thy hand to receive us. O, that we may always remember that we are immortal; and that this remembrance may give seriousness and importance to our present life in the flesh, quicken us to high purposes and aims, inspire within us a true love of thyself and of our fellow-men, prompt an abiding reverence for thy holy law, and keep ever before us the condition of acceptance with thee declared by thy Son, — Not every one that saith unto me, Lord, Lord, shall enter into the kingdom of heaven, but he that doeth the will of my Father who is in heaven. Let the beauty of the Lord our God be upon us, that our souls may be clothed with the graces of purity and charity, and that we may adorn the doctrine of God our Saviour in all things.

Hear us in these our prayers; which we offer in the name of Jesus Christ our Lord. Amen.

VI.

Cheerful Homage.

Give to the Lord, O ye kindreds of the people, give to the Lord glory and strength.

Give to the Lord the glory due to his name; bring an offering, and come unto his courts.

O worship the Lord in the beauty of holiness: fear before him, all the earth.

Say among the heathen that the Lord reigneth: the world also shall be established that it shall not be moved: he will judge the people righteously.

Let the heavens rejoice, and let the earth be glad; let the sea roar, and the fulness thereof.

Let the field be joyful, and all that is in it: then shall all the trees of the wood rejoice before the Lord:

For he cometh, for he cometh to judge the earth: he will judge the world with righteousness, and the people with his truth.

O God our Father, surrounded by the miracles of creation and providence, we would speak of the glorious honor of thy majesty, and talk of thy wonderful works. Thou hast spread out the firmament like a tent to dwell in. Thou hast garnished the heavens by thy Spirit. Thou hast hung the earth upon nothing. Thy way is in the sea, and thy path in the great waters, and thy footsteps are unknown. Lo, these are but parts of thy works. How little do we know of thee! O, the depth of the riches both of the wisdom and knowledge of God! How unsearchable are thy judgments, and thy ways past finding out!

On this bright and beautiful morning, we seem to stand amidst a new creation. The same voice, which in the beginning said, Let there be light, has again spoken, and the earth, lately wrapped in darkness, is filled with morning light. Thy Spirit, which first breathed into human clay the breath of life, and man became a living soul, has recalled our minds from the unconsciousness of sleep, to activity and intelligence. Our bodies, lately exhausted with toil, and our minds, confused with care, are strong and clear, as if received fresh from thy creating hand. Help us to look upon all our faculties, all our blessings, as new gifts from thee. Help us to send out our admiring thoughts over thy works, as the morning light spreads over the earth. Aid us, O Father, to lift up our hearts in gratitude and praise, as the morning vapors rise from hill and stream; and as the sun fills their fleecy skirts with light, so let our thoughts and affections be illuminated by thy love.

Holy Father, more than for this material creation

and all our temporal mercies, do we thank thee for the spiritual creation by Jesus Christ, by which the reign of righteousness and love has been commenced on the earth. To him we owe all the civil, social and religious blessings, that distinguish us from heathen lands. But for him, we should be nurtured, not in Christian homes, but amid the corruptions of paganism; we should be bowing down, not in Christian temples, but in the house of idols; we should be living, not under institutions of learning and liberty, but in the prison-house of ignorance and oppression. O, God! to thy dear Son we owe the blessings of this present life, and the brightness of our immortal hopes. Let our hearts go out in gratitude and love to him who loved us and gave himself for us, and by whose stripes we are healed.

And now, O thou Guardian of our lives, as we again go out unto the duties, trials and temptations, of the day, let thy kind providence be over each one of us. Suffer us not to fall into any temptations greater than we can bear; but, however sudden or unexpected their assaults, wilt thou, by thy Spirit, deliver us from their power. If in the discharge of duty, or in refusing to go with the multitude to do evil, we are reviled, help us to revile not again, but so to conduct as to feel the blessedness of those who suffer reproach falsely for Christ's sake. Give us that spirit of Christian sympathy which rejoices with those that rejoice, and weeps with those that weep Help us, as we have opportunity, to visit the widow and the fatherless, and him that hath no helper, and to keep ourselves unspotted from the world. And when we shall again gather around the altar of our evening sacrifice, O, may we all come with the delightful assurance that the world has left no stain upon our garments, and that for another day of our probation our names are registered in the Lamb's book of life.

In these thanksgivings and supplications we include all our dear absent friends, beseeching thee to bless them according to their several circumstances. Be in all the abodes of suffering this day, to soothe the bed of pain, to cheer the loneliness of age, to lighten the burden of sorrow. Hear and answer us, in the name of thy Son our Saviour, through whom unto thee be the kingdom, the power and the glory Amen.

VII.

Believing and Loving.

My little children, let us not love in word, neither in tongue, but in deed, and in truth.

And hereby we know that we are of the truth, and shall assure our hearts before him.

For if our heart condemn us, God is greater than our heart, and knoweth all things.

Beloved, if our heart condemn us not, then have we confidence toward God.

And whatsoever we ask we receive of him, because we keep his commandments, and do those things that are pleasing in his sight.

And this is his commandment, That we should believe on the name of his Son Jesus Christ, and love one another, as he gave us commandment.

And he that keepeth his commandments dwelleth in him, and he in him: and hereby we know that he abideth in us, by the Spirit which he hath given us.

ALMIGHTY and most merciful God, our heavenly Father, we bow ourselves before thee in all lowliness and reverence of spirit. Thou art God, the Lord of heaven and earth; there is none like unto thee. The angels bow, and archangels veil their faces, before the light of thy glory. The patriarchs and prophets, the apostles and martyrs, the saints of all ages, and our own beloved who have departed in Christ, stand around thy throne, day without night, singing their song, Blessing, and honor, and glory, and power, be unto him that sitteth upon the throne and unto the Lamb for ever and ever. O Lord, we would bring our morning offering of praise and prayer unto thee, humbly imploring a portion of that adoring spirit which shall make us one with them; and though we be yet on earth, shall make us meet to be partakers with them in their blessed service.

Father in heaven, we acknowledge our dependence upon thee. Help us to feel that dependence. There is not a breath we draw, but it is thy gift; not a mo-tion we make, but strength cometh from thee. Thine arm is always beneath and around us; it supports and enfolds us everywhere. Thy bounty supplies our daily returning wants. Thy care is our confidence, thy mercy our refuge, thy love is the light of our countenance and the peace of our hearts. Not an hour, not a moment, that thine hand is lifted from off our heads.

O, what shall we render unto the Lord for all his goodness? We can give thee nothing, for all things belong to thee; and thou seekest no outward sacrifice, else would we give it. But thou dost ask for our hearts. O, may we answer thy call, so tender and paternal, My son, give me thine heart,— Lord, our hearts do we give unto thee. Come and dwell in them. Come and reign in them; seal them as thine own, and from this time forth may we keep them, by the help of the Holy Spirit, consecrated to thy honor and glory. May we feel they are not our own, but thine,— thine by a double claim, because they are thy workmanship, and because we by this solemn act of dedication have given them to thee. Help us, that we may not this day by any forgetfulness, any pressure of earthly care, any force of temptation, by any wrong thought, or feeling, or desire, by any unrighteous word or deed, defile that which is now holy unto the Lord.

God of all the families on the earth, we commend to thee this family now waiting before thee. Look down upon us and bless us. Fill us first with love towards thee and thy dear Son, and then towards one another,— loving not in word and tongue, but in deed and in truth. May we be led by the Spirit of God, that we may be the children of God; and may the fruits of the Spirit— love, joy, peace, long-suffering, gentleness, goodness, faith, meekness, temperance— abound in all our hearts; so may God, who is greater than our hearts, give us confidence and peace. May we be that happy family whose God is the Lord, and upon which thou commandest thy blessing, even life forevermore. Wilt thou take us into thy keeping this day; and if sorrow and suffering, sickness and bereavement, shall fall upon us before its close, may we with calm and steady faith look up and say, Father, thy will be done; even so, for so it seemeth good in thy sight.

And now unto thee, the King eternal, immortal and invisible, the only true and wise God, would we render praise through Jesus Christ, for ever and ever. Amen.

VIII.

Rejoicing Praise.

O God, thou art my God; early will I seek thee: my soul thirsteth for thee, my flesh longeth for thee in a dry and thirsty land, where no water is;

To see thy power and thy glory, so as I have seen thee in the sanctuary.

Because thy loving-kindness is better than life, my lips shall praise thee.

Thus will I bless thee while I live: I will lift up my hands in thy name.

My soul shall be satisfied as with marrow and fatness; and my mouth shall praise thee with joyful lips:

When I remember thee upon my bed, and meditate on thee in the night watches.

Because thou hast been my help, therefore in the shadow of thy wings will I rejoice.

My soul followeth hard after thee: thy right hand upholdeth me.

DIVINE FATHER, who hast again awakened us out of comfortable sleep, the gift of thy mercy, and art granting us the blessing of beholding each others' faces with joy and hope, we unitedly thank thee for thy watchful care of us during the perils of the night, and for all that makes the light of another day welcome to our hearts. With the light of the morning we beg thee to lift upon us the dearer light of thy love, and to refresh our souls by thy grace as thou hast nourished the plants in the earth by the tender dew. O, God, the sweet air we breathe, the cheerful emotions which the day renews, all beautiful objects, and this glorious sun, whose effulgence displays thy greatness and thy goodness, prompt us to gratitude, and call us to give praise unto thee.

We thank thee for restoring us to one another in

the health which gives a relish to every pleasure, and prepares us to undertake with alacrity every duty of life. We thank thee for the happiness we derive from mutual affection, and the ties which bind us together in one family. We thank thee for giving us a pleasant home; for a sheltering roof; for daily food; for means of instruction; for opportunities of usefulness, for the blessings of society; for safety, liberty and peace. Our mouths shall praise thee with joyful lips.

Most holy and merciful God, we desire to call into fresh remembrance the obligations we are under to live soberly, righteously, and godly, in this present world, while we trust in thy mercy through Jesus Christ for that life which is eternal. What manner of persons ought we to be in all holy conversation and godliness, upon whom thou hast bestowed such inestimable benefits; for whom Christ died, and who have the promise and hope of a blessed immortality.

Help us this day to glorify thee, O God, with our bodies and our spirits, which are thine. Into whatever company we may be thrown, let our words, feelings and actions, be blameless, and as far as possible conducive to others' welfare, while they are in strict accordance with our duty. By diligence in our calling, by a vigilant redemption of time, by being continually mindful of our responsibleness for the use we make of all our powers, means and opportunities, may we enable ourselves to give some profitable account of the day when we look back upon it at its close.

O, Thou who art the ever-present witness and the unerring judge of human conduct, may our chief care be to do what is right in thine eyes, and to escape the condemnation of unfaithfulness to thee. To this end we pray for more courage; for resolution and constancy in resisting what is wrong, and cleaving to that which is good; for a heart too pure to desire anything which God has forbidden. Keep and defend, counsel and guide us, O God, and unto thee be all praise forever. Amen.

IX.

Joy and Peace.

Rejoice in the Lord always: and again I say, Rejoice.

Let your moderation be known to all men. The Lord is at hand.

Be anxious for nothing; but in everything by prayer and supplication with thanksgiving let your requests be made known to God.

And the peace of God, which passeth all understanding, will keep your hearts and minds through Christ Jesus.

Finally, brethren, whatsoever things are true, whatsoever things are honest, whatsoever things are just, whatsoever things are pure, whatsoever things are lovely, whatsoever things are of good report; if there is any virtue, and if there is any praise, think on these things.

Those things, which ye have both learned, and received, and heard, and seen in me, do: and the God of peace will be with you.

O, God of the morning, at thy voice creation awakes. Thou kindlest the beams of the rising sun, and causest him to come forth from his chamber in the east, and spreadest the gladness and the glory which we behold. Arise, O Lord, and let there be reverence and gladness in our hearts. We would rejoice in thee always. While we have slept, thou hast guarded our rest, setting thy watch around our lowly habitations, and keeping our souls in their mysterious release from the control of the body; and now when we awake thou art still with us, sending new tokens of thy love, calling us to new duties, and new acknowledgments of thy gracious providence.

Father of the families of the earth, what are we that thou shouldst be mindful of and shouldst visit us, — we the weak, and thou the mighty, — we the ignorant, and thou the all-wise, — we the sinful, and thou the all-perfect? Yet thou art pleased to be near while we bow at this domestic altar, and would breathe into thine ear our gratitude for mercies so free, yet so undeserved. Thou hast even invited us to make our requests known unto thee. It is thou who hast provided for us our home, its shelter, its sanctities and endearments. Bless us, and all who dwell under our roof. Let thy dwelling-place be in our souls. Give us trust and peace. As there is one Lord, one faith, one baptism, may there be only one heart among us, and may the tie which binds us be hallowed by the more sacred tie which should bind all hearts to thee.

We pray for the children whom thou hast given us; that thy most gracious influence may descend upon them; that they may grow up as tender and beautiful plants by our side, full of truth, and gentleness and sweet humility. We pray not that thou wouldst take them out of the world, but spare them and keep them from the evil that is in it; feed their minds with pure and holy thoughts; make them a blessing and ornament in their day, and sharers of thine everlasting favor. So may we be an united, prospered and happy family, on this earth. May we go forth this day in thy strength, and cheerfully do and bear what thou appointest; and at last may we find a home in the heavens from which we shall go out no more forever. And may the peace of God, which passeth understanding, keep our minds and hearts through Jesus Christ our Lord. Amen.

X.

Watchfulness.

Heaven and earth shall pass away: but my word shall not pass away.

But of that day, and that hour, knoweth no man, no, not the angels which are in heaven, neither the Son, but the Father.

Take ye heed, watch and pray: for ye know not when the time is.

For the Son of man is as a man taking a far journey, who left his house, and gave authority to his servants, and to every man his work, and commanded the porter to watch.

Watch ye, therefore; for ye know not when the Master of the house cometh, at even, or at midnight, or at the cock-crowing, or in the morning:

Lest, coming suddenly, he find you sleeping.

And what I say unto you, I say unto all, Watch.

Almighty and most merciful God, we arise from the deathlike insensibility of sleep, to consecrate anew to thee the faculties which thou hast preserved and restored. Thou hast dispersed the shades of night; we pray thee that every shadow of error and unbelief may pass from our minds. We behold the light of a new morning; it is sweet and pleasant to our eyes. Let the light of thy truth shine in upon us, and let there be within us no darkness at all. We feel in our souls and bodies the refreshing influence of our nightly rest. We breathe anew the fresh air of the morning; we are warmed by the beams of the returning sun; may our bosoms glow with a renewed sense of thy love, and our hearts be enkindled with adoring gratitude and affection.

All-merciful Father, we know not what the day may bring forth, but thou seest the beginning and the end. Prepare us, we beseech thee, for the unknown events of thy providence. Watchful at our posts of duty, may we have thee before us all the day long; and whatever thou dost ordain let us receive as from thee, fountain of wisdom and goodness. Prosper us in our lawful pursuits. If success attends our labors, not unto us, but unto thy name, be the praise; if disappointment and calamity overtake us, let us not be cast down nor discomfited, but cheerfully acquiesce, trusting that thou art doing better for us than we can ask or think. Prepare us for life's great changes, and hold us as in the hollow of thy hand. Save us in the hour of sudden temptation; and in the hour of our self-forgetfulness, which, watch as we may, will at times overtake us, do not thou, O God, forsake us. Let no press of business, no fear of loss, no hope of gain, induce us to swerve from thee, our highest good. Under all circumstances of trial let us maintain our integrity, and keep thou our souls in innocency and peace.

We pray for the household into which thou hast gathered us, and the kindred and friends whom thou hast raised up around us; for thy favor to the community in which we live, and thy blessing upon all good enterprises undertaken for the spread of truth and righteousness, and the final welfare of man. With shoes on our feet, and the pilgrim's staff in our hand, with loving words on our lips, and tender sympathies in our hearts, as strangers and sojourners here, knowing not when the Son of man cometh, may we this day press forward towards our final rest and reward, through Jesus Christ our Lord. Amen.

XI.

Heavenly Aspirations.

Blessed are the poor in spirit: for theirs is the kingdom of heaven.

Blessed are they that mourn: for they shall be comforted

Blessed are the meek: for they shall inherit the earth.

Blessed are they who hunger and thirst for righteousness for they shall be filled.

Blessed are the merciful: for they shall obtain mercy

Blessed are the pure in heart: for they shall see God.

Blessed are the peace-makers: for they shall be called the children of God.

Blessed are they who are persecuted for righteousness' sake: for theirs is the kingdom of heaven.

O Thou, whose form the eye seeth not, whose voice the ear heareth not, whom outward sense discerneth not, so near, so inward, art thou to us. The heart pure from sin evermore seeth thee; the soul alive in love and obedience heareth thy voice in its depths; the mind exercised to discern between good and evil perceives thee, with whom evil cannot dwell, Supreme Good, Parent and Centre of All Good. Open our hearts to behold the unseen presence. Open our ears to hear thine everlasting word. Open our whole souls to take in the breath of thy love. Creator of all, with the return of day come new tokens of thy power and providence. Amidst the darkness and the deep silence, thy Spirit hath encircled and filled nature and man; thine the sleep which hath relieved our cares, and soothed our hearts, and repaired us with fresh strength. Thine is the morning which we welcome now; thine the sun calling us forth to work, and to rejoice in its light; thine are the hours rising over us with their invitations to action, and society, and rest. Thine, O God, this great nature which embosoms us in its changing beauty forever. May we love thee; may we live in thee.

Father, reveal the deeper mystery of thy presence in our souls. Those secret aspirations, those silent visions, those living attractions which draw us toward thee, and which seek communion with all pure and holy beings, we confess thee, only thee, their source and their end, ourselves thy children, asking to dwell in thy bosom whence we came. Father, reveal thy love within us; we have nothing else to seek.

We bow before thee now, confessing our weakness, our ignorance, our sin. Amidst the world shining with thy beauty, silent and benignant voices sounding to us through heaven and earth, we have yet forgotten thee many times, and disobeyed thy sweet and holy laws. Among thy children we have lived so long, and so often we have failed to do for them the services which we owe from thee. May the remembrance of our errors check all pride, and keep us in sincere lowliness. May the sense of our need forever urge us to thee; that in thy power we may have strength, that from thy wisdom we may receive knowledge, that by thy Spirit we may be consecrated to holiness of heart and deed. Quicken us with thy life; imbue us with thy love; discover to us the heavenly vision, and help us to obey its teaching. Our Maker, draw us into harmony with thine infinite order. Our Father, unite us to thyself and thy great family in heaven and on earth.

Everywhere may thy children see thee; in thee may they know and love each other. May false gods and false worships perish; live thou, supreme and only true God, who art love, in the worship and service of men on earth, and of all souls throughout the universe. So may violence cease, and peace prevail; so may discord pass into communion of hearts; so may slavery and oppression give place to justice and freedom; so may thy sinning and suffering children all rise into service of each other, into one living church, into thy peace soothing every sorrow, and hallowing every joy. So may all hearts enjoy the blessings pronounced by thy dear Son.

Father, accept this our morning prayer. In its spirit enable us to spend the new day, consecrating each hour and every deed and word to thy service. In its spirit enable us to spend the whole day of life; that when its evening shall come, another morning, fairer and brighter than has now risen upon us, may gladden our everlasting course. And to thee, greater and nearer to us than any thought of ours, may we render glory, worship, service, both now and forever, through Jesus Christ our Lord. Amen.

XII.

Love of God in Christ.

Behold what manner of love the Father hath bestowed upon us, that we should be called the sons of God! therefore the world knoweth us not, because it knew him not.

Beloved, now are we the sons of God; and it doth not yet appear what we shall be: but we know that, when he shall appear, we shall be like him: for we shall see him as he is.

And every man that hath this hope in him purifieth himself, even as he is pure.

Whosoever committeth sin transgresseth also the law; for sin is the transgression of the law.

And ye know that he was manifested to take away our sins; and in him is no sin.

Whosoever abideth in him sinneth not: whosoever sinneth hath not seen him, nor known him.

Little children, let no man deceive you: he that doeth righteousness is righteous, even as he is righteous.

Our Heavenly Father, whose eye of love resteth upon us during our defencelesss hours, and unto whom we are ever present, may thy Spirit witness unto our spirits, as we strive to give thanks and pray. This new day is thy gracious gift; for thou art the fountain of all life, the Creator, the Sustainer, the Sacred Providence. Thine is the sweet and pleasant light; the glow of the heavens and the beauty of the earth are thine; and from thee are all the wisdom of our minds, and all the love of our hearts.

We would pour out our souls in gratitude to thee, the Father of the ever-blessed Redeemer, for the Sun of righteousness which ever shineth down upon us. Through thine infinite mercy these latter days on the earth are days of the Lord, and thou art still offering to reveal thy Son in all willing souls. Thanks be unto the heavenly Father for him who doth go before us in the way, and who doth send to us from thee the Holy Ghost, the Enlightener and Comforter. O God, the strength of the weak, the guide of those who are ready to wander, the teacher of the foolish, and the everlasting friend, may we indeed begin this day in the faith and fear and love of thee. Teach us our entire dependence, that as obedient children we may follow our gracious Father. In past days we have tried to live from ourselves, and have failed. Merciful one, forgive our wickedness and compassionate our folly, and may we be fully reconciled unto him who hath loved us in Christ from the foundation of the world, sending him who knew no sin to be manifested to take away our sins. Enlighten our consciences, and touch our hearts, that we may know what is thine holy will concerning us this day, and may seek with all our strength to accomplish thy great purpose.

In all the relations of life may we be true to our heavenly Master and Redeemer. May the Lord be the light of our household; let it be the home of all pure affections, and in the time of their youth may the young open their hearts unto thee and thy Christ, and enter upon that path of the just which is bright and blessed. In humility and in patience may we do the work and bear the burdens of life. Shield us in the hour of temptation, and enable us to send up from our hearts a faithful prayer unto him who is mighty to succor.

O, God, sustain us out of thy bounty. Bless us in our basket and store. Fill us with a spirit of contentment. In prosperity and in adversity accomplish thy will in us. Enlarge our sympathies, and multiply our charities, and be gracious unto our kindred, and friends, and brethren. Earnestly do we intercede for the ignorant, the poor, and the oppressed; for those who are without thee in the world, and for all who are in any manner tried. In thine own good time may he who was lifted up from the earth draw all men unto him, and thine through the Redeemer shall be the praise evermore. Amen.

XIII.

Dwelling in God and Christ.

Beloved, if God so loved us, we ought also to love one another.

No man hath seen God at any time. If we love one another, God dwelleth in us, and his love is perfected in us.

Hereby know we that we dwell in him, and he in us, because he hath given us of his Spirit.

And we have seen, and do testify, that the Father sent the Son to be the Saviour of the world.

Whosoever shall confess that Jesus is the Son of God, God dwelleth in him, and he in God.

And we have known and believed the love that God hath to us. God is love; and he that dwelleth in love dwelleth in God, and God in him.

Herein is our love made perfect, that we may have boldness in the day of judgment: because as he is, so are we in this world.

There is no fear in love; but perfect love casteth out fear, because fear hath torment. He that feareth is not made perfect in love.

We love him, because he first loved us.

If a man say, I love God, and hateth his brother, he is a liar: for he that loveth not his brother whom he hath seen, how can he love God whom he hath not seen?

And this commandment have we from him, That he who loveth God love his brother also.

ETERNAL and ever-blessed God, who reignest in the heaven of heavens, and whose dominion is over all the earth, hear us graciously when we pray to thee, and grant answers of peace to our supplications. Thanks to thee, O Lord, that thou hast sustained us through another night. As the morning light renews the conscious enjoyment of our blessings, we would praise thee by whom they were all bestowed. Thanks therefore unto thee, O Father, for life and all that makes life happy; for the light that shines upon us, the air we breathe, the food that sustains us, the home that shelters us, and the love that unites us. Thanks to thee for thy holy law, whether in nature or in Scripture; for the teachings of reason, the testimony of conscience, the commandments given of old to thy chosen people, and the grace and truth that came by Jesus Christ.

We bless thy name, that when mankind had forsaken thy ways, thou didst yet so love the world as to raise up a Saviour, to guide and warn, to strengthen and to redeem. We thank thee for the abundant testimony that the Father sent the Son to be the Saviour of the world. Praise to thee, O God, for his holy precepts and his divine example, that, being made perfect through suffering, he has become the captain of our salvation, and having endured temptation, is able to succor them that are tempted. Praise to thee for all the influences of his holy life, his patient death, his glorious resurrection. Grant that these influences may be felt by us in the fulness of their power; that we may be warned and encouraged by his words, excited by his example, softened by the thought of his dying love, made triumphant over the grave by his rising from the dead, so that perfect love may cast out all fear. Grant us, O God, that true and living faith, which shall take hold of the promises of thy grace through him, and shall make us, as his disciples, more than conquerors over all evil. If any injure us, may we exhibit his forgiving spirit; if any are in sorrow, may we like him be prompt to relieve; and if called to reprove the erring, may we unite his hatred of sin with his compassion for the offender. May we never desert the truth, though like him we should suffer for it. May we, as our Saviour taught, love thee supremely, and our neighbor as ourselves. If called to heavy affliction, may we bear it with the meekness of Jesus, saying with him, Not our will, but thine, be done. Thus may we know that we dwell in him because he hath given us of his Spirit, and our life be hid with Christ in God.

Thus, O Lord, we would serve thee; but thus we have not served thee. We have wandered from thy ways, and walked in forbidden paths. O God, have mercy upon us, and forgive our many offences. May we feel them still more deeply, and repent of them still more earnestly. May the remembrance of them warn us against further sin. Be thou near to us in every time of temptation, to strengthen and to save. Be near us in the hour of death, to sustain our failing hearts; and after death, mercifully receive us to thyself.

O God, keep us, we pray thee, this day from outward evil; or, if it must come, make it to produce inward good. Keep us now and ever from sin. Bless all with whom we are connected, and all for whom we should pray, and help us to show our love for thee by loving our brother also. May the kingdom of Christ our Saviour come in our hearts, among those dear to us, and throughout the world. Prepare us, O Lord, for thy kingdom on high; and thine be glory forever, through the same blessed Saviour. Amen.

XIV.

The Pledge of all Mercies.

He that spared not his own Son, but delivered him up for us all, how shall he not with him also freely give us all things?

Who shall lay anything to the charge of God's elect? It is God that justifieth;

Who is he that condemneth? It is Christ that died, yea, rather, that is risen again, who is even at the right hand of God, who also maketh intercession for us.

Who shall separate us from the love of Christ? Shall tribulation, or distress, or persecution, or famine, or nakedness, or peril, or sword?

Nay, in all these things we are more than conquerors through him that loved us.

For I am persuaded, that neither death, nor life, nor angels, nor principalities, nor powers, nor things present, nor things to come,

Nor height, nor depth, nor any other creature, shall be able to separate us from the love of God, which is in Christ Jesus our Lord.

ALMIGHTY GOD, command thy blessing to rest upon us, the members of this family, now that we are assembled for domestic worship. Grant that each one of us may be sensible of the nearness of thy presence, and that we may alike partake of the influences of thy good Spirit. In the name of thy dear Son, who hath taught us how to pray, we would come to thee, "believing that thou art, and art the rewarder of them that diligently seek thee." In no formal service would we address thee; may our worship be of the understanding and the heart. As the preserver of our lives, the giver of our many blessings, the guardian of our souls, who has pledged to us all other mercies in that thou hast spared not thine own Son for our sakes, may we seek to render thee, at all times, an acceptable offering; and wilt thou fulfil in us thy gracious promises to thy saints; help us to enkindle anew the spirit of devotion, and to cherish the heavenly disposition of our Divine Master.

Parent of Good, unite our hearts to fear thy name. May we adopt the resolution of thy pious servant of old, "As for me and my house, we will serve the Lord." May faith, piety and love, pervade all our souls, that as we seek to please thee we may study to promote the happiness of each other. Suffer no one of our number to stray from the true fold, and bring disgrace and sorrow on this family. Let us all take heed to our ways, and at home and abroad be on our watch, "lest when we think we stand, we fall."

O, Father, grant grace unto thy servants who are at the head of this family. Help us to "bring up our children in the nurture and admonition of the Lord." May we so faithfully perform this our duty, that those committed to our care may "rise up and call us blessed," and be "our crown of rejoicing in the day of the Lord." Early may they love and obey thee, and form such characters as shall fit them for all their duties here, and prepare them for the society of heaven. For that heaven, O God, may we all, through thy grace in Jesus Christ, be found at last meet, and may nothing separate us from its everlasting hopes and peace.

Great Benefactor, we now thank thee that thou hast brought us in safety to the beginning of another day. While many have been cut off, some in the morning of life, and others in active manhood, we are still among the living. May we remember that to some of us the night of death may soon come. May every future day, as it will find us one step nearer the grave, so also find us a day's journey nearer heaven.

And in the name of the Mediator, who died for us, but who arose from the dead, and is now at thy right hand, and is our ever-living Saviour, we render to thee honor and glory everlasting. Amen.

XV.

Coming through Christ.

Wherefore, laying aside all malice, and all guile, and hypocrisies, and envies, and all evil-speakings,

As new-born babes, desire the pure milk of the word, that ye may grow thereby:

If indeed ye have tasted that the Lord is gracious.

To whom coming as to a living stone, disallowed indeed by men, but chosen by God, and precious,

Ye also, as living stones, are built up a spiritual house, a holy priesthood, to offer up spiritual sacrifices acceptable to God by Jesus Christ.

Wherefore also it is contained in the scripture, Behold, I lay in Sion a chief corner-stone, elect, precious: and he that believeth on him shall not be confounded.

To you therefore who believe he is precious.

Almighty and most merciful God, we thy children would come close to thee. With the light of this morning, lift upon us the light of thy countenance.

O gracious Father, we thank thee for thy daily goodness; day unto day uttereth speech, and night unto night showeth knowledge,— speech of thy glorious providence, knowledge of thy tender care. By sleep and rest thou hast refreshed our faculties of body and soul; and now thou art opening upon us the wonderful gift — a new day, with its precious hours, opportunities, hopes, and joys, and sorrows. We know not what the day may bring to us; but this we rejoice to know, that if we walk in a religious spirit the day's experience will give us salutary discipline, its joys or its sorrows will deepen our faith, heighten our aspiration, and mature our principles into permanent character.

God and Father of our Lord Jesus Christ, by thy Spirit lead us to the feet of the great teacher, thy messenger and manifestation. Aid us to sound the depths of his truth and love; may his words become spirit and life to us; may the beauty of his holiness be as a heavenly light round about us; and when, as our Mediator, he stands far up on the heights of divine excellence, close to the Father, and takes the things of God and shows them unto men, O, may we see and understand, and come to him as the chosen of God and precious. Impress us, we beseech thee, with the feeling that "we can do all things through Christ who strengtheneth us," and that he that believeth in him shall not be confounded. This day may we be consistent Christians, laying aside every sin, and desiring the word of thy truth that we may grow thereby. Obedient to the authority of Jesus, and in the spirit of confident faith resting in thee, may we be wise, patient, courageous and faithful, and offer to thee a spiritual sacrifice, acceptable through Jesus Christ.

Father Almighty, look in mercy upon the world. May Christ, its true light, scatter the darkness; may ignorance, error and sin, give place to knowledge, truth, and holiness.

We pray for all who are severely tried or strongly tempted; for the aged and the young; for the rich and the poor; for the oppressor that he may repent of his wrong-doing, and for the oppressed that he may be comforted in his sufferings; O, give gracious help to the weary and heavy-laden, and may sinners be converted to righteousness.

Hear us, O our Heavenly Father ; this day may we keep near thee, and may the sense of thy observing presence sanctify us. Hear and bless us as disciples of Jesus, and to thee be glory and thanksgiving forever. Amen.

XVI.

God in Christ.

That was the true Light, which lighteth every man that cometh into the world.

He was in the world, and the world was made by him, and the world knew him not.

He came to his own, and his own received him not.

But as many as received him, to them he gave power to become the sons of God, even to them that believe on his name :

Who were born, not of blood, nor of the will of the flesh, nor of the will of man, but of God.

And the Word was made flesh, and dwelt among us, and we beheld his glory, the glory as of the only-begotten of the Father, full of grace and truth.

O God our Father, blessed be thou. From our inmost hearts we would bless thee now; with our whole hearts quickened to holy worship, may we bless thee forever. All things praise thee; the heavens above us, the earth beneath; the pure air and the gathered clouds; the sun in its brightness, the serene moon, the everlasting stars. Thine are their numberless forms and perpetual courses; unto thee they raise by night and by day the silent hymn.

Our Father, we thank thee that above these manifold orders of existence thou hast made man in thine image, so that he may not only see thy glory through the great nature which surrounds him, but feel thy presence in the love and beauty within his soul. Thou didst of old reveal thyself to him when in innocence he walked in the garden planted by thee with seeds of all which was fair, and fruitful, and full of life. The entrance even of sin severed thee not from thy children: thou art near them still. In all their wanderings, in their diversities of tongue and of thought, thou hast been with them through the ages. Thou hast breathed into their souls the love of wisdom; thou hast shed over their minds the light of truth; thou hast touched their lips with holy fire; thou hast strengthened them to great deeds. The wise thou hast made to shine as the brightness of the firmament; their prophetic words thou hast set in the skies as stars for ever and ever. Open thou the eyes of all thy children to see.

Above them all, our hearts remember him in whom thy fulness dwelleth overflowing evermore, the true light to lighten all that come into the world. Blessed be thou for the power transcending nature, for the wisdom embracing all truth, for the love flowing from thee, for the whole everlasting image of thy being and perfection, embodied in thy Son, our Lord and Saviour Jesus Christ, made flesh and dwelling among us, in the glory of the only-begotten of the Father. For his life, full of grace and truth, unfolding the divine beauty, consecrating childhood and youth and manhood, surmounting temptation, triumphant in death, penetrating into the immortal heart of mankind, and opening the great day of the regeneration, we thank thee, Father, with the words which we can speak: we would thank thee with the love deeper than words, and tears of joy now and forever.

Unto this name, which thou hast exalted above every name on earth and in heaven, may thy children bow with glad obedience and service. As in him thou hast revealed thy saving power, and thy ministries of solace and hope and heavenly peace, so, through his life renewed in all, we pray thee, quicken every man to consecrate himself in holy service to the well-being and the blessedness of others. Out of each heart may living streams flow forth into the whole garden of the Lord, bearing refreshment to the weary, and strength to the weak, solace to the sorrowful, and life to the dead. Through virtue of the Christ in man, the hope of glory, may sin be subdued, and despair rooted out; may selfishness, pride and envy, wrath and revenge, all evil lusts and all their influences, in society, in families, in secret deeds, pass away, supplanted by love, by lowliness and joy in others' good, by gentleness and blessing, by purity of heart, and whatever is good and true, free and peaceful, in all the experiences and relations of human life. So may all that believe on his name have power to become the sons of God.

Father, in this spirit of thy beloved Son may we spend the day to which thy love hath brought us. In this spirit, so pure, so gentle, so sweet, may we spend every day whose morning shall shine upon us. In this spirit which hath outlived death, and opened the sepulchre, and risen to the heavens, may we come forth in that greater morning which shall reveal another sun, and which, in the power of Jesus, shall lead us to his Father and our Father, to his God and our God. Blessed be thou now and forever. Amen.

XVII.

Joy and Victory in Christ.

Blessed be the God and Father of our Lord Jesus Christ, which, according to his abundant mercy, hath begotten us again unto a lively hope, by the resurrection of Jesus Christ from the dead,

To an inheritance incorruptible, and undefiled, and that fadeth not away, reserved in heaven for you,

Who are kept by the power of God through faith in salvation, ready to be revealed in the last time :

That the trial of your faith, being much more precious than that of gold that perisheth, though it be tried with fire, might be found unto praise, and honor, and glory, at the appearing of Jesus Christ :

Whom having not seen, ye love; in whom, though now ye see him not, yet believing, ye rejoice with joy unspeakable, and full of glory:

Receiving the end of your faith, even the salvation of your souls.

Wherefore gird up the loins of your mind, be sober, and hope to the end, for the grace that is to be brought unto you at the revelation of Jesus Christ.

Most Holy and Merciful God, we thank thee for the safe repose of the last night, and that we see the morning light in so much health and comfort. With the light of the morning wilt thou cause the Sun of Righteousness to warm our hearts, and scatter the darkness from our minds by the beams of heavenly truth. We desire to receive a new day as a new gift of thy goodness. The lives which thou hast spared we would consecrate to thee. O, may our hearts glow with a purer purpose of obedience, and be lifted up above all sordid and selfish allurements by the love of goodness and of God. Teach us, Father, how to attain to that holiness which alone can render us fit objects of thy favor. Let thy Holy Spirit help and encourage us in all our struggles against sin, in all our efforts to do our whole duty.

O God, we feel that nothing on earth can be so necessary and important to us as the care and improvement of our immortal souls. Our bodies must soon die. The pleasures and interests of this present world will soon come to an end. But the virtues of the soul can never perish, but shall live forever. The joys of the heavenly world grow more delightful the more we partake of them; and of these nothing but our own sinfulness has power to deprive us.

Aspiring to heaven while we dwell on earth, may we ever seek first the prize of our high calling as Christians, and watch, pray and labor, so as to escape from the doom of corrupt and impenitent souls, and become meet for that inheritance which is incorruptible, undefiled, and that fadeth not away.

Father of Jesus, we can never be thankful enough for thy great goodness in giving thy dear Son to be our Saviour. Blessed be thy name for the precious promises which thou hast made in his Gospel. To him we owe salvation from sin, strength to overcome our trials; to him the hope of pardon, the happiness of a Christian life, and the peace of a Christian death. In what gloom and misery would our souls be sunk but for the mercy of God in Christ Jesus our Lord! For what were it worth while to live if the glorious hope of immortality, brought to light in the Gospel, were taken away, and Jesus to be no longer a Redeemer to lost and guilty men?

In the world if we have tribulation, yet he has taught us how to overcome the world, how to win peace even from the sharpest suffering. O God, permit us not to forsake Jesus for any other leader, to let go the Gospel for any other doctrine. May we cleave to him with joy unspeakable, till we receive the end of our faith, even the salvation of our souls.

Father, grant us thy wisdom and grace, and to thee be all praise and glory forever. Amen.

XVIII.

Following in the Regeneration.

If ye call on the Father, who without respect of persons judgeth according to every man's work, pass the time of your sojourning here in fear:

Forasmuch as ye know that ye were not redeemed with corruptible things, as silver and gold, from your vain conversation received by tradition from your fathers;

But with the precious blood of Christ, as of a lamb without blemish and without spot;

Who verily was foreordained before the foundation of the world, but was manifest in these last times for you,

Who by him do believe in God that raised him up from the dead, and gave him glory; that your faith and hope might be in God.

Seeing ye have purified your souls in obeying the truth through the Spirit unto unfeigned love of the brethren; see that ye love one another with a pure heart fervently:

Being born again, not of corruptible seed, but of incorruptible, by the word of God, which liveth and abideth forever.

For all flesh is as grass, and all the glory of man as the flower of grass. The grass withereth, and the flower thereof falleth away:

But the word of the Lord endureth forever. And this is the word which by the Gospel is preached unto you.

ALMIGHTY and most merciful Father, we approach thee in the name of the glorified Redeemer, in whom thou dost manifest thyself to us in all the mild majesty of thy paternal character. May all our passions be hushed within us, all vain thoughts expelled and driven from us, that we may approach thee with solemnity and stillness of soul, and open our whole mind towards thee, the great and excellent Glory.

We bless thee that thou hast opened our eyes to see the light of another morning; that in those hours when we could take no thought of ourselves we slept securely in the arms of thy providence, and under the guardianship of thy blessed angels, and have now been gently awaked to the duties of another day. We would enter upon those duties with firm resolves and purposes. We would walk this day in the path of thy commandments, keeping Christ ever before us, as the Way, the Truth and the Life, who has redeemed us with his own precious blood. We would here resolve not to offend against thee in word, in thought, in feeling, or in action, but to manifest to all around us the spirit and temper of the Redeemer. O, help us to keep this resolve; for unless thou help us we shall fall. Help us to drive away the tempter when he comes, so that when the hours of the day are ended we may hear thy benediction, "Well done," and have the blessed peace that comes from the smile of thy countenance. Let a light from thy throne fall upon our pathway, and make all our duties plain before us. And when that light comes, give us strength to follow it with a fidelity which danger or death cannot shake or disturb, so that our souls may be purified by our obedience to the truth.

We remember, O our God, how short and fleeting are the days of our probation; for our flesh is as grass, and the glory thereof as the flower of grass. We pray that we may be laying up those treasures that no moth can corrupt and no thieves plunder nor steal, but which live and abide forever. Every day may our understandings be more replenished with thy truth, and our hearts more completely imbued with thy love. Every day may we do something to conquer the evil that is in us, that we may drive out all selfish desires and appetites, and bring down into our souls the angel band of pure affection. We would follow Christ in the regeneration, so that we may rejoice to meet him in the kingdom of thy glory. And to him that is able to keep us from falling, and present us faultless before the presence of his glory, with exceeding joy, to the only wise God our Saviour, be glory and majesty, dominion and power, both now and forever. Amen.

XIX.

Remembrance of Mercies.

I will extol thee, my God, O King; and I will bless thy name for ever and ever.

Every day will I bless thee; and I will praise thy name for ever and ever.

Great is the Lord, and greatly to be praised; and his greatness is unsearchable.

One generation shall praise thy works to another, and shall declare thy mighty acts.

I will speak of the glorious honor of thy majesty, and of thy wondrous works.

And men shall speak of the might of thy terrible acts: and I will declare thy greatness.

They shall abundantly utter the memory of thy great good ness, and shall sing of thy righteousness.

The Lord is gracious, and full of compassion; slow to anger, and of great mercy.

The Lord is good to all: and his tender mercies are over all his works.

All thy works shall praise thee, O Lord; and thy saints shall bless thee.

THOU infinite and eternal Being, Giver of all good, present Helper in all trouble, we call on thy holy name with gladness this morning, and implore thy presence and blessing. We gratefully acknowledge thy goodness to us in the familiar bounties that return to us with the light of day. For the pleasant sunshine, for our daily bread, for our opportunities of usefulness, for our home affections, and our religious hopes, we give thee heart-felt thanks, and beseech thee to make us faithful to thy gifts and stewards of thy trust.

Father of our spirits, abide with us this passing day, and grant that we may give its fleeting hours to precious uses that shall not be fleeting. In heavenly wisdom may we redeem the time, and learn even now to live the life eternal.

Searcher of hearts, reveal to us our sins, and give us grace to put them away, by the power of thy Holy Spirit. Look with thy favor upon all the members of our household, and may each one of us be an earnest doer of thy will in our appointed post of duty. Visit with thy blessing all our kindred and friends. Graciously lift up all who are cast down; strengthen the weak; heal the sick; comfort the afflicted; reclaim the erring; confirm the wavering; edify yet more the faithful. Grant, O Lord of life, that we all may meet at last around thy throne in heaven, and that the love of thee, our God, may be the life of all souls. Hear us, through thine infinite grace in Jesus Christ our Saviour. Amen.

XX.

Faith in the Redeemer.

Jesus cried, and said, He that believeth on me, believeth not on me, but on him that sent me:

And he that seeth me, seeth him that sent me:

I am come a light into the world, that whoever believeth on me should not abide in darkness.

And if any man shall hear my words, and not believe, I judge him not: for I came not to judge the world, but to save the world.

He that rejecteth me, and receiveth not my words, hath one that judgeth him: the word that I have spoken, the same shall judge him in the last day.

For I have not spoken from myself; but the Father who

sent me, he gave me a commandment, what I should say, and what I should speak.

And I know that his commandment is life everlasting: whatever I speak therefore, even as the Father said to me, so I speak.

O God, thou art our life and our health. We bless thee for the renewal of our powers which the night's repose and the morning's freshness bring to us. Creator of our spirits, thou art also the Renewer, and day by day we bless thee for thy renovating grace.

Day by day we need more of thy bounties than we can number, and yet above all others there is one thing that is needful. Give us wisdom and fervor to ask for it as we ought, even for a double portion of thy Spirit; more of thy light in our understandings; more of thy love in our hearts; more of thy strength in our wills. Unite our frail being to thy infinite love through the life of faith and obedience. Graciously open within our hearts the gate of heaven, and may we in all that we suffer, or do, or enjoy, live as subjects of the divine kingdom.

Thanks be to thee, O God, that in Jesus our Redeemer we may behold with joy unspeakable the glory of the only-begotten of the Father, and rejoice in thy grace and truth by him brought near. Lord, we believe; help thou our unbelief. We would look to him, and lean on him, who came as a light into the world, that we should not abide in darkness. By fidelity amid the trials and temptations of the world, as well as by the study of thy word, and prayer at thy mercy-seat, may we strive to go forward in the right path, and enter into life eternal.

Father in heaven, graciously aid us by thy Spirit. Keep our eyes from tears, our feet from falling, and our souls from death. Comfort thy people everywhere with thy love, and renew them by thy grace. Give new power to thy church and word, and let all the people praise thy holy name through Jesus Christ our Lord. Amen.

XXI.

For a Christian Life.

Let brotherly love continue.

Be not forgetful to entertain strangers: for thereby some have entertained angels unawares.

Remember them that are in bonds, as bound with them; and them which suffer adversity, as being yourselves also in the body.

Let your conversation be without covetousness; and be content with such things as ye have: for he hath said, I will never leave thee, nor forsake thee.

So that we may boldly say, The Lord is my helper, and I will not fear what man shall do unto me.

Remember them which have the rule over you, who have spoken unto you the word of God; whose faith follow, considering the end of their conversation;

Jesus Christ the same yesterday, and to-day, and forever.

For here have we no continuing city, but we seek one to come.

By him, therefore, let us offer the sacrifice of praise to God continually, that is, the fruit of our lips, giving thanks to his name.

O God, our Sovereign and Father, it is our joy with every morning's waking to renew the sense of thy presence and the consciousness of thy care. The thought of thee precedes all other thoughts, the love of thee all other affections.

We bless thee, O Lord, that in the wants and capacities of our nature, and by the Gospel of thy Son, thou hast called us to honor, and glory, and immortality. We rejoice in our solemn responsibilities, and accept our duties as the highest proof of thy favor. Suffer not heart and flesh to fail in the glorious service we owe thee. The spirit, O God, is willing, but the flesh is weak. We implore thy divine grace to defend us this day from the dominion of our appetites, the illusions of the world, and the deceitfulness of our own hearts. We have proved the power of temptation, and are afraid of ourselves. Our strength is weakness, our pride is dust. But thou, O Lord, art almighty, and canst make us willing in the day of thy power, and give us the victory in the hour of our conflict.

Clothe us, this day, with all social and domestic graces. Help us to discharge our debt to the world, in the serviceableness of our lives, the benevolence of our sentiments, the gentleness of our manners; and especially uphold us in the exercise of forbearance, tenderness and fidelity, towards those of our own household.

Daily we desire to supplicate thy mercy and protection in behalf of the poor and neglected, the injured and lost. Suffer not our eyes to become used to the sight of injustice, or our ears dull to the cry of misery. May no day pass without thy blessing on some effort we have made for the redemption of our suffering race.

Almighty Judge, as every day brings us nearer to thy bar, may it bring us closer to the requirements of thy Gospel. Rebuke whatever levity, indifference or wilfulness, thou seest in our hearts. May the youngest of us take at once the path to heaven, and the oldest fail not diligently to keep it.

Gracious God, our prayer is before thee. Despise not our offering now, and turn us not away when we seek thine acceptance in the last day. And thine be the kingdom, the power and the glory, through Jesus Christ our Lord. Amen.

XXII.

Social Duties.

Put on, therefore, as the elect of God, holy and beloved, bowels of mercies, kindness, humbleness of mind, meekness, long-suffering;

Forbearing one another, and forgiving one another, if any man hath a quarrel against any: even as Christ forgave you, so also do ye.

And above all these things put on charity, which is the bond of perfectness.

And let the peace of God rule in your hearts, to which also ye are called in one body; and be ye thankful.

Let the word of Christ dwell in you richly in all wisdom, teaching and admonishing one another in psalms, and hymns, and spiritual songs, singing with grace in your hearts to the Lord.

And whatever ye do in word or deed, do all in the name of the Lord Jesus, giving thanks to God and the Father by him.

O Lord, our God, thou art good and ready to forgive, and plenteous in mercy to all them that call upon thee. All thy works and providences speak to us of thee. Our whole lives, from the cradle to this hour, bear witness to thy paternal care and love for us. Our own hearts prompt us to call upon thee. Thy holy Son by his precept and example has enjoined us to draw nigh unto thee in prayer. Through the new and living way consecrated by him we would now approach thee as true worshippers, seeking to worship thee in spirit and in truth.

Guardian and preserver of our lives through the silent night, when there was no eye to watch over us, and no arm to protect us, thou hast preserved us from the pestilence that walketh in darkness, from the assaults of violence, from the flames that might have consumed us and our dwellings. By thy mighty power thou hast again raised us from the temporary death of sleep, and opened our eyes upon the world, fresh and beautiful as on the first morn of creation. Now, also, do the morning stars sing together, and the sons of God shout for joy. Now, as then, thy wisdom, power and glory, are displayed, showing that thou art the same yesterday, to-day and forever.

But in the Gospel, far more clearly and tenderly than in nature, are revealed thy paternal character and providences. We thank thee for the work which Christ has wrought in the world. Especially do we thank thee for that richest fruit of his mission on earth, Christian homes. We bless thee for the spirit which has hallowed the union of husband and wife, parent and child, brother and sister, and made it like the union of Christ and the church. We pray that the spirit of thy holy Son may dwell richly in our hearts this day, and make ours a home of peace, of contentment, of mutual love. Help us to watch over our tempers, that no hasty or unkind word may escape our lips. Give us, we beseech thee, so much of the spirit of our Master, that we may feel it to be more blessed to give than to receive mutual aid and sympathy. Sanctify to us our domestic comforts, duties and affections, that our home may be a school of Christ, to prepare us for our everlasting home in heaven.

O thou Guardian of our lives, as we go forth this day, to the duties, temptations and perils of life, we cast ourselves on thy almighty protection. Dangers may await us which no human wisdom can foresee, changes which no skill of ours can avert. We find comfort in the thought of thy guardian providence over us; we rest in the assurance of thy fatherly protection and love. We may again meet temptations which have so often overcome us. Not in our own strength would we again venture into the scenes of the world. Do thou go with us, upholding us, and providing under every temptation a way of escape. We are again to be brought into relations with our fellow-beings by which we may influence their future course. Give us grace to watch for ways to do them good, to turn their feet to thy testimonies, that they may glorify thy name. We are again to be intrusted, in thy service, with opportunities that may not return. We may this day receive impressions that will give a bias to our whole future lives. Give us grace so to improve these opportunities, and direct these impressions, that the coming evening may find us advanced a day's journey heavenward.

Father of Mercies, we supplicate thy blessing on all classes and conditions of our fellow-beings. Remember in great mercy the poor and destitute, the sick and sorrowful, the tempted and tried, the aged and infirm. Give them all grace to hear and accept the gracious invitation of the Saviour, Come unto me, all ye that labor and are heavy laden, and I will give you rest.

Finally, we commit ourselves and all that are dear

to us into thy merciful hands, beseeching thee to guard, guide, sustain, and sanctify us, this day and all our days; and unto thee shall be all the praise, through Jesus Christ our Lord. Amen.

XXIII.

Joy in God's Compassion.

Bless the Lord, O my soul: and all that is within me, bless his holy name

Bless the Lord, O my soul, and forget not all his benefits:

Who forgiveth all thy iniquities; who healeth all thy diseases;

Who redeemeth thy life from destruction; who crowneth thee with loving-kindness and tender mercies;

Who satisfieth thy mouth with good things; so that thy youth is renewed like the eagle's.

The Lord is merciful and gracious, slow to anger, and abundant in mercy.

He will not always chide: neither will he keep his anger forever.

He hath not dealt with us according to our sins; nor rewarded us according to our iniquities.

For as the heaven is high above the earth, so great is his mercy toward them that fear him.

As far as the east is from the west, so far hath he removed our transgressions from us.

Like as a father pitieth his children, so the Lord pitieth them that fear him.

Our Father, who art in heaven. Hallowed be

thy name. With the light of another day our hearts would ascend in prayer and in praise unto thee, who in the beginning saidst "Let there be light," and who still in thine eternal providence and thy boundless mercy makest the sun to shine on the evil and the good, on the thankful and the unthankful. The heavens declare thy glory. The earth is full of thy goodness. Summer and winter, seed-time and harvest, night and day, speak unto us, each in its turn, of thee, their Maker and Lord. Daily thou crownest us with thy loving-kindness and tender mercies. Bless the Lord, O my soul, and all that is within me bless his holy name!

As a Christian family do we now bow down together before thee, believing what thou hast taught us in Jesus Christ thy Son, believing in thy providential care, believing in thy paternal compassion, believing in the higher life to come, when this corruptible shall put on incorruption and this mortal immortality, and when they that have served or forsaken thee on earth shall pass to their account. As a Christian family, O God, may we begin and may we spend this new day on which we are now entering; being in all things true to our discipleship, and proving by our words and acts, at home and abroad, in the manifold relations of life, that we have a living and not a dead and barren faith in thee and in thy Son. O, help us to finish the work which thou hast given us to do for ourselves. for each other, and for all whom we can serve; remembering the uncertainty of life and the certainty of death.

Father, we commend our bodies and our souls unto thee, confiding in the assurance that thou art gracious and abundant in mercy. Watch over us in every danger, and give us the needed strength for every duty. Make us conquerors over the evil passions that would betray our virtue and our peace, and over the sins of thought, of temper, and of life, which do most easily beset us; and if through the weakness of our nature we at any time fall, deal not with us according to our sins, nor reward us according to our iniquity.

Let this and all our days upon earth be spent in thy fear; and may we live in daily and happy preparation for the last. May the thought of that future life cheer us onward in our earthly pilgrimage, giving purity to our motives and elevation to our aims, and enabling us to bear with serene peace and trust all the allotments of thy holy hand. And having dwelt together in pleasantness and peace during the brief term of our sojourning in these mortal bodies, having been faithful helpers to one another in all the chances and changes of the world, may we at length, in thine infinite grace, be permitted to meet again in a still happier union in thy presence, and in the presence of thy Son, with whom is fulness of joy, through Jesus Christ our Lord. Amen.

XXIV.

For Providential Direction.

Teach me, O Lord, the way of thy statutes; and I shall keep it to the end.

Give me understanding, and I shall keep thy law; verily, I shall observe it with my whole heart.

Make me to go in the path of thy commandments; for in that do I delight.

Incline my heart to thy testimonies, and not to covetousness.

Turn away my eyes from beholding vanity; and revive thou me in thy way.

Establish thy word to thy servant, who is devoted to thy fear.

Turn away my reproach which I fear: for thy judgments are good.

Behold, I have longed after thy precepts: revive me in thy righteousness.

"We praise thee, O God, we acknowledge thee to be the Lord! All the earth doth worship thee, the Father everlasting." "Heaven and earth are full of the majesty of thy glory." The heart of man cannot conceive, much less the tongue of man utter, the greatness of thy power, the depth of thy wisdom, nor the unsearchable riches of thy love. But we give thee thanks that thou hast revealed unto us thy being, that thou hast manifested to us thy power and wisdom, and given such innumerable proofs of thy loving-kindness to us and to all men. We thank thee for the beauty in which thou hast clothed the earth, and the glory with which thou hast filled the heavens. We thank thee that all things minister to our needs, and are adapted to our uses; we thank thee for all the tender ties of friendship and of kindred; for all the privileges of our social state; for the opportunities we have of gaining a knowledge of thy truth; and for the invitation thou hast given us, through thy Son our Saviour, to become fellow-laborers with him and with thee.

O lead us, by all the all-powerful influences of thy Spirit, to accept this invitation, and enter upon the inheritance of our birthright in thy kingdom. Turn away our eyes from vanity, and incline our hearts to thy testimonies. Let us this day be lifted above all low and selfish purposes, and be filled with that divine charity, that holy wisdom, that unconquerable strength, which thou givest to thy saints. Help us to hold fast our integrity; to keep the way of thy statutes, even to the end; and by our communion with thee, and with thy Son, to be made triumphant over all temptation. We would behold thy presence in every work of thy hand. We would find the leadings of thy providence in each event of life. We would give ourselves wholly to thy service, and pray thee to work within us both to will and to do of thy own good pleasure. Make us to go in the path of thy commandment, and may that be our delight.

And as we ask thy blessing upon ourselves, so would we ask it upon all men, and especially upon those whom we each now in silence name to thee. Thou readest our hearts and our silent wishes; grant, O Father, our prayers, if it be best for those for whom we pray.

[Here let there be a few moments' silence.]

Our Father who art in heaven, hallowed be thy name. Restrain thy children from transgression, restore those that wander, lead those that sin unto repentance, give light to those that are in darkness, strengthen them that are weak, and let thy truth and righteousness triumph in all the earth. We believe thine Anointed to be the hope of all nations; may the word of his truth and power fill the hearts of his disciples with the spirit of love, and of wisdom, and of might, that they may so live and labor as to bring all men unto thee through him. And thine be the glory evermore. Amen.

XXV.

Against Distrust.

I say unto you, Take no thought for your life, what ye shall eat, or what ye shall drink; nor yet for your body, what ye shall put on. Is not the life more than meat, and the body than raiment?

Behold the fowls of the air; for they sow not, neither do they reap, nor gather into barns; yet your heavenly Father feedeth them. Are ye not much better than they?

Which of you, by taking thought, can add one cubit unto his stature?

And why take ye thought for raiment? Consider the lilies of the field, how they grow; they toil not, neither do they spin:

And yet I say unto you, That even Solomon, in all his glory, was not arrayed like one of these.

Wherefore, if God so clothe the grass of the field, which to-day is, and to-morrow is cast into the oven, shall he not much more clothe you, O ye of little faith?

O Thou, whose unslumbering providence has kept us another night, and given us refreshing rest, we bless thee for this new day. May our hearts be open to the glad tidings of thy love which it is proclaiming. May we receive it as thy gift, with gratitude for what it speaks to us of thy continued and exhaustless mercy, and with a due sense also of responsibility, in view of the sacred trust thou art again committing to us. We know not what this day may bring forth. Strengthen and prepare us for all that awaits us. Keep us from distrustful thoughts. Give us cheerful and unfailing confidence in that fatherly and all-embracing oversight, without which not a sparrow falleth to the ground. Thou who hast given life, shall we doubt that thou wilt give it meat? Thou who hast given the body, shall we doubt that thou wilt furnish it with raiment? Thou from whom we have received the greater gift, may we not trust thee for the less?

Father in heaven, may no temptation assail us, which the remembrance of thy word, and the communications of thy Spirit, shall not enable us to resist.

May our trials, whether small or great, be borne with Christian meekness, and work out for us some spiritual good. May all our duties be performed in the spirit of him whose meat it was to do thy will; and in memory of his word, that he who is faithful in that which is least, is faithful also in much. May it quicken our good purposes, and encourage us in every right endeavor, to remember that thou lookest upon the heart; and may the thought that thou seest us check every wrong motive and evil impulse. Give us calmness and self-control under every disappointment and provocation. Enable us to meet with gentleness and forbearance any opposition to our wishes, and to strive with patience against our own infirmities and faults, not doubting that success shall ultimately attend our efforts, if we faint not.

Almighty God, may we seek not our own only, but each the other's welfare and enjoyment. May we be ready to deny ourselves every indulgence that would be a disobedience of thy laws. Give us right feelings towards one another, and towards all men. May we come to the close of this day able to look back upon time well spent, opportunities faithfully improved, and progress made in the paths of Christian faith and virtue. And when we shall have fulfilled thy purposes concerning us on earth, may we be received, of thy infinite mercy, to reünion with one another, and to the happiness of the pure and good, in the everlasting mansions revealed to us through Jesus Christ our Lord. Amen.

XXVI.

Relying on God.

Show us thy mercy, O Lord, and grant us thy salvation.

I will hear what God the Lord will speak : for he will speak peace to his people, and to his saints : but let them not turn again to folly.

Surely his salvation is nigh them that fear him ; that glory may dwell in our land.

Mercy and truth have met together ; righteousness and peace have kissed each other.

Truth shall spring out of the earth ; and righteousness shall look down from heaven.

Verily, the Lord will give that which is good ; and our land shall yield her increase.

Righteousness shall go before him ; and shall set us in the way of his steps.

ALMIGHTY GOD, the Source of life, the Giver of all good, help us to draw near to thee, and to hold communion with thee. Waked from the insensibility of sleep, with renewed powers we are about to renew our daily course of duty. But we know, O God, that without thee we can do nothing ; that all our sufficiency is of thee, in whom we live and move and have our being. Before we go forth to our work, we would hear what God the Lord will speak ; and pray that he would speak peace to our hearts, that our strength may be renewed, and that, replenished by thy grace, we may run and not be weary, and walk and not faint.

We bless thee for thy protection through the watches of the night. We bless thee that for us the outgoings of the morning rejoice. Truly the light is sweet; and we bless thee and praise thy goodness unto us, that, while to others the sun is set to rise no more, thou hast preserved our lives, and art multiplying our days on the earth. Thy mercies, O God, are new unto us every morning. We welcome the new day, with its fresh duties and responsibilities, and we await its disclosures in trust and hope. May we meet all changes relying on thee, and keep consciences void of offence toward God and men.

Sustaining to one another the nearest and holiest relations, may our hearts be united in love, and may we be helpers of each others' joy. May this be a household of faith, a Christian home; and may the blessing of Heaven be upon all who dwell within these walls, and upon the absent to whom we are nearly allied. Vouchsafe thy protection and favor to all whom we love; and grant that, however widely we may be separated from one another on earth, our mutual love may remain unchanged, and that in heaven we may meet face to face, to part no more.

Guide us, O Father, by thy counsel: support us by thy care, and from thy inexhaustible stores may all our wants be supplied. May we be contented with that portion of goods that falleth to our share; and when what thou givest is taken away, may our hope and our trust be still in thee. Conduct us, good shepherd, in such a way as thou choosest, and set us in the way of thy steps; and whether it lead to the green pastures, beside the still waters, or to the valley of the shadow of death, be with us in every change, and may thy presence strengthen and gladden our hearts. Show us thy mercy, O God, and finally grant us thy salvation.

Give thy blessing, Holy Father, to our land and to the world. Send forth thy light and thy truth. May truth spring out of the earth, and righteousness look down from heaven, and thy salvation be nigh unto all. To thee, the only living and true God, we render thanks, through Jesus Christ our Lord. Amen.

XXVII.

Faith and Fortitude.

How excellent is thy loving-kindness, O God! therefore the children of men put their trust under the shadow of thy wings.

For with thee is the fountain of life: in thy light shall we see light.

O continue thy loving-kindness to them that know thee, and thy righteousness to the upright in heart.

I laid me down and slept; I awaked; for the Lord sustained me.

I will not be afraid of ten thousands of people, that have set themselves against me on all sides.

O Thou, who hast set the solitary in families, and joined us to each other by the strong bonds of domestic affection and interest, we rejoice to recognize the higher and more sacred ties which bind us to thee and thy service. We regard it as our most precious privilege to come to thee in devout trust and worship, to pour forth our souls to thee, to implore that blessing without which none can be blest. For with thee is the fountain of life, and under the shadow of thy wings the children of men put their trust.

To thy keeping we commit our souls, as to the all-faithful and loving Creator. This day, and all our days, may thy presence go with us, chastening our joys, comforting us in our sorrows, shielding us in hours of peril, protecting from the power of temptation, sanctifying all labors and all events, and imparting a peace which the world cannot give, and cannot take away.

Holy Father, this day may the presence of Jesus, thy chosen messenger and well-beloved Son, go with us, and his parting promise be fulfilled to each of us — "Lo! I am with you alway, even to the end of the world." Attended and inspired by his spirit, may we meet firmly all the conflicts and trials of earth, and be not afraid if ten thousands set themselves against us. Into that spirit of faith and fortitude may we be baptized more and more, and go on our way rejoicing, fearing no evil, and feeling no want.

Command thy blessing, O God, to rest upon us of

this household, as we now bow down before thee, and commit our way to thy hand. And when life's short day is passed, bring us together, a family in heaven, with no wanderer lost, to sit in heavenly places in Jesus Christ. Through him to thee do we ascribe the glory and the praise forever. Amen.

XXVIII.

Love for God and Man.

And one of the scribes came, and having heard them rea soning together, and perceiving that he had answered them well, asked him, Which is the first commandment of all?

And Jesus answered him, The first of all the command ments is, Hear, O Israel; The Lord our God is one Lord.

And thou shalt love the Lord thy God with all thy heart, and with all thy soul, and with all thy mind, and with all thy strength: this is the first commandment.

And the second is like, namely this, Thou shalt love thy neighbor as thyself: there is no other commandment greater than these.

And the scribe said to him, Well, Master, thou hast said the truth: for there is one God; and there is no other but he

And to love him with all the heart, and with all the under standing, and with all the soul, and with all the strength, and to love his neighbor as himself, is more than all whole burnt offerings and sacrifices.

And when Jesus saw that he answered discreetly, he said to him, Thou art not far from the kingdom of God.

O God, Almighty and All-holy, thy children, preserved by thy goodness through the night, look up to thee with grateful hearts, presenting their morning tribute of prayer and praise. Grant us, O Lord, right thoughts and feelings, that we may worship thee acceptably. May we deeply realize that thou art, and that thou art the rewarder of them that diligently seek thee; that thou art not far from every one of us, seeing that thou hast given unto all life, and breath, and all things; that thou art a spirit, unseen by mortal eye, but always near us, observing all that we do, hearing every word that we utter, and familiar with our very thoughts; and that we should love thee with all our heart, and soul, and mind, and strength.

We bless thee, O God, for all the knowledge of thy will imparted by thy voice in nature and in our own hearts; for thy communications to men in ancient times by patriarchs and prophets, and especially for the divine instruction given to us in the fulness of time by our Lord and Saviour Jesus Christ. We bless thee that through him we have access unto the Father; and we pray that, guided and strengthened by our gracious Redeemer, we may more and more steadfastly contemplate thee, the high and holy One, who inhabitest eternity.

We thank thee that thou permittest us to call thee Father. May we ever be thy faithful and loving children. May we be drawn to thy service, and retained therein, alike by reverent fear and grateful love. Knowing that thou discernest all our ways, may we fear to sin against one so great; and receiving alike from nature and from the Gospel assurances of thy goodness, may we with constant care shun to offend against one so kind and bountiful. May we walk with thee, O Lord, this day. If temptation comes, may we meet and conquer it, not in our own strength, but in thine. If sorrow falls to our lot, may we meekly submit, and try to learn thy purpose in the affliction. If crowned by happiness, may we blend thankfulness to thee with humility at the thought of our own deficiencies and sins.

O Lord, forgive, we pray thee, our offences. Grant us true repentance of them, and may sin no more have dominion over us. Deliver us from any danger which may now threaten us; but, above all, keep us, O Father, from the danger of sin, bless us day by day, and at length take us to thyself.

We beseech thee for each other, and for all who are dear to us, imploring for our friends the same blessings we have besought for ourselves, and that we may keep thy commandment in loving our neighbor as ourselves. May we always be united in love here; and at the last be admitted to that holier world, where thy presence shall be more clearly displayed, and where thine accepted servants shall rejoice before thee forever with exceeding joy. May thy blessing be with all mankind; and unto thee, in the holy name of our Saviour Jesus Christ, do we ascribe all praise. Amen

XXIX.

Duties to our Fellow-Men.

Let love be without dissimulation. Abhor that which is evil, cleave to that which is good.

Be kindly affectioned one to another with brotherly love; in honor preferring one another;

Not slothful in business; fervent in spirit; serving the Lord;

Rejoicing in hope; patient in tribulation; continuing instant in prayer;

Distributing to the necessity of saints; given to hospitality.

Bless them which persecute you: bless, and curse not.

Rejoice with them that do rejoice, and weep with them that weep.

Be of the same mind one toward another. Mind not high things, but condescend to men of low estate. Be not wise in your own conceits.

Recompense to no man evil for evil. Provide things honest in the sight of all men.

If it be possible, as much as lieth in you live peaceably with all men.

Dearly beloved, avenge not yourselves, but rather give place unto wrath: for it is written, Vengeance is mine; I will repay, saith the Lord.

Therefore, if thine enemy hunger, feed him; if he thirst, give him drink; for in so doing thou shalt heap coals of fire on his head.

Be not overcome of evil, but overcome evil with good.

ALMIGHTY GOD, by whose paternal care we have been kept through the darkness of another night, we bless thee for the light of this day, and for all the mercies it reveals. From thy hands we receive afresh the lives which thou first bestowed. We enter again into possession and enjoyment of the world which thou didst build and furnish for our habitation. We behold anew the faces of the friends whom thou hast made dear. We feel within us the motions of that understanding which thine inspiration hath given us. Creator and preserver of our lives, Giver of every good and perfect gift, we adore thy nature and thy providence.

Consecrate now, O Lord, to thine own service, the powers thou hast created, the possessions thou hast conferred. We dare not go forth to our labors and enjoyments without thy direction and blessing. Shine in so vividly upon our hearts, that nothing we behold this day may cloud thy presence. Draw us so near to thyself that the world may find no room to come between us and thee. Fortify us by thy Spirit against the temptations that await us, and spare us trials greater than we can bear.

Animate us this day, O Lord, with the spirit and example of thy Son, for whom we ever bless his Father and ours. May his words and works, his life and death, his commandments and promises, dwell in our thoughts, possess our affections, and shape our behavior.

And while we invoke his spirit, we confess our own unworthiness. O Lord, suffer not our sins to hinder our prayers; take not thy Holy Spirit from us, who so often have grieved it. Withhold not that Saviour we have so many times denied. Leave us not to ourselves. Be kinder to us than we are to each other, or to our own souls.

Command thy special blessing, gracious Parent, upon this family. Help us to dwell together in unity and mutual helpfulness. As parents, may we imitate the universal Father; as children, the Son of God. Teach us in the government of our household to unite the goodness and the severity of God, and incline the hearts of our children to submit to authority and welcome instruction.

Enlarge our hearts, thou universal Parent, towards our race. We pray for all men, but especially for those less happy than ourselves; for the poor and oppressed, the sick and solitary. Inspire us with reverence for humanity as made in thy likeness, and hallowed in thy Son. Hasten our feet at its cry, open our hand to its want, and sweeten our lips for its consolation.

Grant, O God, that these the words of our mouths may this day be established in the works of our lives; and thine be the glory and the praise, through Jesus Christ our Lord. Amen.

XXX.

Use of Daily Blessings.

The heavens declare the glory of God; and the firmament showeth his handiwork.

Day unto day uttereth speech, and night unto night showeth knowledge.

There is no speech nor language, where their voice is not heard.

Their line hath gone out through all the earth, and their words to the end of the world. In them hath he set a tabernacle for the sun,

Which is as a bridegroom coming out of his chamber, and rejoiceth as a strong man to run a race.

His going forth is from the end of the heaven, and his circuit to the ends of it: and there is nothing hid from his heat.

The law of the Lord is perfect, converting the soul: the testimony of the Lord is sure, making wise the simple.

The statutes of the Lord are right, rejoicing the heart: the commandment of the Lord is pure, enlightening the eyes.

The fear of the Lord is clean, enduring forever: the judgments of the Lord are true and righteous altogether.

Who can understand his errors? cleanse thou me from secret faults.

Keep back thy servant also from presumptuous sins; let them not have dominion over me: then shall I be upright, and I shall be innocent from the great transgression.

Let the words of my mouth, and the meditation of my heart, be acceptable in thy sight, O Lord, my strength, and my redeemer.

God over all, forever blessed, we would worship thee in reverence, and gratitude, and joy. As the sun in the heavens doth rise and shine down upon our dwellings, so may the light of thy truth and thy love rise and shine upon our souls. Thou dost bring the dawn out of darkness; grant unto us also that true knowledge of thee which shall enlighten us in all our ways. Thou dost beset us behind and before, numbering the very hairs of our heads, giving unto us discerning minds, and offering unto us that Spirit which maketh us truly free. Praise unto thee, thou everlasting Helper, for thine infinite compassions. May they entreat us every day to consecrate ourselves unto thee, and may they remind us that our life is a solemn trust.

Known unto thee, Father, are all thy works from the foundation of the world,—the duties, the perplexities and the joys, which are appointed for each day of thy children's lot. Prepare us, O thou, who knowest our mortal frame, for all that shall befall us, that in our prosperity we may not be high-minded; that in our adversity we may be drawn very closely unto him who pitieth us every day, and doth encompass our weakness with his almighty power. Earnestly do we seek of thee the forgiveness of those sins that have darkened our past lives. Enable us, in the humblest reliance upon the only Mediator, to build again that which is fallen down, and to walk in ways more excellent. Keep us from presumptuous sins, and cleanse us from secret faults. Establish us in that law of the Lord which converts the soul, and in those statutes of the Lord which rejoice the heart. Let there be health and peace in this dwelling. Save us from foolish anxieties. May we believe that the Lord will provide. Striving each one of us to bear his own burden, may we do good to our brethren as we shall have opportunity, and freely give as we have freely received.

We commend the young to him who, whilst he was yet with us in bodily presence, took little children into his loving arms. May they feel that the gracious Lord still loveth them, and is ready to send to their hearts the Holy Spirit of consolation and peace. O God, be very near to our kindred and friends. We would ever remember them in our morning prayer. O thou, unto whom all souls are present, hear the prayers of the afflicted; watch over those who travel by land or by water, and may the sweet influences of the Gospel gladden and redeem many hearts. We ask it through him who is evermore the way. Amen

---

XXXI.

Faithfulness in Duty.

Now we exhort you, brethren, warn them that are unruly, comfort the feeble-minded, support the weak, be patient toward all men.

See that none render evil for evil to any man; but ever follow that which is good, both among yourselves and to all men.

Rejoice evermore.

Pray without ceasing.

In everything give thanks: for this is the will of God in Christ Jesus concerning you.

Quench not the Spirit.

Despise not prophesyings.
Prove all things; hold fast that which is good.
Abstain from all appearance of evil.
And the very God of peace sanctify you wholly; and I pray God your whole spirit and soul and body may be preserved blameless, to the coming of our Lord Jesus Christ.

O Thou, in whom we live, and move, and have our being. Unto thee, the giver of every good gift to the body and the soul, we lift up our hearts in gratitude and in love. Every day would we bless thee, and we would praise thy name for ever and ever. We would fervently thank thee for life, for health, for the pleasures of the senses; for the various enjoyments of our nature; for the manifold privileges of our lot; for the holy and tender ties which bind us to each other; above all, for the means of spiritual progress offered unto us by thy providence and thy grace; for the heavenly mission of thy Son; for the sanctifying, cheering and comforting truths of his word; for the quickening example of his life; and for all the blessed influences which are ever flowing out from him upon the hearts and lives of his disciples.

And now, O God, God and Father of our Lord Jesus Christ, as we enter on the duties of another day, may we go to them in the spirit of our Master; in a devout, pure, faithful spirit; abhorring that which is evil, cleaving to that which is good; in love to thee, in love to each other, in love to our neighbors, in love to our fellow-men. And wherever we are, whatever we do, whatever we suffer, may we remember that thou, God, seest us. In all our temptations, and in all our trials, may the thought of thy presence be as a light to our feet and a lamp to our path. Be with us in our daily labors, and crown them with thy blessing. May they be hallowed by fidelity, and truth, and kindness; and may we look through them to thee, and above them to the prize to which, in the midst of all, thou art ever calling us from on high, through Christ Jesus.

O thou who knowest the secrets of all hearts, forgive us, in thine infinite mercy, the sins of the past. Strengthen our good purposes for the future. Lead us not into temptation, but deliver us from evil. Prepare us for the changes that are before us, hidden from our sight, but known unto thee. Prepare us for prosperity and for adversity, for health and for sickness, for life and for death.

O thou who art our God and the God of all the families of the earth, bless this our home, and make it a Christian and a happy home, consecrated to thee. Bring our souls more and more into harmony with all truth and goodness. Unite them to thyself in the bonds of a filial piety, and to each other in a true affection, and to all men in a large and tender-hearted charity and good will; that so we may be indeed the children of our heavenly Father, and the disciples of him whose love was the image of thine. And through him to thee be all glory and praise forever. Amen.

XXXII.

Preservation from Sin.

Hear, O my son, and receive my sayings; and the years of thy life shall be many.

I have taught thee in the way of wisdom; I have led thee in right paths.

When thou goest, thy steps shall not be straitened; and when thou runnest, thou shalt not stumble.

Take fast hold of instruction; let her not go: keep her; for she is thy life.

Enter not into the path of the wicked, and go not in the way of evil men.

Avoid it, pass not by it, turn from it, and pass away.

For they sleep not, except they have done mischief; and their sleep is taken away, unless they cause some to fall.

For they eat the bread of wickedness, and drink the wine of violence.

But the path of the just is as the shining light, that shineth more and more to the perfect day.

O, HOLY FATHER, who art the author and the giver of every good gift, we bless thee for the renewed light of this day, and for all the hopes and opportunities which it sets before us. We give thee thanks that thou hast watched over us during the past night, and kept all harm from us; and we would show our thankfulness for the gift of life thus renewed, by dedicating that life unto thy service. We therefore pray thee, help us each one to keep ourselves this day without sin. Thou needest nothing at our hands; show us, therefore, how we may serve thee, by showing us how we may serve the best interests of thy children. Banish from our hearts, O God. every selfish and unworthy thought. Give us a perfect mastery over every appetite and passion. Keep us from the path of the wicked, and from the way of evil men. Rule thou in our hearts, and fill us with holy thoughts and noble desires. Let us find in all the duties of the day the guidance of thy grace, and have the hope of thine acceptance. Help us to keep thy commandments, and fulfil for us the promise of our Lord, that thou and he will dwell in the hearts of them that obey thee, and make their path to shine more and more to the perfect day. Thus lift us by thine indwelling presence above the power of temptation, and let it become the joy of our lives to be co-workers with Christ and with God.

And, as we ask these blessings for ourselves, so would we pray in behalf of those whom we love, in behalf of our neighbors and friends, and in behalf of all men. Let the word of Christ become the salvation of all nations. Give this day wisdom to every counsel of the good, courage and strength to every Christian heart, and success to every Christian effort. But let thy good providence baffle every wicked design, and bring evil counsels to naught. Thus hasten the coming of the kingdom of our Lord, in whose name we offer our prayer, beseeching thee to forgive and to accept us, and to deal with us not according to our feeble words or cold desires, but according to our needs, and according to thine infinite mercy. Amen.

XXXIII.

For Christian Growth.

Grace and peace be multiplied unto you through the knowledge of God, and of Jesus our Lord,

According as his divine power hath given unto us all things that pertain unto life and godliness, through the knowledge of him that hath called us to glory and virtue :

Whereby are given unto us exceeding great and precious promises; that by these ye might be partakers of the divine nature, having escaped the corruption that is in the world through lust.

And, besides this, giving all diligence, add to your faith, virtue; and to virtue, knowledge;

And to knowledge, temperance; and to temperance, patience; and to patience, godliness;

And to godliness, brotherly kindness; and to brotherly kindness, charity.

For if these things be in you, and abound, they make you that ye shall neither be barren nor unfruitful in the knowledge of our Lord Jesus Christ.

Wherefore the rather, brethren, give diligence to make your calling and election sure; for if ye do these things ye shall never fall:

For so an entrance shall be ministered unto you abundantly into the everlasting kingdom of our Lord and Saviour Jesus Christ.

O, MAKER of the world, we bless thee that the light is sweet, and that it is a pleasant thing for the eyes to behold the sun, and that our eyes again behold it. O, Preserver of men, we bless thee that by night and day thy providential care is the same. We have laid us down and slept, because thou hast sustained us. We have awaked, and are still with thee. Thou compassest our path and our bed. We have reposed under the shadow of thy protection, and we have risen up with the strength that thou hast renewed. We thank thee that once more we see the forms of the world, and hear the voice of the morning. Our early offering would be praise to thee, who alone causest us to dwell in safety. Unto thee will we direct our prayer, and will look up. We would employ in an act of worship the powers which thou hast given back to us refreshed; that we may set forward with new resolves, and with thy continued help.

Make us truly grateful to thee for all the blessings that stand revealed to us in the returning light. We thank thee that we are still among the living, the living to praise thee with conscious faculties and active service, as we beseech thee to grant us grace to do this day. For every power, privilege and opportunity of good, for the sight of thy works and the experience of thy mercy, for all the bounties that we partake, and all the hopes that we cherish, we would give thee humble and hearty thanks. And we pray that this gratitude may inspire an earnest purpose of heart, leading us to strive to be less unworthy than we now are of all thy benefits. Enlighten our darkness, O Lord, and mercifully guide our way for us, for it is not in man that walketh to direct his steps. Guard us against every evil to which we may be exposed from abroad; and may our hearts be kept above all other keeping, since out of them are the issues of life.

Vouchsafe, O Lord, to preserve us this day without sin. May we be in thy fear all the day long. Since we know not what a single day may bring forth, prepare our minds for whatever thy will may ordain; and since each one lays its own obligations upon us, make us faithful to the duties of each, as its hours are passing away. May we not be slothful in business, but fervent in spirit, serving thee in the common occupations of the world, and doing all things heartily as unto the Lord, giving all diligence that we be not barren or unfruitful in the knowledge of our Lord Jesus Christ. May we be kind and just in our intercourse with others, and gain a more perfect rule over our own spirits. Keep us mindful of thy constant presence, that we may not sin against thee.

Make this day a good day to us, by ordering the events of it graciously. Make it good for us, whatever may betide us in it, by ordering our dispositions and deeds aright. May we use wisely its opportunities, and confirm ourselves in faithful habits, and put further away besetting sins, and advance nearer towards the fulfilment of the true ends of our being. And so enable us to number all the days that we have here to live, that, when they come to an end, our spirits may be ready, and may depart in peace, and find forgiveness of sin, and grace with thee, through thine infinite mercy in Jesus Christ our Lord. Amen.

XXXIV.

Against Worldliness.

But godliness with contentment is great gain.

For we brought nothing into this world, and it is certain we can carry nothing out.

And having food and raiment, let us be therewith content.

But they that will be rich fall into temptation, and a snare, and into many foolish and hurtful lusts, which drown men in destruction and perdition.

For the love of money is the root of all evil; which, while some coveted after, they have erred from the faith, and pierced themselves through with many sorrows.

But thou, O man of God, flee these things; and follow after righteousness, godliness, faith, love, patience, meekness.

Fight the good fight of faith, lay hold on eternal life, whereunto thou art also called, and hast professed a good profession before many witnesses.

I give thee charge in the sight of God, who quickeneth all things, and before Christ Jesus, who before Pontius Pilate witnessed a good confession,

That thou keep this commandment without spot, unrebukable, until the appearing of our Lord Jesus Christ.

OUR Father in heaven, we thank thee that thou hast watched over us during the past night, and that we are preserved to behold the light of another morning, and to enter upon the duties of another day, in circumstances so encouraging to our hearts, so full of promise and hope. May we feel that this great blessing of continued life is thy gift; that the strength which we have derived from sleep is thy bestowment. Fill our hearts with gratitude, that we have slept in peace and safety; that no peril has overtaken us; that no harm has come nigh our home; and that with the morning there have come to us means of usefulness and growth in goodness. We pray, our Father, that these means of improving ourselves and of helping others may be so used by us, that when the day shall close we can look back upon its hours with satisfaction, and look up to thee with thankfulness. O, may not our hearts be pierced with many sorrows by the consciousness of having neglected or misused these precious opportunities of being co-workers with thee in doing good. May the law of love abide in our hearts, and words of kindness be upon our lips, this day. As parents and children, as brothers and sisters, as members of one household, may we be mindful of each other's wants, careful not to wound each other's feelings, and rejoice to make each other happy. May we strive to lead each other to love thee, our Father, who hast made us capable of so tenderly loving each other.

We pray that we may carry this spirit of love and good will into all our intercourse with those around us. May we seek to promote kindness, forbearance, forgiveness, among our companions and friends. May we seek opportunities of doing good. May we feel that there are none so young that they cannot be useful and good, and make others happy; that none are so old that they may not make life attractive by patience and gentleness; that none are so strong that they do not need sympathy and the help of others. Wherever we are, and whatever we do, may we feel that thou art with us, and may this sense of thy presence keep us from sin, and inspire us to faithfulness. May we not be eager for worldly things, for honor, and fame, and riches; but, having food and raiment, may we be content, seeking to do well what we find to do, to provide for our temporal comfort without show and excess, to guard against foolish and hurtful lusts, and to follow after righteousness and godliness, until the appearing of our Lord Jesus Christ. Thus may we witness a good profession, and fight the good fight of faith, and lay hold on eternal life.

Father, we pray that thou wilt bless our kindred and friends from whom we are separated. If they are sick, heal them; if they are in trouble, deliver them; if they are needy, supply their wants; if they are prospering, fill their hearts with gratitude, and a sense of their dependence upon thee.

We pray not for these alone. Our Father, we seek thy blessing for all men, our brethren. May the ignorant be enlightened; the sinful, converted; the oppressed, liberated; till everywhere, all over the earth, thy children shall know thee and love thee, Fountain of all good, Giver of all blessings, to whom be thanksgiving forever through Jesus Christ our Saviour. Amen.

XXXV.

For Diligence.

But ye, brethren, are not in darkness, that that day should overtake you as a thief.

Ye are all children of light, and children of the day: we are not of the night, nor of darkness.

Therefore let us not sleep, as do others; but let us watch and be sober.

For they that sleep, sleep in the night; and they that are drunken, are drunken in the night.

But let us, who are of the day, be sober, putting on the breastplate of love; and for a helmet, the hope of salvation.

For God hath not appointed us to wrath, but to obtain salvation by our Lord Jesus Christ,

Who died for us, that, whether we wake or sleep, we should live together with him.

Wherefore, comfort yourselves together, and edify one another, even as also ye do.

OUR FATHER who art in heaven, hallowed be thy name. Thy kingdom come. Thy will be done on earth as it is in heaven.

Thanks we give to thee for the sleep and rest of the past night. Filled with new vigor, we rejoice in the waking hour; and with the return of consciousness we would recognize thee ever present and blessing us. The world is filled with thy glory; and the great providence is the manifestation of thy goodness; and here at the family altar, here especially, would we render to thee unfeigned thanks for thy care of each one of us. Impress us with the thought of our entire dependence upon thee. Every pulsation of our hearts, every thought of our minds, every feeling of our souls, every breath and sensation, are so many witnesses to thy quickening Spirit. We live, and move, and have our being, in thee.

O God, help us to understand the great significance of life; created in thine image, and called to be fellow-laborers with thee, and taught to aspire to glory, honor and immortality, aid us, we beseech thee, to comprehend such a privilege and destiny, and to press forward to it with the awakened and resolute powers of our souls. This day may we be wise, sober, and diligent. May the powers of the world to come touch the springs of present action. O, may we make no work for repentance, ever mindful that as we sow we must reap. Warned of sin and its dreadful consequences, may we abhor evil and cleave to that which is good, looking with prayerful hope to the open heavens, and arming ourselves to engage with vigor in thy service.

Bless each one of us before thee. May peace and love fill this home with grateful happiness. May we be wise unto salvation. Lead the young in paths of innocence; cheer the days of old age; and guide all hearts to thee.

O Thou, who didst so love the world as to give thine only Son to reclaim man from sin, and open before him the way of life, we thank thee that thou hast appointed us to obtain salvation through our Lord Jesus Christ. Convinced of our need of a Saviour, may we seek and find Christ, hear his word, obey his precepts, and have him formed and living in our hearts. This day may we be children of the light, Christians in every thought and deed, and come one day's journey nearer to a glorious and blessed immortality; so that the day of our death, even should it be this day, may not overtake us as a thief, and whether we wake or sleep we may live with Christ.

Graciously hear us, O Father of our spirits, for thine is the kingdom, and the power, and the glory, forever. Amen.

XXXVI.

For Self-Control.

My son, attend to my words; incline thy ear to my sayings.

Let them not depart from thy eyes; keep them in the midst of thy heart.

For they are life to those that find them, and health to all their flesh.

Keep thy heart with all diligence; for out of it are the issues of life.

Put away from thee a froward mouth, and perverse lips put far from thee.

Let thy eyes look right on, and let thy eyelids look straight before thee.

Ponder the path of thy feet, and let all thy ways be established.

Turn not to the right hand nor to the left: remove thy foot from evil.

ETERNAL GOD, we adore thee as the sovereign Lord over all beings and in all worlds. None can dispute thy authority, resist thy will, or deny thy right to reign supreme. But we rejoice and are comforted to know that thy power is not more absolute than are thy wisdom and thy goodness, and that thy mercy endureth forever.

O God, grateful for thy continual care, we would feel that it is our duty and our happiness alike to submit ourselves to thy will. O, teach us to obey thee as we ought. Let not the evil that is in our own hearts, nor the evil that is in the world around us, beguile us to our ruin. May we keep thy sayings in the midst of our heart, remembering that we can be safe, innocent and happy, only as we are guided, controlled and disposed of, according to thy holy will. Be thou, O God, our counsellor, guardian, sanctifier, and comforter. With filial reverence, gratitude and love, we would commit to thee the keeping of our souls, as to a faithful Creator, who does all things well, and cannot lay upon man more than is right.

If it be our lot this day to endure hardship, loss or pain, to be wounded in our affections, or injured in our interests, then, O Father of mercies, do thou help us to keep our hearts with all diligence, and in patience to possess our souls. Blessed by thee in all time past, we would never repine at thy chastisements, or doubt thy future care and kindness. Let not one murmuring thought or feeling arise within us in the hour of our chastening. But may the sorrows we experience be mitigated by the remembrance of all thy past mercies, and soothed by the hope of good yet to come after sorrow may have purified and made us better. If the events of this day shall be conducive to our prosperity, replete with joy, and our hearts exult in the attainment of some good we have desired, then, O Father, may thy Holy Spirit graciously move each better feeling within us, prompt us to render the thanks due for thy merciful goodness to us, and repress every impulse which might tend to convert to evil what is designed for our improvement. Thus may we use all sublunary things with pious wisdom, nor turn to the right hand nor to the left in the path of thy service.

Great God, we beseech thy blessing on us and on all who are dear to us. Let this be a day well spent. May the light of thy presence shine around our paths.

Let thy peace dwell in our hearts. Let integrity and justice, truth and innocence, purity and charity, distinguish and adorn our characters. May we honor Christ before men by a conduct consistently Christian. To thee, O Father, we yield ourselves, to be thine now and forever. Amen.

XXXVII.

Mutual Affection.

Let no corrupt communication proceed out of your mouth, but that which is good to the use of edifying, that it may minister grace to the hearers.

And grieve not the Holy Spirit of God, whereby ye are sealed to the day of redemption.

Let all bitterness, and wrath, and anger, and clamor, and evil-speaking, be put away from you, with all malice :

And be ye kind one to another, tender-hearted, forgiving one another, even as God for Christ's sake hath forgiven you

ALMIGHTY GOD, it is owing to thee that we have been preserved through the past night. It is through thy goodness that we have been refreshed with sleep, and that our eyes are now opened to the light of another day. Accept, we beseech thee, our grateful praise; and grant that this day we may be upheld by thy power, and led by thy hand, and kept from danger, from sin, and from pain. With the return of each morning may our thoughts and affections rise to thee; and as one day succeeds another, so may our love to thee be perpetually renewed in our hearts, and our service of thee be constant.

Help us, O God and Father, to love one another. Let thy love be shed abroad upon this family, and may each member of the same walk in the light of thy favor. May children know thee to be their God, and their father's God; and may they seek thy blessing as their greatest happiness, and make it their first duty and find it their highest pleasure to keep thy commandments.

O God, we commit our ways to thee. To thee we commend all whom we love. Be with them and with us, by day and by night, in sorrow and in joy, in time and in eternity. Forgive us all our sins, and accept us freely through Jesus Christ our Lord and Saviour. Amen.

XXXVIII.

Submission and Peace.

My son, despise not the chastening of the Lord; neither be weary of his correction:

For whom the Lord loveth he correcteth; even as a father the son in whom he delighteth.

Happy is the man that findeth wisdom, and the man that getteth understanding.

For the merchandise of it is better than the merchandise of silver, and the gain of it than fine gold.

She is more precious than rubies: and all the things thou canst desire are not to be compared to her.

Length of days is in her right hand; and in her left hand riches and honor.

Her ways are ways of pleasantness, and all her paths are peace.

ALMIGHTY and eternal God, our Creator, Preserver and Benefactor, we desire to begin this day with the acknowledgment of thy power and goodness, and of our obligation to love and serve thee; and we beseech thee to grant us grace to pass the whole of it in thy fear, and in the fulfilment of thy commandments.

O Lord, enable us diligently to perform our respective duties. Let us not waste our time, nor be unfaithful to any trust. Let us have the testimony of our consciences that in simplicity and sincerity we have our conversation in the world. Let truth be ever on our lips. May we perform a kind and Christian part to all who come within our influence.

We also beseech thee to give us patience to bear the several trials and vicissitudes of life with an equal and contented mind. Let us not be perplexed with the cares of this world, nor overwhelmed with unnecessary fears; but let us ever trust thy gracious providence, and hope in thy goodness and mercy.

Bless unto us the afflictive circumstances through which we may pass. May we see thy hand in all thy various dispensations, and know that if we truly love and serve thee all things shall work together for our good.

While we recognize thy loving-kindness in the fair

scenes through which we walk, and amid the bounties of thy liberal hand, may we feel that our trials come from the same infinite goodness from which our blessings flow; may we not be weary of thy correction, nor ever doubt thy love.

We commend to thy fatherly care all our friends and relations. We pray for the rising generation; that thou wouldst be their hope, their refuge, and their strength. Hear the cry of the sick, and the aged, and the afflicted; and grant help and peace to all thy needy and dependent creatures, and pardon to sinful and sinning men, through Jesus Christ our Saviour. Amen.

XXXIX.

Domestic Relations.

I write unto you, little children, because your sins are forgiven you for his name's sake.

I write unto you, fathers, because ye have known him that is from the beginning. I write unto you, young men, because ye have overcome the wicked one. I write unto you, little children, because ye have known the Father.

I have written unto you, fathers, because ye have known him that is from the beginning. I have written unto you, young men, because ye are strong, and the word of God abideth in you, and ye have overcome the wicked one.

Love not the world, neither the things that are in the world. If any man love the world, the love of the Father is not in him.

For all that is in the world, the lust of the flesh, and the lust of the eyes, and the pride of life, is not of the Father, but is of the world.

And the world passeth away, and the lust thereof: but he that doeth the will of God abideth forever.

O Thou that hast placed the solitary in families, and made our domestic relations so tender and blessed, unto thee we gather at the beginning of this day. Amid the dark and silent watches of the night our eyes have been closed, and we have rested in refreshing sleep under thine all-present and ever-wakeful care. Peace and safety have been within our habitation; and with renewed strength we, thy children, come to thee with our thanksgivings, confessions, and prayers.

We thank thee, O God, for all the blessings, personal, domestic and social, which we enjoy. We thank thee for health, and soundness of body and mind; for the delights of home; for the blessed bonds which bind us together; for the tender friendships we have formed, and the kind friends thou hast given us; and for the innocent recreation and pleasures which relieve the labors of life. But, above all, we thank thee for the gift of thy Son Jesus Christ; for his spotless life and his divine example; for his death endured for us; for his glorious resurrection and ascension; and for all the spiritual light and instruction, aid and guidance, rich promises and precious hopes, of his Gospel.

Forgive us, O our Father, that we have not cherished the gratitude due for all thy mercies; that we have too often forgotten the great Giver; that we have surrendered so often and so easily to temptation; that we have been so disobedient to thy laws; that we have been so deficient in the true spirit of thy children, rendering at times not only evil for evil, but evil for good, and living too exclusively for the world and the things of the world. Help us, gracious and holy Being, in our repentance, that it may bring forth in us the good fruits of amendment unto everlasting life.

While this day encircled in the embrace of our beloved home, may our affection for one another be sanctified by an abiding love of thyself and of thy Son; so that we may aid one another on earth in whatever will make us acceptable to thee, and fit us to enter and dwell together in heaven. When separated to our various cares and duties, may thy Holy Spirit enable us to be true to our obligations unto thee, faithful to our engagements, just and diligent in our use of time, conscientious in improving our talents and privileges. May we be forbearing and patient under provocation; gentle and generous in our tempers; inflexible in every good purpose; and alike through good report and evil report firm and resolved in our adherence to rectitude and truth. May we always bear in mind that thine all-seeing eye is upon us, and that thou judgest not as man judgeth, but judgest the heart.

May we be, therefore, pure in heart, shunning even the appearance of evil, and growing this day and every day in the divine life, according to the perfect pattern of our blessed Saviour.

We pray, heavenly Father, that thou wouldst send down thy best and choicest blessings upon our kindred and friends; and that our friends may be the friends of our God, and true disciples of thy Son. Bless thy church universal. Pity the poor and the afflicted. Heal the sick. Strengthen the weak and the tempted. Deliver the oppressed. Reclaim the sinner. Hasten the time when all men shall know thee the one living and true God, and Jesus Christ whom thou hast sent.

All which we ask through him who hath taught us in praying unto thee to say,

"Our Father which art in heaven, hallowed be thy name. Thy kingdom come. Thy will be done in earth as it is in heaven. Give us this day our daily bread. And forgive us our debts, as we forgive our debtors. And lead us not into temptation, but deliver us from evil. For thine is the kingdom, and the power, and the glory, forever. Amen."

XL.

Triumph of the Gospel.

For the grace of God that bringeth salvation hath appeared to all men,

Teaching us, that denying ungodliness, and worldly lusts, we should live soberly, righteously, and piously, in this present world;

Looking for that blessed hope, and the glorious appearing of the great God, and our Saviour Jesus Christ;

Who gave himself for us, that he might redeem us from all iniquity, and purify to himself a peculiar people, zealous of good works.

These things speak, and exhort, and rebuke with all authority. Let no man despise thee.

O Thou who alone hearest prayer, and unto whom all flesh should come, in the name and as the disciples of Jesus Christ, whom thou hearest alway, and with whom thou art ever well pleased, we would present ourselves before thee this morning, and in the spirit and with the confidence of children would offer thee our humble sacrifice of prayer and praise.

We thank thee, O thou preserver of men, for thy kind and paternal care of us during the silent and defenceless hours of the last night. We would rejoice in the pleasant light of another morning. We thank thee for the providence that preserves our lives, for the food that nourishes our bodies, for the relationships that cheer and gladden our hearts, and, above all, for the religion that animates and confirms our hopes. Continue these blessings to us, give us grace to improve them aright, and make us worthy of enjoying them.

Help us to realize our dependence upon thee for all the privileges, blessings and comforts, of this life, and for all the hopes and prospects of a better. May we improve the blessings of a common providence, as the gifts of a munificent Benefactor; and our Christian privileges, as the exceeding riches of thy grace in thy kindness towards us, through Jesus Christ. To this end may we receive with meekness the engrafted word, which is able to save our souls. Help us to open our minds and hearts to the light and influence of the truth as it is in Jesus, thanking thee that thy grace, which bringeth salvation, hath appeared to us in him.

We supplicate thy presence, protection and blessing, during the day on which we have entered. Spread over us the wing of an ever guardian providence, and shield us from every danger and from every casualty. Prosper us in every lawful undertaking, and bring us to the close of the day still surrounded with thy mercies, and still among the living to praise thee.

We look to thee for a blessing upon the inhabitants of this town, and all our towns. We pray for those who are languishing on beds of sickness, and have wearisome days and nights assigned them. Comfort all who mourn with the consolations of the Gospel, which hath abolished death, and brought life and immortality to light. Show thyself to be a Father of all the fatherless, the Judge and husband of the widow, the rod and staff of the aged, who tremble on the edge of the grave. Give repentance unto sinners; give comfort, confidence and hope, to the penitent; and bring all to the knowledge and obedience of the truth, that they may be saved. Denying ungodliness and worldly lusts, may they live soberly, righteously and piously, in this present world; looking for that blessed hope, the glorious appearance of our Lord Jesus Christ.

And wilt thou hasten the time when the mild and pacific principles of the Gospel of Jesus Christ shall take possession of all hearts, and unite the whole family of mankind in one great brotherhood, where there shall be no contest but for a crown of glory; no strife but to excel in deeds of benevolence, philanthropy and charity; no triumph but the triumph of truth; when the last universal empire shall be the empire of the Prince of peace, of the increase of whose government, and the duration of whose reign, there shall be no end. Thus throughout the world may he redeem from all iniquity, and purify unto himself a peculiar people, zealous of good works. And unto thee, the ever-living and only true God, through Jesus Christ would we ascribe everlasting praise. Amen.

XLI.

Daily Virtues.

Let love be without dissimulation. Abhor that which is evil; cleave to that which is good.

Be kindly affectioned one to another with brotherly love in honor preferring one another ;

Not slothful in business ; fervent in spirit ; serving the Lord ;

Rejoicing in hope ; patient in tribulation ; continuing instant in prayer ;

Distributing to the necessity of saints ; given to hospitality.

Bless them who persecute you ; bless, and curse not.

Rejoice with them that rejoice, and weep with them that weep.

Be of the same mind one toward another. Mind not high things, but condescend to men of low estate. Be not wise in your own conceits.

Recompense to no man evil for evil. Provide things honest in the sight of all men.

If it is possible, as much as lieth in you, live peaceably with all men.

Dearly beloved, avenge not yourselves, but rather give place to wrath : for it is written, Vengeance is mine ; I will repay, saith the Lord.

Therefore if thy enemy hunger, feed him ; if he thirst, give him drink : for in so doing thou shalt heap coals of fire on his head.

Be not overcome by evil, but overcome evil with good.

Most High and Mighty Lord, our God, to thee we owe again the pleasant light of the sun, the renewed strength of the morning, and the hopes of day. How benevolent is thy providence, and how rich is thy grace ! In thy light may we see light, and walk as children of the day, and shun all the works of darkness. Let it please thee to take us, and all things belonging to us, this day under thy fatherly care, and guide and bless us in all our ways. May we bear on our hearts a grateful sense of thy many mercies; and may we love as well as fear thee. May we suffer no cloud of unbelief or sin to come over us this day, to darken the sunlight of thy love.

Help us, O God, to improve our time and opportunities as gifts from thee. Make us diligent in business, fervent in spirit, serving the Lord. Aid us in keeping the body pure as the temple of the soul, and in consecrating the soul as the shrine of thine indwelling Spirit. Sanctify all our aims and wishes by a filial submission to thy holy will. May thine exceeding peace rule in our hearts; and may we possess our souls in the patience of faith and hope.

Endue us more and more, we pray thee, with the spirit of thy blessed Son, that we may dwell in him, and through him in thee, that we all may be one. Knowing that our life is but a vapor, may we so number our days as to apply our hearts unto wisdom. Prosper us as thou seest best in our lawful undertakings, but above all fit and prepare us, by all we do or suffer, for the everlasting blessedness of heaven. Forgive us our sins, and wean our hearts from them, that we may sin no more. As we go forth to the cares and labors of this day, may we carry the spirit of our blessed faith into every scene, and may it be a bright and beautiful light around our daily paths. In forbearance, generosity, sympathy and brotherly love, may we have our walk with our fellow-men, and may our example and influence be a blessing to all whom we may meet.

Most merciful God, may thy blessing rest on this household, and on all our absent friends. Take under thy benign care the poor, the sick, the afflicted, the oppressed and the dying, and let the deliverance of the Gospel come unto all men our brethren. These things we ask and offer in the name, which is above every name, of Jesus Christ thy well-beloved Son. Amen.

XLII.

Sunday Morning.

Open to me the gates of righteousness: I will enter them, and I will praise the Lord:

This gate of the Lord, into which the righteous shall enter.

I will praise thee: for thou hast heard me, and art become my salvation.

The stone which the builders refused is become the head stone of the corner.

This is the Lord's doing; it is wonderful in our eyes.

This is the day which the Lord hath made; we will rejoice and be glad in it.

Blessed be he that cometh in the name of the Lord: we have blessed you out of the house of the Lord.

God is the Lord, who hath shown us light: bind the sacrifice with cords, even to the horns of the altar.

Thou art my God, and I will praise thee: thou art my God, I will exalt thee.

O give thanks to the Lord; for he is good: for his mercy endureth forever.

Our Father who art in heaven, again the sun has risen at thy command. Through thine unsleeping providence, refreshed by slumber, we stand upon the threshold of another day,—a day of rest, of meditation, of worship, and of prayer. May it be sanctified in the outward observance, and in spirit, and in truth. Let that holy light, of which the sun shining in the firmament is but a dim symbol, dawn upon our souls, dispelling unhallowed thoughts, revealing thy glorious presence, and leading us onward to that better life upon which, through thy grace, may we enter. May this day, by the use which we make of its opportunities, by the answers of peace which it brings to our prayers, by the cleansing influences which it dispenses, prove a day never to be forgotten, a day worth ten thousand spent in the ways of the world.

O God, our Maker, who alone canst give us the light we need, unseal our spiritual vision. Make us to discern the greatness which this day commemorates. It speaks of thine abundant mercy; of that best gift of thine, thy holy child Jesus, who appeared among men in the power of thy Spirit, and in the fulness of thy divinity, and in whom the world saw the glory as of thy only-begotten Son. Glad tidings of great joy he brought from heaven to earth. Teach us the value of those gracious messages, that we may know how to thank thee, and that the hymns and praises that we sing this day may be the prompting and the tribute of our souls.

O God, let our faith be not in word only, but in power. May the spirit of thy Son be our spirit, the spring of our conduct, giving us strength to avoid every form of evil, and to cleave, amidst all temptations, to thy law. Thus open to us the gates of righteousness, that we may enter therein and praise the Lord. Then shall we know its priceless worth, when we have once tasted, by personal experience, of the heavenly gift. Then shall we bring no dead offering, but a living sacrifice, and our praises shall rise like incense up to the throne of God, and thou, ever more ready to give than we are to ask, wilt delight to pour down upon us more abundant measures of truth and holiness. So by true spiritual worship, by the private meditations and the public services of this day, may we go from grace to grace, and from strength to strength, until we stand forever in thy presence.

Merciful Father, we mourn that these our best desires are so faint; that we are so fondly attached to the things that perish, to the lust of the eyes and the pride of life; so seldom and so faintly impressed with the guilt of our ingratitude and disobedience, and that we live so willingly without God and a true hope. Increase our sorrow for our unworthiness, and make it that godly sorrow which will quicken us to instant and thorough amendment. Encompass our minds this day with thoughts of heaven. Give thine angels charge concerning us, that our feet may never more stumble, that we may run with patience the race that is set before us, in the straight and narrow way, looking unto Jesus, the author and finisher of our faith. O come, thou Spirit of truth, come and take up thine abode evermore in our souls! Be the life of our lives, a fountain springing up within us to everlasting life, that we may never thirst again, and that these waste places, our hearts, may become like the garden of the Lord!

Almighty God, may thy kingdom be advanced in all hearts this day. We pray for our brethren of every order and denomination. Dwell in the midst of all worshipping people. Let not this day be abused into an occasion of selfish indulgence, but may men hearken to the strong cries of their immortal souls, and be fed this day with bread from heaven. May the truth as it is in Jesus be everywhere faithfully proclaimed and received into honest and good minds, where it shall spring up and bring forth the immortal fruits of holy living. Send its blessed consolations into afflicted souls; let it bind up the broken-hearted, and give liberty to the captive. May it be like a sword to pierce the hearts of the thoughtless and rebellious; and let all who profess and call themselves Christians depart from iniquity, and lead godly and peaceable lives, glorifying thy Son, and thee the God and Father of all. To thee shall be the praise for ever and ever. Amen.

XLIII.

Sunday Morning.

God be merciful to us, and bless us; and cause his face to shine upon us.

That thy way may be known upon earth, thy saving health among all nations.

Let the people praise thee, O God; let all the people praise thee.

O let the nations be glad and sing for joy: for thou wilt judge the people righteously, and govern the nations upon earth.

Let the people praise thee, O God; let all the people praise thee.

Then shall the earth yield her increase; and God, even our own God, will bless us.

God will bless us, and all the ends of the earth shall fear him.

God of the Sabbath, we thank thee for this day of sacred rest. We welcome it with grateful hearts. Wearied with the cares and duties of another week, we need its calm repose, its holy quiet. May it be a sacred season to us all, a sabbath of the soul. May our bodies and spirits be refreshed. May this blessed day come freighted with good for our souls. While it reminds us of the blessings of the past week, may it also speak to us of Christ, whose resurrection sanctifies it, and makes it holy to Christian faith.

O, that the spirit of the risen Saviour might penetrate our hearts; that we might rise with him above all that is low and gross, impure and sinful, and sit with him in heavenly places this day! O, that his love might fill our hearts, and mould our spirits, and color every thought of our minds, and every act of our lives! Forgive us that we do not open our hearts more fully to his spirit and truth. Forgive us for every violation of that spirit during the past week. And now that a new week has opened upon us, now while we stand upon its threshold, help us to consecrate ourselves afresh to thy service.

We thank thee for all our Christian privileges. May we improve them wisely. We thank thee for the Bible. Make us to understand its teachings; to love its sacred truths. Aid us to a clear knowledge of the office and mission of thy Son. May we read his words with an understanding heart and an applying conscience. May the divine truths that fell from his lips dwell in our hearts by faith. May we love them; obey them; feed upon them as the bread of heaven.

We thank thee for the opportunities of public worship. May we go to the house of prayer this day with a reverent and worshipful spirit. May our thoughts and our conversation be such as become the Gospel. Save us from making our Father's house a house of merchandise. Make it indeed the house of God, and the gate of heaven to our souls. In sincerity and in truth let the people praise thee, O God, let all the people praise thee, that God may bless us, that thy saving health may be known among the nations.

Bless, we pray thee, our minister. May he be a true minister of Jesus Christ. May he be filled with the Master's spirit. May he be faithful in applying Christian truth to the sins of our own times, and of our own hearts. May he not shun to declare the whole counsel of God. May he speak the truth in love. May he win souls to Christ. May his words this day be fruitful of good to the souls of his flock; and may we all, pastor and people, be laborers together in our respective spheres of duty for the advancement of the Redeemer's kingdom.

Bless our Sunday-school. May it be a true school of Christ. May it lead children to the Saviour, and fill their young hearts with his love. Bless the teachers. May they feel the sacred character of their work. May its sacredness not discourage but inspire them. May they never grow weary in well-doing, but diligently scatter the good seed in faith and prayer.

Bless all the ministers of Christian faith and love everywhere. May the living word have free course, and be glorified, until all evil, wrong and sin, shall cease; until thy kingdom shall come, and thy will be done on earth as it is done in heaven, and thy way shall be known upon the earth, thy saving health among all nations. This we pray in the name of thy beloved Son. Amen.

XLIV.

Sunday Morning.

How amiable are thy tabernacles, O Lord of hosts.

My soul longeth, and even fainteth for the courts of the Lord; my heart and my flesh crieth out for the living God.

O Lord God of hosts, hear my prayer: give ear, O God of Jacob.

Behold, O God our shield, and look upon the face of thy anointed.

For a day in thy courts is better than a thousand. I would rather be a door-keeper in the house of my God, than to dwell in the tents of wickedness.

For the Lord God is a sun and shield: the Lord will give grace and glory: no good will he withhold from them that walk uprightly.

O Lord of hosts, blessed is the man that trusteth in thee.

Almighty God, our Heavenly Father, fill our hearts with joy that the light of another sacred day has risen upon us; a day of rest from our usual labors, a day of repose from our usual cares. How pleasant is this light to our eyes! how grateful is this rest to our hearts! Thou hast, in thy great goodness, our Father, caused this day to be set apart for worship, for religious meditation and spiritual communion. May its sacred hours be precious to us, and may we so improve them as to make a Sabbath-day's journey heavenward.

Aid us, Heavenly Father, as we study thy word, as we meditate upon thy truth at home. May we be comforted and strengthened by the promises con tained in the Gospel of thy Son. May we desire to partake more and more of his spirit; to be conformed more and more to his likeness; to become one with him as he is one with thee. We thank thee for the words of truth which he spake; for the life of holiness which he lived; and for the death of triumph which he died. May we be inspired with a deeper love of goodness as we read of his works of patience, and trust, and self-sacrifice; and, as we remember that this day is made dear to our hearts by his resurrection from the dead, may our faith in the future life be strengthened; may the spiritual world become to us a reality, since he has entered it.

Go with us, our Father, as we go to thy house to worship thee, with thy people. May we enter thy courts with thanksgiving, and thy gates with praise. May we bear to thine house the sacrifice of grateful and penitent hearts. And may those who worship with us worship in spirit and in truth. May we all leave our worldly cares behind us, and during the season of worship may our whole hearts be in communion with thee.

Give thy grace to the preacher of thy word, that he may so conduct the services of thy house as to make them a joy to our souls. May our pastor be helped by thee in the discharge of his arduous and responsible duties. Give him deep insight into thy truth. Give him a fervent spirit, that he may speak thy truth with power. And to all who hear give teachable, devout hearts, so that all thy people may offer to thee acceptable service this day. Revive, O our Father, pure and undefiled religion in this congregation. Arouse the church to a sense of their great obligations to live soberly, righteously and godly, so that others shall take knowledge of them that they have been with Jesus, and thus be won from sin to holiness. May worldliness and coldness and indolence disappear, and may thy people give themselves for a triumphant conflict with sin and ignorance.

And may a knowledge of the truth as it is in Jesus be spread abroad in all the churches in all the world. May those who love thee labor to send a knowledge of thee to those who know thee not. May those who now worship idols which their own hands have made, soon be taught to worship thee, the only living and true God. May the time be hastened when thy kingdom shall come and thy will be done on earth as it is in heaven, and thy name, O Father, shall have the praise through Jesus Christ evermore. Amen.

Evening Prayers.

EVENING PRAYERS.

I.

The Sure Defence.

The Lord hear thee in the day of trouble; the name of the God of Jacob defend thee.

Send thee help from the sanctuary, and strengthen thee out of Zion.

Remember all thy offerings, and accept thy burnt sacrifice

Grant thee according to thine own heart, and fulfil all thy counsel.

We will rejoice in thy salvation, and in the name of our God we will set up our banners: the Lord fulfil all thy petitions.

Now know I that the Lord saveth his anointed: he will hear him from his holy heaven with the saving strength of his right hand.

Some trust in chariots, and some in horses: but we will remember the name of the Lord our God.

Eternal God, Father of the family on earth and in heaven, we bless thee for our homes, and for the countless mercies which surround us now as we bring our evening offering to thine altar. Thou dost set the solitary in families, and it is thy love that inspires every true human affection. Thou hast ordained all the precious relations of the household. Thou hast established the ties of husband and wife, parent and child, brother and sister, and these ties are truly blessed when consecrated by thy grace. Enable us, O Lord, to bring all our thoughts, affections and purposes, to thee, and to order our whole plan of life within the courts of thy kingdom.

Teach us to look to thee for light and strength in the least and the greatest of our duties, that the whole round of our existence may be ruled by thy truth, and that our whole being may centre in thy love. May we learn to rule our children by ruling our own tempers through a divine faith, and thus bring the strength of heavenly grace to work upon their wayward impulses. Open thou within our household the springs of spiritual life, and may we all, both young and old, day by day, refresh ourselves by the living water. In our home may we rejoice to give the cheerfulness and strength of our affections to the service of religion, and deem no day so dark as that which shuts out the light of God from our souls, or closes our minds to the love unspeakable that dwells in our Lord and Saviour Jesus Christ.

Help us, O God, to remember wisely the former times; to gather cheerful wisdom from the remembrance of the by-gone years; to cherish with tender faith and affection the memory of departed kindred and friends, and from our experience of vicissitude and decay win new motives to hope and fidelity in years to come.

We pray for our friends now absent, and bless thee that all who love thy truth are in one favored fellowship, in one spiritual household, wherever they journey. Into that household lead us ever in more close and hallowed relations. Grant that even now our earthly home may open into heavenly mansions. And as we now rely on thy defence, and in thy name set up our banners, may we rejoice that the Lord sendeth help, and strengtheneth out of Zion, and will remember all our offerings and accept our evening sacrifice. To thy holy name be all glory forever. Amen.

II.

Looking Up.

Unto thee, O Lord, do I lift up my soul.

O my God, I trust in thee: let me not be ashamed; let not mine enemies triumph over me.

Yea, let none that wait on thee be ashamed: let them be ashamed which transgress without cause.

Show me thy ways, O Lord; teach me thy paths.

Lead me in thy truth, and teach me: for thou art the God of my salvation; on thee do I wait all the day.

Remember, O Lord, thy tender mercies, and thy loving-kindnesses; for they have been ever of old.

Remember not the sins of my youth, nor my transgressions:

according to thy mercy remember thou me, for thy goodness' sake, O Lord.

Good and upright is the Lord: therefore will he teach sinners in the way.

The meek will he guide in judgment, and the meek will he teach his way.

All the paths of the Lord are mercy and truth unto such as keep his covenant and his testimonies.

FATHER, the day which thou hast given us is spent. We thank thee for the good which it hath borne to us, and for the quietness with which it is closed. For the strength and the health which we have enjoyed, for the powers and the opportunities of labor, and for the fruit growing and gathered of our efforts, we render thanks to thee. From thee cometh all; by thee the whole is preserved continually; to thee let each return. When through the day perils have been near us more than we could see, only thy power hath saved us. When joys have gathered over us, these are thine, and the feeling of thy love is their crown. Father, we thank thee for thy gifts.

O Thou, to whom the depths of our hearts are open, we need not declare the sins which thou seest, and which we mourn. We would not forget the beauty of the soul even in us; through all stains and defilements help us to perceive thine image in which man is made, that we may know thee with us and in us, that we may feel the unspeakable worth of our being and that we may be raised through love and sorrow to repentance, to purity, to communion with thee. Whatever in the unceasing currents of our thought, whatever in the changing excitements of our feeling, whatever in our words spoken or suppressed, in our deeds done or omitted, contrary to the conscience of good, darkening to the soul, unkind to thy children, disobedient to thee, strengthen us to see with clear insight, incline us to confess with free penitence, quicken us to throw from us hereafter and forever. Thou askest neither penance nor sacrifice; thou puttest us not in anger away from thee; thy mercy is near to us every hour; greater than the number or the guilt of our sins is the love in which thou dost call and welcome the sorrowing soul. Father, we come unto thee; thy peace is over us, an infinite Sabbath.

Thine hath been the day; thine is now the night. While thou art opening other lands and seas to the beams of thy rising sun, thou hast brought to us the hour of its decline. In stillness thy twilight has come and gone; in stillness thy night is passing, thy stars are shining, thy creatures are at rest. Now that we lay us down to sleep, we trust ourselves to thy care. Pour through us gentle and refreshing influence. If it be thy will that we live through these hours, protected only by thee, prepare us for truer and holier service on the morrow. Even if our waking should be where this sun of ours cometh not from its east, we would not fear; thou art with us; take thou these waiting souls.

Soon the last evening shall spread over us from thee. Father, may we be ready. We have wept for the dear ones whom thou hast withdrawn from us; our eyes shall overflow with new joy that thou keepest them in safety and peace. They live in thee; may we live in thee the short day we are spending on earth; may we live in thee through the life which transcends earth and overcomes death. With the great multitude which no man can number, of all nations, and kindred, and people, and tongues, standing before the throne and before the Lamb, may we join the loud voice — Salvation to our God who sitteth upon the throne, and unto the Lamb! Amen.

III.

God our Portion.

The day is thine, the night also is thine: thou hast prepared the light and the sun.

I am continually with thee: thou hast held me by my right hand.

Thou wilt guide me with thy counsel, and afterward receive me to glory.

Whom have I in heaven but thee? and there is none upon earth that I desire besides thee.

My flesh and my heart faileth: but God is the strength of my heart, and my portion forever.

For lo, they that are far from thee shall perish : thou hast destroyed all them that go astray from thee.

But it is good for me to draw near to God : I have put my trust in the Lord God, that I may declare thy works.

O LORD GOD, Father of all Mercies, we desire to offer up to thee, before we seek repose, our evening sacrifice of prayer and praise. We bless thee for thy goodness to us during the past day, and we beseech thee to continue to us thy gracious protection during this night. Thou sustainest us, though we see thee not. Whom have we in heaven but thee? Whom on earth shall we desire beside thee? Thou art our support in trouble; our guide in difficulty; our best consolation in time of sickness; our only refuge in the hour of death.

Thou knowest our ways and our hearts. Pardon, we beseech thee, whatever evil we have said, or thought, or done, this day. Teach us continually to examine our hearts by the light of thy holy word; and grant unto us true repentance and faith in our Lord and Saviour. May we manifest those tempers, and abound in those works, which his Gospel requires. May we be full of meekness and patience, of kindness and forbearance, of benevolence and charity; and, being established in the love of God, may we also love our neighbors with a pure heart fervently.

We beseech thee to bless unto us the events of thy providence; and so to order all things, during the remainder of our lives, that they may issue in our eternal good. We know not what a day may bring forth; but thou knowest all things, the strength of our hearts, and our portion forever from the beginning to the end. O, sanctify unto us our prosperity and our adversity, our sickness and our health, and in all conditions grant unto us grateful and contented minds. While we live on the earth guide us by thy counsel, and afterward receive us to thy glory.

We commend to thee the young and the old, the strong and the feeble, the happy and the afflicted. Grant unto all the needful spirit of thy grace, the remission of sins, and life everlasting, through Jesus Christ our Lord. Amen.

IV.

Seeking a Clean Heart.

Create in me a clean heart, O God; and renew a right spirit within me.

Cast me not away from thy presence; and take not thy Holy Spirit from me.

Restore to me the joy of thy salvation; and uphold me with thy free Spirit.

Then will I teach transgressors thy ways; and sinners shall be converted to thee.

O Lord, open thou my lips; and my mouth shall show forth thy praise.

For thou desirest not sacrifice: else would I give it: thou delightest not in burnt-offering.

The sacrifices of God are a broken spirit: a broken and a contrite heart, O God, thou wilt not despise.

O LORD, our Heavenly Father, the day is thine, and the night also thine. The light and the darkness, thou hast created them. They are both alike unto thee, who seest through the thickest shades, and whose care never slumbers nor sleeps; and they both alike unto us reveal thy gracious providence. We would show forth thy loving-kindness in the morning, and thy faithfulness every night.

We thank thee for thy goodness to us during the day that is now past. We thank thee that we have been preserved from its various perils, seen and unseen, and kept in our going out and our coming in; that no calamity has befallen our condition, and no burthen more than we could bear been laid upon our strength. We thank thee for all the instruction we have received, whether through our outward experience or thy good Spirit; for all that we have tasted of thy bounty, and seen of thy truth. We thank thee for every social and domestic comfort that we have enjoyed; for every faithful exercise in which we have been allowed to partake; for every good purpose that thou hast strengthened us to fulfil; for whatever blessing has flowed through the senses, or been imparted to the soul. We owe all to thee, on whom we absolutely depend, and in whom alone we truly live.

O Lord, who searchest the hearts of the children of men, with the acknowledgment of thy constant favors it becomes us to mingle the feeling of our sinfulness and ill-desert. We are not worthy of the least of thy mercies, though thou passest before us in innumerable benefits, and carest for us with all this care. May thy goodness lead us to repentance, that we may be ashamed of our unthankfulness, and turn from every thought of disobedience unto thee. Forgive us, we beseech thee, whatever we have done amiss this day, and whatever we have failed to do which thy law within us enjoined.

And now, Searcher of hearts, we would enter into a solemn self-examination. If we have indulged any evil habit or passion, if we have dealt unreasonably with our brother, or lost the control of ourselves, if we have allowed the hours of this opportunity and probation to run to waste, or if we have abused them to any corrupt affection or evil design, we entreat of thee, O Father, the pardon of these sins. Create within us clean hearts, and renew a right spirit within us; and let this entreaty fill us with earnest resolutions for the time to come, if we are permitted to see it, that it shall find us more truly inclined to thy will, and walking in thy way.

And now, Lord, we commit ourselves to thee this night. Draw around us with its shadows the peace of thy Spirit, and the strength of thy defence. When we can do nothing for ourselves, do all for us. Before we lose all will of our own in dreams and unconsciousness, we would solemnly renounce every intention of wrong; we would cast out from our hearts every disposition of enmity; we would be of a forgiving spirit; we would have no variance with the world that is soon to become to us for a season as if it were not; we would repose ourselves upon thy sovereign will, even thine only. And when we come to lie down in the last sleep, may thy mercies surround us with their security, and enfold us in their peace, and crown us with the redemption that has been revealed to us by Jesus Christ our Lord. Amen.

V.

Encouragements to Pray.

Ask, and it shall be given you; seek, and ye shall find, knock, and the door shall be opened to you:

For every one that asketh, receiveth; and he that seeketh, findeth; and to him that knocketh, the door shall be opened.

Or what man is there of you, who, if his son shall ask bread, will give him a stone?

Or if he shall ask a fish, will he give him a serpent?

If ye then being evil know how to give good gifts to your children, how much more shall your Father who is in heaven give good things to them that ask him?

Therefore all things whatever ye would that men should do to you, do ye even so to them: for this is the law and the prophets.

Now the God of peace, that brought again from the dead our Lord Jesus, that great Shepherd of the sheep, through the blood of the everlasting covenant,

Make you perfect in every good work to do his will, working in you that which is well-pleasing in his sight, through Jesus Christ; to whom be glory for ever and ever. Amen.

FATHER of our spirits, we bless thee that the peaceful hour of evening has come to us once more, and that we may hear the voice of thy mercy in the invitation to rest. In thee may we find rest to our souls. Without trust in thy love there is no true peace for us upon our pillow, and with thy presence only can we know the true refreshing of our souls. Lord, draw near to us now, and keep us within the shadow of thy wings. We thank thee that a Father's ear is opened to the cry of thy children, and that there is no truly good thing which thou wilt not give to the asking soul.

We would solemnly review the experience of this day. We would bless thee for whatever good we have been enabled to do or enjoy. We implore thy forgiveness for all our transgressions of thy holy will. We beseech thee to bestow upon us thy grace to enable us to overcome our peculiar faults, and to grow in the true life of children of God. Let our own earnest self-examination bring this day's record before the throne of thy judgment. May every day find us more obedient to the golden rule of our great

Teacher. Thus help us to prepare ourselves for the day of account.

We commit to thy guardian care all our kindred and friends, imploring for them the blessings of health of body and peace of mind. We pray for the poor, and sick, and bereaved; for the oppressed, the benighted, the lonely, and the abandoned, we implore thy grace. Lord, forgive our sins, and teach us true forgiveness of those who sin against us. Bring on the blessed time when every wanderer shall return to the Father, and shall come to himself in coming to his God.

Now that we are to give ourselves to refreshing slumber, may we wisely interpret its solemn meaning, and own the divine power that continues within us the motions of healthful life whilst we are wholly unconscious. May it be to us an image of the blessed rest in God which the soul shall know when her weary strivings are ended, and we may hope to enter upon the perfect peace that lives, and moves, and has its being, in God. Lord, rebuke our wilfulness, and win us unto the blessed subjection of thy holy will. In our labor and in our rest, work thou in our souls to do and to will that which is pleasing in thy sight, till we are made perfect through Jesus Christ. In the name of that great Shepherd of the sheep, who through the everlasting covenant offered himself for us, do we ascribe unto thee, the God of peace, glory for ever and ever. Amen.

VI.

Grateful Confidence.

O give thanks unto the Lord; for he is good: because his mercy endureth forever.

Let Israel now say, that his mercy endureth forever.

Let the house of Aaron now say, that his mercy endureth forever.

Let them now that fear the Lord say, that his mercy endureth forever.

The Lord is on my side; I will not fear: what can man do unto me?

It is better to trust in the Lord than to put confidence in man:

It is better to trust in the Lord than to put confidence in princes.

The Lord is my strength and song, and is become my salvation.

The voice of rejoicing and salvation is in the tabernacles of the righteous: the right hand of the Lord doeth valiantly.

We humbly thank thee, merciful Father, for thy goodness in conducting us to the close of this day, and for all thy mercies bestowed upon us from day to day. Add this to all thy favors, we beseech thee, that we may never forget to be thankful, but may constantly acknowledge thee as the source of all our blessings, and praise thee, our strength, and song, and our salvation. Write thy law upon our hearts, that all our desires, words and actions, may be conformable to thy holy will.

And now, remembering thy mercies hitherto vouchsafed to us, we do entirely trust thee for the time to come. Thy mercy endureth forever. The Lord is on our side, and we will not fear. For this only we are anxious, and do earnestly pray, that we may, all our days, serve and please thee in such a constant practice of piety, righteousness and mercy, of temperance, meekness, patience, truth and fidelity, that the voice of rejoicing may ever be heard in our tabernacle, and we may commend the religion and name of our Lord and Master, Jesus Christ, unto all.

Accept, O God, as the testimony of our love and charity, our hearty intercessions for all mankind. Let the glorious light of thy Gospel shine upon all nations; and grant that all who have already received it may adorn its doctrine in all things.

O Lord, by thine own right hand, which doeth valiantly, continue thy gracious protection to us this night. Into thy care we commend ourselves, our souls and bodies, and all things belonging to us. Long continue to us our domestic prosperity, and let not this circle be invaded by sickness or death. Bind our hearts to thee by ties of which the ties of earth are but feeble types. And make us mindful, we pray thee, of that time when we shall lie down in the dust, and grant us grace always to live in such a state that we may be a family in heaven. And now to thee, our God and Father, we ascribe all honor and glory through Jesus Christ. Amen.

VII.

The Giver and Preserver.

Preserve me, O God: for in thee do I put my trust

O my soul, thou hast said unto the Lord, Thou art my Lord: my goodness extendeth not to thee;

But to the saints that are in the earth, and to the excellent, in whom is all my delight.

The Lord is the portion of mine inheritance, and of my cup: thou maintainest my lot.

The lines are fallen unto me in pleasant places; yea, I have a goodly heritage.

I will bless the Lord, who hath given me counsel; my reins also instruct me in the night-seasons.

I have set the Lord always before me: because he is at my right hand, I shall not be moved.

O God our Father, thou causest thy sun to rise, and we go forth to our work until the evening. Thou makest darkness, and it is night, wherein all lie down to rest. Brought safely through the dangers and experiences of another day, we lay on our family altar the evening sacrifice of prayer and praise. Holy Father, how sweet this rest, after the toils and fatigues of the day! How grateful this domestic peace, after the noise and confusion of the world! How delightful the confidence and affections of home, after the competitions and rivalries of business! To thy fatherly care and love we owe all these provisions of mercy. Thou maintainest our lot, and givest us lines that have fallen in pleasant places, and our goodly heritage.

And when we look back on the past day, amidst all its toils and cares, how many mercies of thine have crowned it with blessings! Thou hast given relish to our food, zest to our pleasures, and pleasure even to our toils. While others have fallen into sorrows, and would give worlds if they could regain what they have lost, thou hast kept our feet from falling, our eyes from tears, and our souls from death. Thou hast given invention to our minds, cunning to our right hands, and success to all our labors. Thou hast surrounded us with friendly counsel and sympathy, and by thy Holy Spirit rebuked every wrong desire, and promoted holy aspirations. For these, and the other mercies of the past day, which are more than we can number and richer than we can estimate, we would render thee the homage of grateful and adoring hearts.

O God our Judge, another day has gone, with its solemn account, to bear witness for or against us at thy tribunal. We confess, with sorrow, that we have done many things which we ought not to have done, and left undone many things which we ought to have done. For all our misspent time and neglected opportunities; for all our wrong motives and unchristian feelings; for all our irregular desires, vain hopes, and foolish fears, we would supplicate thy pardoning mercy. We fear that pride and moral insensibility have concealed from our view many sins which have been open to thine all-seeing eye. Open our eyes to behold our moral condition; touch our hearts with true penitence, that we may not lie down to rest with the burden of unrepented sin upon our consciences, and the frown of thy displeasure on our slumbers, O thou in whose protection is all our hope.

To thee, who dost never slumber, and to whom the darkness is as the light, as we lie down to rest and resign ourselves to unconsciousness, do we now commit our bodies and spirits. Defend us, we implore thee, from the devouring flames, from the assaults of violence, from the attacks of disease. And as sleep brings refreshment to our toil-worn bodies and care-worn minds, let rest from earthly cares and passions renew a tenderness of spirit, a sensibility to conscience, a sense of thy presence and love. And as the dew refreshes the parched earth and revives the drooping plants, so may the dews of thy grace refresh our hearts, and revive our best affections and desires. Keep us in safety through the silent watches of the night, and open our eyelids on a morning filled with holy thoughts, and consecrated to thy service. Or, if our bed should prove our grave, awake us at the glorious morn of the resurrection, with spirits disenthralled, and prepared to enter thy service, and behold thy glories, and enjoy thy love. These thanksgivings and supplications we offer in the name of Jesus Christ our Lord, through whom unto thee we ascribe all glory, and honor, and praise. Amen.

VIII.

Continual Praise.

I will bless the Lord at all times: his praise shall continually be in my mouth.

My soul shall make her boast in the Lord: the humble shall hear thereof, and be glad.

O magnify the Lord with me, and let us exalt his name together.

I sought the Lord, and he heard me, and delivered me from all my fears.

They looked unto him, and were lightened; and their faces were not ashamed.

The poor man cried, and the Lord heard him, and saved him out of all his troubles.

The angel of the Lord encampeth round about them that fear him, and delivereth them.

O taste and see that the Lord is good: blessed is the man that trusteth in him.

O LORD, Maker of heaven and earth, we cast ourselves on thy care for this coming night. Weary with the labors to which thou grantest our daily bread, and filled with the experience of many lessons of thy providence, we seek the wonderful refreshment thy wisdom has prepared for our bodies and our souls. We bless thee for the grateful vicissitudes of day and night, labor and rest, wakefulness and sleep. Thou sendest us forth into the world thou hast made, to the society thou hast ordained for us. We thank thee for the provision thou hast made for our necessities, knowledge for our minds, friends for our hearts, obstacles to strengthen our will, trials to deepen our faith, successes to cheer our hope. In all we perceive and adore our great Taskmaster's faithfulness, and bless the gracious hand with which he mingles our cup. Thy praise shall be continually in our mouths.

And now that we commit ourselves to thy care during the darkness that gathers round us, we desire to review our lives, to confess our sins, and implore thy forgiveness. We look back upon many omissions of duty, on many acts of careless or wilful offence against thy holy law. We have allowed the world too much room in our hearts. We have yielded to the seductions of sloth or of pleasure, and to the love of money or the fear of man. O God, rescue us from the bondage of iniquity. Break this tyrannous sceptre of the world which usurps thy throne in our hearts. Suffer not the convictions and desires of our better hours, when thy Spirit is nigh, to expire in the moment of temptation, and the season of trial.

We fervently pray, O God, that thy kingdom may come, thy will be done in earth as it is done in heaven. We deplore the unchristian customs, the negligent ways, the cruelties and wrongs, of society; and especially ask thy pardon for whatever we are doing, by our sloth or our activity, to perpetuate their existence, or delay their extinction. Give new power to thy Gospel over our hearts and throughout the world, that its blessed Spirit may overcome every high thing that is set against it, and establish the pure worship of thy holiness, the love of Christ, and the brotherhood of our race, in all parts of the earth.

Father of our spirits, we adore thee with the last strength of this day. We worship thee, not for what thou canst do for us, but for what thou art in thyself. Source of all truth, beauty and goodness, in our deep sleep steal thou into our unresisting hearts, and impress thine image freshly on our souls. We would rest in thy arms, and awake in thy likeness.

And when, O Lord, our day of life is over, and the great night cometh, may a glorious resurrection bring us to the light of the everlasting morning of thy presence. We ask it in the name of thy Son our Saviour. Amen.

IX.

Trust and Courage.

The Lord is my light and my salvation; whom shall I fear? the Lord is the strength of my life; of whom shall I be afraid?

One thing have I desired of the Lord, that will I seek after; that I may dwell in the house of the Lord all the days of my life, to behold the beauty of the Lord, and to inquire in his temple.

For in the time of trouble he will hide me in his pavilion: in the secret of his tabernacle will he hide me; he will set me up upon a rock.

Hear, O Lord, when I cry with my voice: have mercy also upon me, and answer me.

When thou saidst, Seek ye my face; my heart said to thee, Thy face, Lord, will I seek.

Hide not thy face from me; put not thy servant away in anger: thou hast been my help; leave me not, neither forsake me, O God of my salvation.

I had fainted, unless I had believed to see the goodness of the Lord in the land of the living.

Wait on the Lord: be of good courage, and he will strengthen thy heart: wait, I say, on the Lord.

O God, the strength of our life, and our help in all time. Another day of our life on earth bears testimony to thy loving-kindness and tender mercy. We have gone out and come in before thee. Thou compassest our path and our lying down. What shall we render unto thee for all thy immeasurable goodness, which is new every morning, and fresh every evening? Every day may we do good, and not evil, in the world. Every day may we love thee more, and serve thee better. Accept whatever thou hast seen to be right, and pity and pardon whatever thou hast seen to be wrong. Confirm all that thou seest to be good, and cleanse us of all that is evil.

Since in thee we live, and move, and have our being, may we rest by night and by day in the arms of thy protection, and fear not. Let a devout and cheerful confidence take entire possession of our souls, that we may have no undue anxiety for the future, and dread no evil so much as the evil of sinning against thee. To thee the darkness shineth as the day, and thou keepest watch round about our pillow. We sleep in thee, and when we awake we are still with thee.

Graciously guard us and our dwelling this night from all manner of harm, and open upon us the light of another day, if it be thy pleasure, in peace and safety. While we here this night wait on the Lord, wilt thou strengthen our hearts, and give us to see yet more of the goodness of the Lord in the land of the living. And when we sleep the sleep of death, may it be in the full and sustaining hope of our resurrection from the night of death, and our entrance into the light of the everlasting day. Through him who loved us and gave himself for us, our Lord and Master, we give thee all praise and glory forever. Amen.

X.

Safety in God.

The Lord hath set apart him that is godly for himself: the Lord will hear when I call unto him.

Stand in awe, and sin not: commune with your own heart upon your bed, and be still.

Offer the sacrifices of righteousness, and put your trust in the Lord.

There be many that say, Who will show us any good? Lord, lift thou up the light of thy countenance upon us.

Thou hast put gladness in my heart, more than in the time that their corn and their wine increased.

I will both lay me down in peace, and sleep: for thou, Lord, only makest me dwell in safety.

Eternal God, whose gracious hand has led us to the close of another day, before we shut our eyes upon the world, and lose the sense of ourselves and thee, we would acknowledge thy love, and confide ourselves to thy care. We come to offer thee nightly sacrifice, and to put our trust in the Lord.

We bless the goodness that has crowned this day, and gratefully recognize in its events the boundless extent of thy providence. How manifold the experiences, how numerous the teachers, how varied the blessings, of our human lot! Whether thou sendest joy or sorrow, health or sickness, we desire to submit our souls to thee as to a faithful Creator, who knowest all thy children's wants, and art ever studying their highest good.

With the thought of thy daily goodness we would join the remembrance of our neglects and sins. O God, subdue the wilfulness, scatter the blindness, and correct the levity, of our hearts. And as with every setting sun our time of probation draws towards its close, deepen our sense of accountability, and prepare us for the judgment-seat of thy Son. O, how shall we appear! We implore thy grace to wash away our sins, thy Holy Spirit to touch and heal our hearts. O Lord, hear the voice of our complaint.

Have compassion on our weakness, and suffer us not to waste our fleeting lives in folly, or to meet our approaching fate without preparation.

We commend ourselves as a family to thy protection and blessing, praying that thou wouldst make us to dwell in safety. Increase our love to each other and to thee. Forgive our offences against the law of kindness; our parental negligence; our filial disobedience; our weaknesses of temper, deviations from truth, or lack of love. Make our home the threshold of heaven, and grant that our love towards those we have seen may grow into a perfect love for Him who is invisible.

Heavenly Father, watch our slumbers; renew our lives; put the gladness of a new day into our hearts, and from day to day lift upon us the light of thy countenance, till we shall see thee face to face, when suns shall no more go down. And to thy holy name be all glory. Amen.

XI

The Shadow of the Almighty.

He that dwelleth in the secret place of the Most High shall abide under the shadow of the Almighty.

I will say of the Lord, He is my refuge and my fortress: my God; in him will I trust.

Surely he will deliver thee from the snare of the fowler, and from the noisome pestilence.

He will cover thee with his feathers, and under his wings shalt thou trust: his truth shall be thy shield and buckler.

Thou shalt not be afraid for the terror by night; nor for the arrow that flieth by day;

Nor for the pestilence that walketh in darkness; nor for the destruction that wasteth at noon-day.

Because thou hast made the Lord who is my refuge, even the Most High, thy habitation;

There shall no evil befall thee, neither shall any plague come nigh thy dwelling.

For he will give his angels charge over thee, to keep thee in all thy ways.

Because he hath set his love upon me, therefore will I deliver him: I will set him on high, because he hath known my name.

He shall call upon me, and I will answer him: I will be with him in trouble; I will deliver him and honor him.

With long life will I satisfy him, and show him my salva tion.

ALMIGHTY and ever-blessed Father, guided by thy gentle hand, we have reached the close of another day. May all that is within us praise and magnify thine holy name. Thanks be unto thee for this new experience of life, for all the light which thou hast poured upon our various paths, and for that patience which hath borne with our great unfaithfulness. We cannot number up the mercies which have made these hours profitable and glad; yet would we strive to feel and confess that thou hast been a father unto us. In all our successes and in all our trials, in all our joys and in all our sorrows, thou hast blessed us;

for in all ways thou hast sought to save our souls alive, and establish us in the heavenly dwelling-places.

Unto every open heart thou hast drawn very near this day in the Gospel of thy Son; and if at any time we have been weary and heavily-laden, his cross hath spoken to us his sweet and comfortable words. It is of thy goodness that we are still gathered in this earthly household, for thine is the breath of every living thing. O Lord, when we examine ourselves whether we be in the faith and love of the Gospel, we must confess our short-comings. How far we are from thee! How often we forget the Master! Blessed be thy name for the covenant of forgiveness in his precious blood. Fill us with a godly sorrow and a saving hope. Forgive us through him who died, and let us be renewed in the spirit and temper of our minds.

O Lord, who through thy Son hast bound us anew together, and appointed for us a new law of brotherly love, may we be indeed a Christian household, and may our prayers go up unto thee for kindred and brethren. Be very near unto those for whom the watches of this night shall be hours of pain. May their thought be of thee, and of him who was a man of sorrows, and of that rest which remaineth for the children of God.

O thou everlasting Friend, enlighten our darkness; let the close of each day find us nearer to thee, and in more perfect fellowship with those holy ones who, having lived and died in thy faith and fear, have entered into the joy of their Lord. O Father, watch over us during the hours of slumber. Let us abide this night under the shadow of the Almighty. Under the shelter of thy wings let us trust, and be thou our shield and buckler. And when our last day shall come, may no night gather about our souls, but may the Lord of life be our light and guide. To thee through him shall be the praise. Amen.

XII.

The Deliverer from Peril.

And straightway Jesus constrained his disciples to get into a ship, and to go before him unto the other side, while he sent the multitudes away.

And when he had sent the multitudes away he went up into a mountain apart to pray: and when the evening was come he was there alone.

But the ship was now in the midst of the sea tossed with waves: for the wind was contrary.

And in the fourth watch of the night Jesus went unto them walking on the sea.

And when the disciples saw him walking on the sea they were troubled, saying, It is a spirit; and they cried out for fear.

But straightway Jesus spake unto them, saying, Be of good cheer: it is I; be not afraid.

And Peter answered him and said, Lord, if it be thou, bid me come unto thee on the water.

And he said, Come. And when Peter was come down out of the ship, he walked on the water to go to Jesus.

But when he saw the wind boisterous he was afraid; and, beginning to sink, he cried, saying, Lord, save me.

And immediately Jesus stretched forth his hand, and caught him, and said unto him, O thou of little faith, wherefore didst thou doubt?

O, OUR GOD, again, as the thick shades of night fall on us, and, after the cares and toils of the day, we seek the refreshing sleep thou hast provided for tired man, we would devoutly commend ourselves to thy sovereign keeping. Through all the perils of this night wilt thou preserve us, in the time of our necessity sending us a divine help like that which walked in the night on the waves of the sea to sustain the sinking disciple. May we this night hear the voice of a like watchful love say to us, Be of good cheer; and neither now nor ever may that voice ask us, Wherefore didst thou doubt, O thou of little faith?

For what we have done amiss forgive us, merciful Lord. If we have strayed from thee, or forgotten thee, O now, in this silent and secluded hour, help us to repent, to resolve anew with better and firmer vows. Let us feel thy Spirit breathing love and serenity into our hearts.

And now, Almighty God, as the favored children of heavenly grace, let our sleep be sweet, and thy banner over us be love. We pray for others, our dear ones at home and abroad. May they lie down in innocence, sleep in peace, and awake in grateful joy. And when our days and nights on earth are ended, O take us all to thyself in the immortal blessedness of heaven. We offer this prayer most humbly in the name of our Lord and Master Jesus Christ. Amen.

XIII.

The Lord our Shepherd.

The Lord is my shepherd; I shall not want.

He maketh me to lie down in green pastures: he leadeth me beside the still waters.

He restoreth my soul: he leadeth me in the paths of righteousness for his name's sake.

Yes, though I walk through the valley of the shades of death, I will fear no evil: for thou art with me; thy rod and thy staff they comfort me.

Thou preparest a table before me in the presence of my enemies: thou anointest my head with oil; my cup runneth over.

Surely goodness and mercy shall follow me all the days of my life: and I will dwell in the house of the Lord forever.

Our Father and our God, all honor, and glory, and dominion, and power, be given unto thee for ever and ever. All thy works praise thee, and may all thy saints bless thee. The mercies, deliverances and blessings, of another day, demand our gratitude. In going out and in coming in, thou, the good Shepherd, hast led our steps, and our paths have been in green pastures, and beside the still waters. We have lived upon the bounties of thy love, and been satisfied; for goodness and mercy have followed us all the day. Thou hast breathed upon our souls, and thine inspiration hath given us understanding. Thou hast opened the whole creation of heaven and earth to our view, that we might be led by what is seen and temporal to thee the Unseen and Eternal.

Thou hast visited us this day, and tried us every hour, that our hearts might incline to follow the Lord our God. Have mercy upon us that we receive in no wiser or better spirit the ceaseless lessons of thy love. But as the day is now gone, and its opportunities can never be recalled, we would gather up in this evening hour all it has given us and taught us, and erect a new memorial of praise. Forgive us, O God, if in aught we have been blind to the glories of the day which thou hast made, or careless of its duties, or deaf to its invitations, or ungrateful for its benefits, or forgetful of its everlasting consequences. May the deep consciousness that thou, our heavenly Father, hast made and given us all these things, abide evermore in us.

And now, as thou dost draw the curtains of darkness again around us, may we rest in thee and fear no evil. Grant us, if it be thy holy pleasure, quiet and refreshing repose, and a glad awakening on the morrow. And as by the close of the day thou remindest us of the end of all earthly things, and gently callest on us to prepare for the final sleep of death, O God, fit us for that solemn event, that we may enter the shades of the tomb without fear or doubt, having thy presence with us, and thy rod and thy staff to comfort us. With our sins forgiven and our souls sanctified, may we meet thee in peace, and dwell in the house of the Lord forever. We ask it, through thine abounding mercy, in Jesus our Lord. Amen.

XIV.

Israel's Shepherd.

Give ear, O Shepherd of Israel, thou that leadest Joseph like a flock; thou that dwellest between the cherubim, shine forth.

The day is thine, the night also is thine; thou hast pre pared the light and the sun.

Look upon us, we beseech thee, O Lord God of hosts, cause thy face to shine, and we shall be saved.

Help us, O God of our salvation, for the glory of thy name, and deliver us, and purge away our sins, for thy name's sake

I am continually with thee. Thou hast holden me by thy right hand.

Thou shalt guide me with thy counsel, and afterward receive me to glory.

So we thy people, and sheep of thy pasture, will give thee thanks forever; we will show forth thy praise to all generations.

O Thou who alone art good, it is very sweet and

our bounden duty, when we rest from the service and joy of the day, to come into thy gracious presence, and meditate at the feet of the blessed Lord. Let this be peace and refreshment unto us as we journey through the world.

Thanks be unto thee, O thou who leadest us like a flock. Thou hast heard our prayers, thou hast supplied our wants, and even when we have forgotten thee thou hast not forgotten us. We have labored and enjoyed under thy blessing. If we have been patient in tribulation, if we have followed after charity, if we have obeyed the Master in any good measure, it was thy Spirit in our hearts. Thou hast opened the door of the everlasting life unto all who knocked. Father, we thank thee; make us more thankful.

O Lord, we need to be forgiven; let thy mercies abound towards us. Let us not say we were tempted of thee, but may we take unto ourselves guilt and shame, and in all sorrow of heart confide only in that great love wherewith thou dost love us in the dying Lord. Purge away our sins, for thy name's sake. May we henceforth so strive against evil that we shall make each new day better than the past. As our day passes into night, we would call to mind the night of death and the morning of resurrection.

Father, station thine holy angels about the sick and the dying; turn the wicked from his purpose; be with the tempted, the friendless, the disconsolate; raise up guides for poor wanderers. Shield us all this night from harm. May our rest prepare us for new faithfulness in our various stations; and when for us this sun in the heavens shall be clouded, and these stars shall withdraw their shining, may we pass out into an unclouded day, through the riches of thy grace in Christ Jesus our Lord. So we thy people, and the sheep of thy pasture, will give thee thanks forever, and show forth thy loving-kindness to all generations. Amen.

XV.

Pardon and Protection.

Be merciful to me, O Lord : for I cry to thee daily.

Rejoice the soul of thy servant : for to thee, O Lord, do I lift up my soul.

For thou, Lord, art good, and ready to forgive ; and abundant in mercy to all them that call upon thee.

Give ear, O Lord, to my prayer ; and attend to the voice of my supplications.

In the day of my trouble I will call upon thee : for thou wilt answer me.

Among the gods there is none like thee, O Lord ; neither are there any works like thy works.

All nations whom thou hast made shall come and worship before thee, O Lord ; and shall glorify thy name.

For thou art great, and doest wondrous things : thou art God alone.

Teach me thy way, O Lord ; I will walk in thy truth : unite my heart to fear thy name.

I will praise thee, O Lord my God, with all my heart: and I will glorify thy name forevermore.

O Thou who art the Father of mercies and the Giver of all good, the day is thine, with its powers of action and its opportunities of good: the night also is thine, with its welcome rest to the body and the soul. Thanks be unto thee for the ever-varied, daily-multiplied gifts of thy paternal love. O, that we might be more worthy of thy care; more alive to thy goodness; more faithful to thy law; more diligent in the right use of the time and the talents committed to our trust!

Lord, thou knowest how the hours of this day, given us by thee, have been spent; how its duties have been done; how its temptations have been met; how its trials have been borne. If in aught we have failed or fallen, God of mercy, forgive us; and grant that wherein we have done wrong we may do so no more; but with a holy steadfastness of purpose may we choose and follow that which is good, and make the future redeem the past.

Be merciful unto us, O God; for unto thee do we cry. Help us in our weakness. Help us to do thy will, and to be what thou lovest, followers of thy dear Son. May we be fellow-workers with him and with thee in doing good, as we have opportunity, unto all. And may it be our joy and crown to promote the happiness and peace, the present and the eternal good, of those who are near and dear to us. If it please thee, O God, who alone knowest what is best, we beseech thee long to preserve their lives to be the blessings of ours; and may we be ever faithful both to them and thee; and may the blessed memory of those who have gone before us to their rest abide in our souls, and be as a light shining from heaven to lead us onward and upward in the way of duty and the way of peace.

Father, into thy hands we commend ourselves, our friends, our kindred, our country. We pray for the sick, the suffering, the needy, and the distressed. We pray for all who are in danger, by land or by sea. We would pray more fervently for them that have fallen, or are falling, into the bondage of sin. Save them, O God, and as far as in us lieth help us also to save them, by the word of truth, and the labor of love, and the patience of hope. May thy kingdom come; may the Gospel of thy Son prosper in the thing for which it was sent. We pray for the triumph of freedom, temperance, peace, and every good cause, in our country and the world; that thy will may be done on earth as it is done in heaven, and all nations may come and worship thee, and glorify thy name, forever.

O Thou whose unslumbering eye watches over thy people by night and by day, in time and through eternity, preserve us by thy good providence from all evil, and bring us to the light and the duties of another morning refreshed in body and in mind, rejoicing in thy love, and prepared for thy service; which we ask as disciples of Jesus Christ our Lord. Amen.

XVI.

The Divine Shelter.

Hear my cry, O God; attend to my prayer.

From the end of the earth will I cry to thee, when my heart is overwhelmed: lead me to the Rock that is higher than I.

For thou hast been a shelter for me, and a strong tower from the enemy.

I will abide in thy tabernacle forever: I will trust in the covert of thy wings.

For thou, O God, hast heard my vows: thou hast given me the heritage of those that fear thy name.

Truly my soul waiteth upon God: from him cometh my salvation.

He only is my rock and my salvation; he is my defence; I shall not be greatly moved.

So will I sing praise to thy name forever, that I may daily perform my vows.

FATHER of all the families of the earth, and in whom all are ever blessed, we come again to thee, delighting to gather around the domestic altar, and offer the evening sacrifice. May it ascend as fragrant and holy incense, and draw down thy best blessing. In the stillness of this hour we would be still and know that thou art God, the God of the universe, its Author and Father; from whom all souls pro ceeded, and in whom they live, the Giver of every good gift. We rejoice that thou art the rock higher than we, in whose shadow we may rest; and that now, shut out from all human eyes, we may gather ourselves together under the covert of thy wings, and beneath thy sheltering care.

And now, as another day is added to our existence, may we remember who it is that lengthens out our days. Let not the continual reception of thy sure mercies render us insensible or unthankful. Rather let it excite in us profoundest gratitude, and deepest sense of obligation and responsibility to him by whom they are bestowed.

We lament our past insensibility to thy goodness, and all in thought, feeling, word or deed, that was inconsistent with our relation to thee, unworthy the natures made in thine own image, and opposed to the excellence after which we were formed to aspire. From the depths of our souls do we lift the prayer, God be merciful to us sinners, and lead us to newness of life, and to the practice of every virtue, of purity, self-denial, active benevolence, enlightened and exalted faith, fervent and living piety.

May the members of this household be drawn nearer continually to each other by the cords of a tender sympathy and affection, at the same time that they are brought nearer to thee. After they shall have accomplished their respective courses on earth, may they be reünited in a heavenly home. We pray for all thy children. For them and for ourselves would we offer the all-comprehending petition, "Thy will, O Father, be done!" And to thy holy name, through Jesus Christ, be the glory and the praise forever. Amen.

XVII.

Evening Sacrifice.

Let my prayer be set forth before thee as incense; and the lifting up of my hands as the evening sacrifice.

The Lord is righteous in all his ways, and holy in all his works.

The Lord is nigh to all them that call upon him, to all that call upon him in truth.

He will fulfil the desire of them that fear him: he also will hear their cry, and will save them.

The Lord preserveth all them that love him: but all the wicked will he destroy.

My mouth shall speak the praise of the Lord: and let all flesh bless his holy name for ever and ever.

Almighty God, our heavenly Father, by whose kind providence we have been guided and preserved this day, unto thee would we return our thanksgiving for all thy mercies, and from thee beseech protection and defence this night. Let our prayer come before thee. If we have this day offended against thy holy laws, and been filled with any other spirit than that of Christ our Master, show us, O Father, our sin, and lead us to a heart-felt repentance. As we now, in silence, recall our actions during the day, may thy Holy Spirit guide our thoughts, helping us to judge soberly of ourselves, that we may see our sins, and gain wisdom and strength even from our failures.

[Here let there be a few moments of silence.]

Blessed Lord, who dost freely offer forgiveness to the penitent, and newness of life to them that believe in Jesus, accept our confessions, and heal us from our sins. Let the word of Christ be our consolation and our strength, and in him lead us hereafter to a better life, to the glory of thy holy name.

We give thee thanks, O Father, for the mercies of the past day, and we give thee thanks for the blessings of the night; for the rest which thou dost daily grant us; rest from labor of the hands, and rest from cares and anxiety of spirit. We thank thee that after the toils and trials of the day we have the privilege of coming, in the quiet hours of evening, to cast our cares upon thee, and to put our trust and confidence in thy mercy. Our souls shall speak the praise of the Lord, and bless his holy name for ever and ever. Thus, O Father, would we now come; forgive our sins, pardon our follies, dispel our fears, fill us with joy and peace in believing, and grant us such quiet and refreshing sleep that we may gain new strength to serve thee acceptably in whatever way thou shalt appoint.

"Our Father which art in heaven, hallowed be thy name. Thy kingdom come. Thy will be done on earth as it is in heaven. Give us this day our daily bread. And forgive us our debts, as we forgive our debtors. And lead us not into temptation, but deliver us from evil. For thine is the kingdom, and the power, and the glory, forever. Amen.

XVIII.

All from God.

The Lord looketh from heaven; he beholdeth all the sons of men.

From the place of his habitation he looketh upon all the inhabitants of the earth.

He fashioneth their hearts alike; he considereth all their works.

There is no king saved by the multitude of a host: a mighty man is not delivered by much strength.

A horse is a vain thing for safety: neither shall he deliver any by his great strength.

Behold, the eye of the Lord is upon them that fear him, upon them that hope in his mercy;

To deliver their soul from death, and to keep them alive in famine.

Our soul waiteth for the Lord: he is our help and our shield.

For our heart shall rejoice in him, because we have trusted in his holy name.

Let thy mercy, O Lord, be upon us, according as we hope in thee.

Our Father who art in heaven, hallowed be thy name. Another day thou hast added to our lives. Its rapidly passing hours have come and gone, freighted with blessings from thee. Through its seen and unseen perils thou hast safely borne us. Under the burden of its trial and discipline thou hast been near us, and under the pressure of its responsibilities and constantly recurring duties thou hast helped us. For what we have this day enjoyed, for the boundless entertainments of thy providence, for the blessed light of the sun on which we have looked, the healthful air that we have breathed, the habitations that have sheltered, the food that has nourished, and the garments that have covered us, for these renewed opportunities for the exercise and improvement of our talents, the success which has attended our labors, the pleasures of our social intercourse, and the delights of our home, here, in the midst of that home which thou hast spared to us, would we pour out our hearty gratitude to thee. How can we number one in a thousand of those mercies which thou hast showered upon us! We have been out, and we have come in, and thou hast been doing us good continually. Impress upon our hearts a deep sense of thine unbounded goodness; and if we have ever forgotten thee, pardon our weakness and folly, and, for thy mercy's sake, do thou not forget us.

We ask thy blessing upon us this night. Let thy peace be to this habitation. Let us go to our rest with a conscience void of offence towards thee and all mankind. If any have injured us, may we forgive as we hope to be forgiven. If we have injured any, may our regrets secure thy compassion, and may we have the dispositions to make all the amends in our power. We commend ourselves to thee. During our defenceless hours do thou defend us. As we lie upon our beds and meditate, let us remember the darkness and the light are both alike to thee, and may we enjoy continued tokens of thy favor. Under thy sheltering wing we lay ourselves down. May sweet sleep visit our eyelids. May we enjoy invigorating and healthful repose; and in the morning when we awake may our thought be still of thee. And unto thee will we render the praise and the glory forever. Amen.

XIX.

Searching our Ways.

The preparation of the heart in man, and the answer of the tongue, are from the Lord.

All the ways of a man are clean in his own eyes; but the Lord weigheth the spirits.

Commit thy works to the Lord, and thy thoughts shall be established.

Every one that is proud in heart is an abomination to the

Lord: though hand join in hand, he shall not be unpunished.

By mercy and truth iniquity is purged: and by the fear of the Lord men depart from evil.

When a man's ways please the Lord, he maketh even his enemies to be at peace with him.

Better is a little with righteousness, than great revenues without right.

A man's heart deviseth his way: but the Lord directeth his steps.

O God, who dwellest in the sanctities of heaven, and among the children of men, once more do we gather around our domestic altar to remember the loving-kindness which visited us in the morning, and which has attended us all the day long. Thou hast been with us, the members of this favored family, giving us the activity of our bodies, the vigor of our minds, and the strength of our affections. Thou hast ordered for us the events of the day. It has spoken to us of thy goodness; we will praise thee continually. Thou hast this day called us into the field of duty. Thou hast spread before us the exalted privileges and the precious hopes of Christians. Means, motives, encouragements, without number, thou hast afforded us, and nothing hast left undone which thou couldst have done for any. This day, in every scene through which we have passed, thou hast been calling us to glory, honor, and immortality.

And what, O God, have we rendered thee for thy boundless blessings? We would search our ways, remembering that though clean in our eyes, thou, O Lord, weighest the spirit. We confess our blindness, and weakness, and sinfulness. We mourn the strength of our passions, and the feebleness of our resolutions. We fear that the objects and the interests of time, by which thou wouldst try us, and mould us into thy likeness, have too much absorbed us, and won the affections which belong unto thee. We feel that in the eagerness of our pursuits we have given to things seen and temporal that which belongs only to things unseen and eternal. We mourn that we have not better improved thy gifts, and that we have not a better account to render of the day that has passed over us. Pardon, good Lord, thy children, and may our watchfulness witness to the sincerity of our regrets, and a more vivid sense of thine unbounded goodness animate our zeal, and prompt us to new fidelity, every day that thou shalt spare us.

Remember us and those whom thou hast given us this night. Look down upon our unprotected dwelling, and guard our pillow. May the angel of the Lord encamp round about us, to deliver us from all evil. Let us behold the light of another morning, if it seemeth good to thee; or, if in thine infinite wisdom this repose shall become the repose of death, let us behold that glorious morning of the resurrection which no night shall follow. For which we pray ever to be prepared, in the name and as disciples of Jesus Christ. Amen.

XX.

Praise and Trust.

Blessed be the name of the Lord from this time forth and forevermore.

From the rising of the sun to the going down of the same the Lord's name is to be praised.

O Israel, trust thou in the Lord: he is their help and their shield.

O house of Aaron, trust in the Lord: he is their help and their shield.

Ye that fear the Lord, trust in the Lord: he is their help and their shield.

The Lord hath been mindful of us: he will bless us; he will bless the house of Israel; he will bless the house of Aaron.

He will bless them that fear the Lord, both small and great.

Ye are blessed by the Lord who made heaven and earth.

The heaven, even the heavens, are the Lord's: but the earth hath he given to the children of men.

The dead praise not the Lord, neither any that go down into silence.

But we will bless the Lord from this time forth and forever. Praise the Lord.

Father, ever-kind and ever-merciful, we thank thee, as the day is closing, for the blessings which its hours have brought to us. How good, how mindful of our wants, thou hast been! Thou hast spread the table of thy bounty, and we have had food convenient for us. Thou hast surrounded us with friends, and we have been encouraged by their words of sympathy and counsel. Thou hast given us labor to perform, and strength to perform it. Forgive us, we pray thee, if we have been slothful servants. Forgive us, our Father, if amidst all the enjoyments and labors of this day we have been unmindful of thee; for in thee we live, and move, and have our being. Every good gift and every perfect gift cometh down from thee. Without thee we can do nothing. Accept, we pray thee, our endeavors to do thy will this day.

We thank thee that thou didst not forget us, if we have forgotten thee; that thou didst help us in the hour of temptation, so that we did not yield; that thou didst direct our inquiries, as we were seeking our duty, so that we found it; that thou hast watched over us in our words and acts, in our hours of labor, and in our hours of repose, and brought us in health, and strength, and happiness, to the close of another day. How deeply should our hearts be moved with gratitude when we call all these blessings before us, and think of their value! We thank thee that by these daily labors and toils we may purify our souls and become like thee, and like Jesus Christ thy Son our Saviour. We thank thee that in the cares and obligations of our condition in life there is afforded us such an opportunity of becoming one with thee and one with Christ. May this day's experience give us courage for future labor and watchfulness. May every day's attempt to conform our lives to thy law incite us to still greater diligence in the work of life.

Our Father, we pray that before we close our eyes in sleep this night we may be at peace with all men. If any one has wronged us, may we freely forgive the wrong, as we hope and pray that we may be forgiven by thee. If an unkind feeling has been in our bosoms, Father, forgive us; if an unkind word has been upon our lips, Father, forgive us; if we have performed an unkind act, forgive us; and breathe into our hearts a spirit of love to our enemies, if we have any.

And now, as the period of rest draws nigh, we ask thy protection during our hours of sleep. Watch over us, O thou who never slumberest nor sleepest, and give us that refreshing repose which we need, that when the morning dawns we may be strong in thy strength, to do thy work and perform thy will. Father, we commit ourselves to thy care. In thy keeping we shall be secure. In thy arms we are safe. Do with us and for us, our Father, as thou seest we need now and evermore. We resign ourselves to thy care, thankful that with the house of Israel and of Aaron, and with thy sainted children in all ages, we may trust in the Lord, who is our help and our shield. From the rising of the sun to the going down of the same be thy name praised, through Jesus Christ, to whom be glory in his church forever. Amen.

XXI.

Daily Gratitude.

Praise ye the Lord. Praise the Lord, O my soul.

While I live will I praise the Lord : I will sing praises unto my God while I have any being.

Put not your trust in princes, nor in the son of man, in whom there is no help.

His breath goeth forth, he returneth to his earth ; in that very day his thoughts perish.

Happy is he that hath the God of Jacob for his help, whose hope is in the Lord his God ;

Which made heaven and earth, the sea, and all that therein is ; which keepeth truth forever ;

Which executeth judgment for the oppressed ; which giveth food to the hungry. The Lord looseth the prisoners.

The Lord openeth the eyes of the blind : the Lord raiseth them that are bowed down : the Lord loveth the righteous.

The Lord preserveth the stranger ; he relieveth the fatherless and widow : but the way of the wicked he turneth upside down.

The Lord shall reign forever, even thy God, O Zion, unto all generations. Praise ye the Lord.

O Thou all-bountiful Giver of our enjoyments and our privileges, at the close of a day which thy goodness has crowned with blessings, we offer unto thee the prayer of gratitude. What are we, O Lord, that thou shouldst be mindful of us? Creatures of a day, feeble alike in our powers and in our purposes of good, wandering often from thy holy ways, and walking in forbidden paths, it becomes us not to boast ourselves as though we had attained aught by our own strength or our own merit. It is of thy goodness that we live, and enjoy life's blessings. All the gifts of this world are from thee,—health, competence, success in life, the happy home, the company of friends, and whatever else makes pleasant this earthly state of being. We thank thee, O God, for the share of these blessings thou hast granted to us. May we enjoy them with that moderation of spirit which, gratefully recognizing thee as the bestower, shall be prepared to submit if at any time thy gifts should be withdrawn. May we use the means of good thou givest us, not for our own advantage only, but for that of others, and thus for thy glory. May we feel that it is a blessed privilege to make others partakers in our happiness.

O God, we pray that thou wouldst guard us, as against the trials of adversity, so also against the temptations that attend a prosperous state. Keep us from pride. Knowing that there is nothing we have but we have received it from thee, may we not glory as though we had it of ourselves; but rather be more truly humble, as we contemplate thy goodness on the one hand, and our deficiencies on the other. Keep us from indolence. If we are not excited to industry by the pressure of want, may we be by the sense of duty to others and to thee. Keep us from selfishness. May we sympathize with others in their distress, and rejoice in their good fortune. Keep us from too great devotedness to this world. May we remember that a time must come when all earthly possessions will be of no avail, but when we must part from this life and all its pleasing pursuits, and go where the only distinction recognized will be that of piety and virtue. May we by good conduct and humble faith lay up for ourselves treasures in that unseen and eternal world; and at length, O Father, may thy forgiving mercy receive us there.

We pray for our friends; bless them, O Lord, with this world's gifts, but still more with those of the life to come. Bless thou the poor and needy, and open the hearts of the prosperous for their relief. Comfort those in sorrow; restore the sick, or prepare them for the last great change; receive the dying to thyself. Recall the sinful from their wanderings, and confirm thy servants in their faithfulness. Bless all and each according to thine infinite wisdom and perfect love. May the Gospel of Christ our Saviour be honored in our hearts and lives, and made triumphant through the world; and now and evermore to thee, O God, be praises in his holy name. Amen.

XXII.

Cheerful Thanks.

It is a good thing to give thanks to the Lord, and to sing praise to thy name, O Most High.

To show forth thy loving-kindness in the morning, and thy faithfulness every night.

For thou, Lord, hast made me glad through thy work: I will triumph in the works of thy hands.

Ye that love the Lord, hate evil: he preserveth the souls of his saints; he delivereth them out of the hand of the wicked.

Light is sown for the righteous, and gladness for the upright in heart.

Rejoice in the Lord, ye righteous; and give thanks at the remembrance of his holiness.

We come to thee, Father in heaven, spared and blest as we have been through another day, that we may thankfully testify to thy goodness and loving-kindness towards us, and confidingly commit ourselves to thy protection through the night. Dangers seen and unseen have been in our path, but thou hast been our shield. We have gone out and come in, in safety beneath thy care. Thy bounty hath spread our board; thy strength has sustained, and thy blessing crowned, our labors; thy Spirit hath helped our infirmities; and, surrounded by the innumerable mercies of our daily lot, we are brought to the hour of rest. And as we would show forth thy loving-kindness in the morning, so would we speak of thy faithfulness every night.

What thanks can we acceptably render unto thee, O thou ever good and gracious Being? May we remember that the best proof that we are sensible of thy great and unmerited goodness to us is our daily conformity to thy will, and obedience to thy commandments; the daily consecration of ourselves to thy service; withholding ourselves from sin, resisting temptation, controlling passion, doing good to others, and in all things imbibing the spirit, and copying the life, of the Lord Jesus. Thus may we prove that we love the Lord, by hating every evil.

Merciful Father, forgive us that we have not thus shown forth our gratitude, but have been too thoughtless of thine untiring love, too careless of our constant obligations, too ready to sin. Forgive us, we implore thee, all our sins of thought, word, and deed; and grant us thy Holy Spirit to aid and strengthen us in all time to come, that we may become with every added day more devoted to thy will.

Father, help us to grow in thy divine image. Help us truly to love thee, and thy dear Son. Help us more and more to appreciate thine inestimable love towards us, in sending him to be our Saviour. Help us more entirely and gratefully to accept his mediation, and become reconciled to thee. Help us to make our home on earth a Christian home. Through our pure and disinterested affections, and our right, tender and respectful treatment of each other, may it aid to fit us for a better home in heaven. Help us to renounce every evil word and work; to avoid the seductions of vicious pleasure; to overcome all temptation, and keep ourselves unspotted from the world. Help us, even in our sorrows and trials, to rejoice in thee as the all-wise disposer of our earthly lot, who will, in thine own time, prove that light is sown for the righteous, and gladness for the upright in heart, and that they shall triumph in the work of thy hand. Help us to cultivate ever a spirit of benevolence, and to have warm hearts and ready hands for its offices. Help us to cherish a sense of true devotion and piety Help us to live as seeing things invisible; as immortal beings, who know they are to account to thee for the deeds done in the body, and receive according thereto, whether good or evil.

And now, Father, in peace and charity with all men, and in peace with thee, we commend ourselves, our kindred and friends, to thy ever-watchful care. May we sleep in safety, and awake beneath thy smile. While thine all-enfolding wing protects us in the darkness, may the morning light welcome us to new activity, and new devotedness to thee.

This we ask through Jesus Christ our Mediator and Redeemer, for whom we ever bless thee, and in whose name ascribe to thee, Father everlasting, all glory and praise forever. Amen.

XXIII.

Wonders and Bounties.

O Lord our God, how excellent is thy name in all the earth! who hast set thy glory above the heavens.

When I consider thy heavens, the work of thy fingers; the moon and the stars, which thou hast ordained;

What is man, that thou art mindful of him? and the son of man, that thou visitest him?

For thou hast made him a little lower than the angels, and hast crowned him with glory and honor.

Thou hast made him to have dominion over the works of thy hands; thou hast put all things under his feet:

All sheep and oxen, yea, and the beasts of the field;

The fowl of the air, and the fish of the sea, and whatever passeth through the paths of the seas.

O Lord our God, how excellent is thy name in all the earth!

O God, our Creator, our guide in life, our support in death and our portion forever, brought safely through the perils of the day, a happy family circle, we would again surround thine altar with grateful, confiding, adoring hearts. How many and how rich are the mercies which have crowned another day! The sun has lighted us on our paths of duty and enjoyment; and night draws around us its sheltering wings, to soothe us to rest. Business has opened to us the means of support and usefulness, and society has cheered us with its intercourse. Home has cherished us in its love, and friendship surrounded us with its sympathy. Wisdom has counselled us out of thy word, and out of the teachings and lives of the good and wise. Thy Holy Spirit has been moving on our hearts, rebuking every wrong impulse, and prompting holy desires. And now thou hast set thy glory in the heavens, and called out the moon and the stars the work of thy hand. O Lord our God, how excellent is thy name in all the earth!

For all these blessings, so rich, so unmerited, so exclusively thy gift, we would render thee humble and hearty thanks. But not as the beings of this world do we owe thee the deepest gratitude. More than for all temporal mercies do we thank thee for the gift of thy Son. Without the light which he has shed on nature, on human life, on the grave, they would be dark indeed. As the gifts of thy love, our daily blessings have a new value. As a discipline of character, life, with all its trials and sorrows, has a high and holy meaning. As the gate of immortal life, the grave has a solemn, but sublime and inspiring hope. With all these blessings and encouragements of thy providence and grace, what manner of lives ought we to lead in all holy conversation and godliness! Our hearts should be filled with love, and our hands with deeds of kindness. Nature should be alive with thy presence, and our homes hallowed by thy love. Every business and every pleasure should be holy to those whom thou hast made but a little lower than the angels, and hast crowned with glory and honor.

We are humbled, O God, when we think how greatly we have fallen short this day. Forgive us, in thy great mercy, all forgetfulness of thee in the past day, all unfaithfulness in business, all unkindness in society, every hasty word in our home.

And grant that we may not lie down on our pillows with one unrepented sin. Give us forgiving and loving hearts, that we may be at peace with each other, and humble and contrite spirits, with which thou dost delight to dwell. Under the shelter of thy wings may we rest sweetly, and rise to a better and happier life on earth than we have before known. And should this prove the night of death to any of us, may our parting be blessed; and may we at the morn of the resurrection be prepared for thy presence, and the society of the saints in light.

Holy Father, to thy kind protection we commend all our absent friends. Let no evil come nigh their dwellings, and no disease invade their frames. Let thy sheltering providence and thy forgiving love wrap them as in a mantle of safety and peace.

Father of mercies, we supplicate thy blessing upon those tossed on beds of pain, struggling with disease, and especially those who are this night to pass through their last mortal agony. Beyond the reach of human aid, help them to lean on thine almighty arm and find rest. Give them the faith and peace of thy holy Son, when he said, Father, into thy hands I commend my spirit.

Finally, we commit our all into thy merciful hands this night, and through the changes of life, trusting in thy protection, and fearing no evil. And unto thee we will ever render the homage of adoring hearts, through Jesus Christ our Lord. Amen.

XXIV.

Self-Examination.

Thou art my portion, O Lord: I have said that I would keep thy words.

I entreated thy favor with my whole heart; be merciful to me according to thy word.

I thought on my ways, and turned my feet to thy testimonies.

I made haste, and delayed not to keep thy commandments.

At midnight I will rise to give thanks to thee, because of thy righteous judgments.

I am a companion of all them that fear thee, and of them that keep thy precepts.

The earth, O Lord, is full of thy mercy: teach me thy statutes.

O Thou the preserver of our lives, our Father which art in heaven, our grateful hearts would praise thee in this evening hour. The labors of the day finished, we would lay aside the cares and anxieties of life, and here at our family altar, united in loving harmony, commit ourselves to thee.

We thank thee, O Father, that thou dost bow thy heavens and graciously hear when we devoutly make known our wants and aspirations. Especially do we thank thee that now, at the close of this day, we may come as children, and speak to thee the thought of our hearts, and invoke the assistance of thy Spirit. O lead us to self-examination. Aid us to see ourselves as thou seest us. In thy light may we see light. Cleanse our sight that we may discern the secrets of our hearts, and know the motives which prompt us to action. Help us to try our ways to see if we have this day served thee, made thy will our rule, and thy work our employment; if we have lived mindful of the momentous concerns of the life eternal.

O Thou whose mercy is over all thy children, forgive our sins. We would arise and come home to thee. We hear the gracious call of thy messenger-Son, Come unto me, all ye that labor, and are weary and heavy-laden, and I will give you rest; and we would come with open hearts and penitent confessions, and say, Father, forgive us. May we so live in all purity, honesty and love, that when all our days on earth shall have passed, and the shadows of our life-evening shall be gathering round us, we may hear benign voices, angels of peace, saying, Fear not, for you there remaineth a rest in heaven.

O God, these days and nights are passing rapidly, and time makes his mark upon these mortal tabernacles; may we be prepared to live in that house not made with hands, eternal in the heavens.

O Father of infinite love, help us to keep our minds and hearts in the glorious faith and cheering hope of Christ Jesus our Lord, that whether we wake or sleep we may live with him, through whom to thee be rendered praise and thanksgiving, world without end. Amen.

XXV.

The Searcher of Hearts.

O Lord, thou hast searched me, and known me.

Thou knowest my down-sitting and mine up-rising; thou understandest my thought afar off.

Thou compassest my path, and my lying down, and art acquainted with all my ways.

Whither shall I go from thy Spirit? or whither shall I flee from thy presence?

If I ascend up into heaven, thou art there; if I make my bed in hell, behold, thou art there.

If I take the wings of the morning, and dwell in the utter most parts of the sea;

Even there shall thy hand lead me, and thy right hand shall hold me.

If I say, Surely the darkness shall cover me; even the night shall be light about me.

Yea, the darkness hideth not from thee; but the night shineth as the day: the darkness and the light are both alike to thee.

Search me, O God, and know my heart; try me, and know my thoughts;

And see if there be any wicked way in me, and lead me in the way everlasting.

ALMIGHTY GOD, our heavenly Father, we would again adore thy goodness, and seek thy forgiving mercy, and commit ourselves to thy watchful care. Thy kind providence has guarded and guided us through another day. Thou hast graciously continued our powers of body and of mind, and hast surrounded us with a multitude of blessings. What thanks shall we render unto thee for all thy mercies? If it hath pleased thee to mingle cares and afflictions with the brightness of our lot, we know that they come from a Father's hand, and are working out for us a Father's purposes of love.

Almighty Parent, teach us to enjoy thy favors with a filial gratitude, and to meet thy sanctifying chastisements with a filial submission and a filial trust. May the remembrance of thy constant goodness cheer and sustain us amidst the labors and perplexities, the changes and disappointments, of life. May we do our best, looking unto thee; and having done our best, in a calm and cheerful faith, we will leave the issue unto thee, knowing that in thy hands we are forever safe. Let thy will be done on earth as it is done in heaven.

O God, the searcher of hearts, as we look back on the day that is now drawing to its close, we would examine ourselves as in thy sight, and try our hearts and our ways by the word and the life of Christ; and if in aught we have been wanting in his spirit, or have been violating his law, God be merciful to us sinners. Awaken us to a deeper sense of our dangers and of our duties. Help us by thy Holy Spirit to forsake the sins which we confess, and to carry out the good purposes which we now form in thy presence. Help us to see the wrong, to abhor and to shun it; help us to see the right, to love and to pursue it. May it be our great aim, the one thing which we keep ever before us, that which we first and most earnestly seek, to be religiously faithful to the duties of our lot, both the little and the great.

O God, our heavenly Father, thou hast made our life on earth a pilgrimage brief and uncertain: and now we are a day's march nearer to the grave and to eternity. We know that the time is short to us and to all. May we live, while we live; live as thy true children and servants, made for nobler pleasures than those of sense, for higher glories than any which men can offer, for sweeter rewards than those of earthly gain.

And now, O God, who compassest our path and our lying down, to whom the darkness and the light are both alike, we would seek the blessing of sleep, reposing now, as always, in the arms of thy protecting providence, and committing ourselves and all whom we love to thy fatherly care. We would go to the slumbers of this night, as we hope to go to the slumbers of the last, in peace with thee, in harmony with our friends, in charity towards all, in a Christian faith and a Christian hope, looking up to heaven and to thee. We pray for thy blessing upon our neighborhood, our country and the world, upon every righteous cause and every quickening truth in its struggle with the old evil that is in the world; we ascribe unto thee the kingdom, the power and the glory, for ever and ever. Amen.

XXVI.

Confession of Sin.

I will arise, and go to my father, and will say unto him, Father, I have sinned against Heaven, and before thee,

And am no more worthy to be called thy son: make me as one of thy hired servants.

And he arose, and came to his father. But when he was yet a great way off his father saw him, and had compassion, and ran, and fell on his neck, and kissed him.

And the son said unto him, Father, I have sinned against heaven, and in thy sight, and am no more worthy to be called thy son.

But the father said to his servants, Bring forth the best robe, and put it on him; and put a ring on his hand, and shoes on his feet:

And bring hither the fatted calf, and kill it; and let us eat and be merry:

For this my son was dead, and is alive again; he was lost, and is found.

O, ALMIGHTY and everlasting God, for all the blessings which we every day receive from thy bounty, for all the known and all the unobserved favors, deliverances, visitations and graces, of thy Holy Spirit, we bless thy good providence; beseeching thee still to continue thy fatherly care over us, for we need thy constant protection and guidance.

God be merciful unto us, who have broken thy laws, abused thy patience, wasted thy time, sinned against thy light, and resisted thy good Spirit. In thy plenteous tender mercies pardon all that we have done or thought amiss during the past day. Now, when we draw nigh to thee, confessing that we have sinned against thee, wilt thou draw nigh to us, and embrace us in the arms of thy forgiving grace. We rejoice before thee in what our divine Master, thy chosen messenger, hath taught us of thy readiness to forgive, and thank thee that in the father welcoming the returning prodigal we may see thy own tender love. When we lie down, may it be as pardoned children. Grant us grace that we may render ourselves more worthy of thy favor for the time to come. Let us be excited to serve thee, our heavenly Master, with fidelity, and finish our work with diligence, before that night overtakes us wherein no man can work.

O Thou who never slumberest nor sleepest, but both by night and day dost watch over thy people, keep and defend us, we pray thee, this night. Let the shades which encompass us be as the shadow of thy wings. May our sleep be quiet and refreshing; and may we rise in the morning prepared and invigorated to serve thee in the duties of the day. May all our nights on earth be hallowed by thy blessing, and all our days devoted to thy service, so that when we have slept the sleep of the grave we may awake to the resurrection of the just.

Hear us, we beseech thee, in thy Son's name, as whose disciples we approach thee, our Father, and ascribe unto thee all honor and glory forever. Amen.

XXVII.

Seeking Pardon.

That which we have seen and heard we declare to you, that ye also may have fellowship with us: and truly our fellowship is with the Father, and with his Son Jesus Christ.

And these things we write to you, that your joy may be full.

This then is the message which we have heard from him, and declare to you, that God is light, and in him is no darkness at all.

If we say that we have fellowship with him, and walk in darkness, we lie, and do not the truth:

But if we walk in the light, as he is in the light, we have fellowship one with another, and the blood of Jesus Christ his Son cleanseth us from all sin.

If we say that we have no sin, we deceive ourselves, and the truth is not in us.

If we confess our sins, he is faithful and just to forgive us our sins, and to cleanse us from all unrighteousness.

If we say that we have not sinned, we make him a liar, and his word is not in us.

O Thou infinite and eternal God, the framer of our bodies and the Father of our spirits, in whose hands our times are, and whose are all our ways. We bless thee for the powers of our minds, and for the affections and sympathies of our hearts. We bless thee that thou hast made us capable of contemplating thine adorable nature and character; capable of knowing thy will and our duty in all the relations of life;

capable of serving thee in some acceptable, though imperfect, manner in this world; and capable of being prepared, by the aid of thy grace in Jesus Christ, for the more perfect service and the more sublime enjoyment of thee in the world to come.

We thank thee that thou hast added another day to our earthly life. We bless thee for every token of thy merciful kindness manifested towards us; that thou hast kept our feet from falling, our eyes from tears, and our souls from death; and hast brought us to the close of the day and of the evening still surrounded by the tokens of thy love, and still sustained by the power of thy grace. Serenely would we now look up to thee; for thou art light, and with thee there is no darkness at all.

Wilt thou, who art faithful and just to forgive us our sins, pardon the transgressions and imperfections of this day, and of our whole life. Create in us clean hearts, and renew a right spirit within us. Through that blood of Jesus which cleanseth from all sin, wilt thou blot out all our transgressions. Suffer them not to rise in this world to our shame, nor in the world to come to our condemnation. May the mind and spirit of Jesus, the Master, be received into our hearts, and nurtured and cherished there, until, bearing something of his image and likeness, we are prepared to join the spirits of the just in that world where our fellowship, in the purest and holiest sense, will be with the Father, and with his Son Christ Jesus.

May thy blessing ever rest upon this family. May each member of it, whether present or absent, be an object of thy protecting care and kindness, and a subject of redeeming love and grace. We commend ourselves, and all that we have, to thy holy protection and keeping this night. May we lie down in the fear and love of God. May our sleep be quiet and refreshing to us; and may we awake to behold the light, to partake of the blessings, and to perform the duties, of another day, in health and in peace.

Be with us while we shall continue in the world. Mete out our trials in great mercy to us. Lay not more upon us at any time than thou wilt give us strength to bear, and to bear patiently, with filial submission to thy will, with improvement to our own souls, and with glory to thy great and holy name. And when we shall have borne, and done, and suffered, according to thy whole will, in this our earthly life, may we be found meet to be partakers of that rest which remains for the people of God.

We look to thee for a blessing upon the whole human family. Hasten the time when pure religion, and rational liberty, and equal laws, and righteous government, shall enlighten, protect and bless, the world. May every nation, kindred and tongue, unite with the heavenly hosts in ascribing glory to God in the highest, because there is peace on earth, and good will to men.

Hear us, O our Father in heaven, and when thou hearest, answer, and forgive, and accept us, in the name and as the disciples of Jesus Christ. Amen.

XXVIII.

Born of the Spirit.

Jesus answered, Verily, verily, I say to thee, Except a man be born of water, and of the Spirit, he cannot enter into the kingdom of God.

That which is born of the flesh, is flesh; and that which is born of the Spirit, is spirit.

Marvel not that I said to thee, Ye must be born again.

The wind bloweth where it will, and thou hearest the sound of it, but canst not tell whence it cometh, and whither it goeth: so is every one that is born of the Spirit.

Verily, verily, I say to thee, We speak what we know, and testify what we have seen; and ye receive not our testimony.

If I have told you earthly things, and ye believe not, how will ye believe if I tell you heavenly things?

And no man hath ascended to heaven, but he that came down from heaven, even the Son of man who is in heaven.

And as Moses lifted up the serpent in the wilderness, even so must the Son of man be lifted up:

That whoever believeth in him should not perish, but have eternal life.

For God so loved the world, that he gave his only-begotten

Son, that whoever believeth in him, should not perish, but have everlasting life.

For God sent not his Son into the world to condemn the world, but that the world through him may be saved.

INFINITE and holy One, with thee there is no darkness. The shadows of evening cannot hide us from thy presence. Thóu art with us still. Thine eye has been upon us through all the day. Thou hast watched over us, shielded us from harm, and brought us to the close of another day laden with fresh experience of thy love and care.

Forgive all that has been wrong in our actions, our words, or the spirit we have cherished. If we have yielded to temptation; if we have not been watchful against besetting sins; if we have been unfaithful in any of the relations and duties of life; if we have swerved from Christian integrity; if we have been untruthful, unkind, or ungenerous; if we have given way to petulance, or passion; if we have shown a retaliatory or unforgiving spirit; if we have grieved or wounded trusting affection; if we have betrayed or disappointed the confidence of friendship; or in any way disobeyed thy will, and grieved thy Holy Spirit, Father, forgive us, and help us to see and feel our sins, and inspire us with a new spirit, that we may live more as becometh thy children.

And now, O Father, we would listen to those words of Jesus which unfold the need of a spiritual birth. Sitting at the feet of that Teacher from heaven, may his voice fall on our ears in the tender and earnest accents once heard on earth. While he takes the things of God and shows them unto us, may the reality and hopes of a spiritual life be by us discerned. O, that the work of regeneration might ever be going on in our souls. O, that each day might witness some progress in the divine life. O, for a living faith, strong and victorious, that shall open our souls more fully to thy Holy Spirit, and bring our inmost natures into harmony with thy will. Help us to look to thine only-begotten Son, who was lifted up that all men might be drawn unto him, and give us that saving faith in him which is unto everlasting life.

For all the good gifts of thy providence this day we thank thee; for food, and raiment, and shelter, and friends; for protection from sickness and casualty, and for all the enjoyments of social and domestic life. Sanctify our home. May it be a Christian home; a home of love, of faith, of hope, and prayer. And may all its influences, through thy rich grace, fit us for a home in heaven.

May we lean trustingly upon thine everlasting arm this night. May a sense of thy presence and love give peace to our slumbers. May we be refreshed and strengthened by needful repose. And if it shall seem good to thee to wake us to the light of another day, may our souls wake to new emotions of gratitude, and new purposes of living to thy glory. This we humbly ask, through Jesus Christ our Lord. Amen.

XXIX.

For the Comforter.

If ye love me, keep my commandments:

And I will pray the Father, and he shall give you another Comforter, that he may abide with you forever;

Even the Spirit of truth; whom the world cannot receive, because it seeth him not, neither knoweth him: but ye know him; for he dwelleth with you, and shall be in you.

I will not leave you comfortless; I will come to you.

Yet a little while, and the world seeth me no more; but ye see me: because I live, ye shall live also.

At that day ye shall know that I am in my Father, and you in me, and I in you.

These things have I spoken unto you, being yet present with you.

But the Comforter, which is the Holy Ghost, whom the Father will send in my name, he shall teach you all things, and bring all things to your remembrance, whatsoever I have said unto you.

Peace I leave with you, my peace I give unto you: not as the world giveth, give I unto you. Let not your heart be troubled, neither let it be afraid.

Ye have heard how I said unto you, I go away, and come again unto you. If ye loved me ye would rejoice, because I said, I go unto the Father: for my Father is greater than I.

O God, how infinite art thou! How far beyond the reach of our thoughts, beyond the grasp of our understandings! We adore thine almighty power, which created and sustains the world; we are lost in wonder at that wisdom which guides all the course of nature, and of providence; and our whole hearts are filled with thankfulness for the numberless tokens of kindness which thou givest us from the inexhaustible treasures of thy love. We thank thee for our creation, for our preservation, and for all the blessings of this life; and especially for the kind providence which has this day guarded us from evil, and given us opportunities to gain knowledge, and wisdom, and virtue.

We confess, O Father, our unworthiness to receive these gifts of thy love; we acknowledge that our obedience is imperfect, and that our sins are many. We are the more deeply ashamed of them because of thy forbearance and kindness; and the more touched by thy goodness, because thou dost bestow it upon us in our unworthiness. Let thy goodness lead us to repentance; let thy love strengthen us in a better life. Show us, O God, our sins; let us know wherein we have failed, and let us henceforth be more true to thee, and to Jesus our Redeemer. May that Holy Spirit which he promised to send as the Comforter from thee descend upon us, to convict us of sin, to lead us to repentance, to teach us all truth, to assure us of forgiveness, to work in us the fruits of righteousness, and to abide with us forever.

We give thanks unto thee, O, Father, for these precious hopes and promises of our Lord Jesus Christ. Trusting in him for the forgiveness of our sins, and for the acceptance of our prayers, we rest on thine almighty arm, and know that thou wilt keep them in perfect peace whose hearts are stayed on thee. May the peace of Jesus, given not as the world giveth, be our blessed portion. Dwelling in him even as he dwelt in thee, thou wilt keep us evermore in safety. No harm can befall us by night or by day, since the darkness and the light are both alike to thee.

Let thy blessing be upon each member of this household, upon all who are dear to either of us, and upon all to whom thou hast bound us by any ties. Bring sinners to repentance, lead thy saints to holier living, and hasten the day when all men shall serve thee acceptably, through Jesus Christ our Lord, through whom unto thee would we give honor forever. Amen.

XXX.

Spiritual Worship.

Our fathers worshipped in this mountain ; and ye say, that in Jerusalem is the place where men ought to worship.

Jesus saith to her, Woman, believe me, the hour cometh, when ye shall neither in this mountain, nor yet at Jerusalem, worship the Father.

Ye worship ye know not what : we know what we worship, for salvation is of the Jews.

But the hour cometh, and now is, when the true worshippers shall worship the Father in spirit and in truth : for the Father seeketh such to worship him.

God is a spirit : and they that worship him, must worship him in spirit and in truth.

Almighty Parent, we have walked by thy light and thy strength through whatever dangers, seen or unseen, have been about us, until the curtains of the night have been drawn around us, inviting us to repose. How hast thou watched over us and guarded us in all our paths! In every step we have taken, every breath we have inspired, every beating of our pulses, we have drawn from thine everlasting strength and love. Now that the evening shadows are laid upon all outward things, and we are invited by the still and solemn hour to look in upon our own hearts, we implore thine all-revealing Spirit to show us to ourselves. We look up to thee in thy dazzling purity and holiness, and our own imperfection and corruption come more fully into light. Forgive us the sins we have this day committed, and enable us so to see the secret springs of all our corrupt life, that we may present our whole soul to be now visited and cleansed by thy Spirit, so that all things may be created new within us. Thou art our Father-Spirit, and may our nightly worship of thee be in spirit and in truth.

Our Father in heaven, our eyes wait upon thee with unutterable longings. We have tried all other good, and still our souls hunger and thirst. Thou alone canst fill the void that is in us, and satisfy the cravings of our immortal minds. If deprived of all things else, we are still rich if only we have the experience of thy grace. But if we lose thee we lose all things else, for the whole world is naught bereft of thee. Therefore we pray, above all things, that thou mayst come within us, and we beseech thee to lead us through all that we need to prepare the way for that blessed and glorious coming. If we need prosperity, we pray for it that it may bring us to thee. If we need adversity and privation, we would rather have these than spiritual death. Whatever it may be that shall raise us, O, send us that which shall bring us nearer to thee, and reveal thee through our whole nature as our unfailing light, our never-setting sun.

As we lie down to sleep, we resign all that we are into thy hands. May we be embosomed in thy love. Keep away all evil thoughts and fancies, and may we repose like infancy in thee. And may all our days and nights prepare us for that world where our sun shall no more go down, neither shall our moon wane, but where the Lord shall be our everlasting light, and our God our glory. Through Jesus Christ. Amen.

XXXI.

Help in Trouble.

God is our refuge and strength, a very present help in trouble.

Therefore we will not fear, though the earth shall be removed, and though the mountains shall be carried into the midst of the sea;

Though its waters shall roar and be disturbed, though the mountains shake with the swelling of it.

The Lord of hosts is with us; the God of Jacob is our refuge.

Come, behold the works of the Lord, what desolations he hath made in the earth.

He maketh wars to cease to the end of the earth; he breaketh the bow, and cutteth the spear asunder; he burneth the chariot in the fire.

Be still, and know that I am God: I will be exalted among the heathen, I will be exalted in the earth.

The Lord of hosts is with us; the God of Jacob is our refuge.

O OUR Lord God, almighty and all-merciful, thou hearest the cry of those who are in affliction; thou knowest our frame; thou rememberest that we are but dust. O Lord our God, in the midst of life's sorrows and trials our strength is in thee. We know that sorrow springeth not from the ground, that it cometh not without thy divine command; grant us therefore, O Father, to submit to the rod, and to him who hath appointed it. Thou, Lord, dost not willingly afflict or grieve the children of men; aid us, therefore, to discern in the present and in every time of trial the beneficent end thou hast in view, that we may derive from affliction the means of amendment. Grant us that we may not be overmuch bowed down by any burden of sorrow, so as to forget that resignation to thy will, that courage, and that faith in thee, which become us as thy children, and as disciples of our Lord Jesus Christ.

May we with grateful hearts recount the blessings

we still enjoy, and if reminded of happier times in the past, look forward to the enjoyment, through thy blessing, of happiness in the future; and above all to that heavenly world, where there shall be no more sorrow nor sighing, but where the light afflictions which are but for a moment here shall work for us a far more exceeding and eternal weight of glory. May the sorrows we here endure, and all the varied discipline of thy providence, aid us in our endeavors to attain that world, and the glorious resurrection from the dead.

Grant us, O Lord, ever to keep in remembrance, and place before us as the model of our conduct, that holy and divine Saviour, who though he was rich yet for our sakes became poor, that we through his poverty might be rich. May we follow his example in the patience with which he endured affliction, in the firmness which resisted all temptation, the love that returned good for evil and prayers for curses, and the trust in thee which gained the victory over death.

O Lord, while we deplore outward sufferings, may we not be insensible to the sins which have deserved severer chastisement at thy hand. We lament our unworthiness, and pray that thou wouldst grant us still deeper repentance, a clearer view of our own transgressions, and a firmer purpose of heart to turn from them all. In thy mercy, O God, forgive them, and strengthen us that we may fall into them no more. Let us examine our own hearts and lives, and root out from them every beginning of evil. Nor let us make the effort to resist temptation in our own unaided strength, but trusting to the assistance of thy heavenly grace.

O Lord, as the night has gathered round us, so do shadows and darkness veil the light of thy countenance from thy children's eyes. Yet grant us to commit ourselves calmly to rest, knowing that thou, though unseen, watchest over us. May we rise in safety with another day, consoled, refreshed and strengthened, for the duties to which it calls us. So, too, may every shadow of distress pass from us, and the light of happiness shine upon our path; and at length, when the last shade shall gather, grant us, O God, to sink submissively and peacefully to rest, and to rise accepted in the image of our God when the light of eternity shall dawn upon us. We offer these our petitions, O Lord, as a united though suffering family of thy children, in the name of thy blessed Son, our Saviour, Jesus Christ, ascribing unto thee, our heavenly Father, glory and blessedness forevermore. Amen.

XXXII.

The True Rest.

At that time Jesus answered and said, I thank thee, O Father, Lord of heaven and earth, because thou hast hid these things from the wise and prudent, and hast revealed them to babes.

Even so, Father, for so it seemed good in thy sight.

All things are delivered to me by my Father; and no man knoweth the Son, but the Father; neither knoweth any man the Father, save the Son, and he to whomsoever the Son will reveal him.

Come unto me, all ye that labor, and are heavy-laden, and I will give you rest.

Take my yoke upon you, and learn of me: for I am meek and lowly in heart; and ye shall find rest to your souls.

For my yoke is easy, and my burden is light.

Blessed art thou, O God, our great Preserver and Benefactor, our Father in heaven. Another day closes upon us in the midst of countless mercies. Throughout its various scenes, at home and abroad, thou hast been with us in thy providential care. In every joy it has brought, in every success we have met, in every act of kindness we have experienced; in the air we have breathed, in the food which has nourished us, in the occupations which have exercised our minds and bodies, in our continued health, in the comforts and endearments of home; we acknowledge thee, and gratefully adore thy love. And above all, in the advent, mission and ministry, of thy Holy Child Jesus, our Redeemer, Saviour and Lord; in the precious revelation he has made of thee as a Father; in his great sacrifice for our sins; in all that he taught and all that he suffered, that he might bring us into living communion with thyself, save us from the power and degradation of sin, and prepare us for death and judgment.

Hear our prayer, O God, that we may come to him who is the only true rest for our souls. Through his grace may we break the hard yoke of our passions, and leave the heavy burden of our sins, and learn of him who was meek and lowly, whose yoke is easy and whose burden is light. Weary and heavy-laden, may we find in him a peace which the world cannot give and cannot take away.

Before we lie down to rest, we would commune with thee, and with our own souls. We would lay open to thee, and examine for ourselves, our own hearts. In the review of the day, we humble ourselves before thee. Thou hast not been to us a conscious, cherished abiding presence, and therefore we have sinned. The fear of God has not always been before our eyes, and therefore we have forgotten and broken thy holy law. Truly we have done those things which we ought not to have done, and have left undone those things which we ought to have done. Forgive us, we beseech thee, for thine own mercy's sake, as thou hast promised by thy Son; and may the sweet assurance of thy pardon take possession of our hearts, and give us abiding peace. We would retire to our chambers at peace with thee, at peace with the world, at peace with our own souls.

Watch over us, O God, this night; and protect us and our habitation, and all who are dear to us, while we sleep. And should another day dawn upon us, may we awake in safety, with minds and bodies refreshed, ready to go forth to our respective duties, and faithfully serve thee and our fellow-men.

Which we ask in the name and as the disciples of Jesus Christ, our most blessed Lord and Saviour. Amen.

XXXIII.

The Bread of Life.

And Jesus said to them, I am the bread of life: he that cometh to me shall never hunger: and he that believeth on me shall never thirst.

But I said to you, That ye also have seen me, and believe not.

All that the Father giveth me, shall come to me; and him that cometh to me I will in no wise reject.

For I came down from heaven, not to do my own will, but the will of him that sent me.

And this is the Father's will who hath sent me, that of all which he hath given me, I should lose nothing, but should raise it up again at the last day.

And this is the will of him that sent me, that every one who seeth the Son, and believeth on him, may have everlasting life: and I will raise him up at the last day.

Almighty God, our heavenly Father, who daily loadest us with benefits; we would come to thee at the close of this day to express our grateful sense of thy great and manifold mercies.

At home and abroad, in our several ways and amid varied exposures, thou hast kept us from dangers and from death. Thou hast continued to us the use of our powers and faculties, and enabled us to go through the toils required by duty and necessity without injury to mind or body. Thy bounty has supplied our wants. Thy loving hand has tenderly smoothed for us the rough and thorny paths. In thee we have found an unfailing support, when, wearied and fainting, we had felt our own strength insufficient to our need. Most humbly and fervently we thank thee, O God, for these and all the manifestations of thy unmerited goodness.

And now that we are about to retire to our rest, we would beseech thee to continue to bless us, and to take care of us. If in the day that has just past we have been successful in our endeavors to control our tempers, appetites and passions, wilt thou accept this as a proof of our sincere desire to abstain from what is evil, and by thy grace confirm and fortify within us the same holy resolution, so that on the morrow we may begin again the like efforts of self-government with yet greater zeal. If we have tried to be of use to any of our fellow-beings, to do them good, to lighten their burdens and assuage their griefs, O Father, do thou crown what we have imperfectly attempted with thine own efficacious blessing. May the happiness of others become yet dearer to our hearts with each succeeding day.

But, O God, thou knowest that we too often fail to do even what we have most sincerely desired, and that many errors and sins remain in us to make us afflicted and ashamed before thy holy eyes. O, may thy mercy pardon what we have done amiss. Make us truly contrite in view of all our transgressions. Let thy Holy Spirit help our infirmities, purify our affections, and give new moral force to our best purposes and desires. May our souls be led to him who alone can feed them, so that they will hunger no more. To him may we go who will in no wise reject those who seek him, but will give them everlasting life, and raise them up with him at the last day.

And now may we lie down upon our beds in peace. Be thou our guardian and deliverer. Keep far from us and our habitation every evil; and grant us, in thy mercy, the joy of a happy reünion around this family altar in the morning, if it be thy will that we open our eyes to the light of another day. Amen.

XXXIV.

Mental Rest.

Therefore take no thought, saying, What shall we eat? or, What shall we drink? or, Wherewithal shall we be clothed? (For after all these things do the Gentiles seek;) for your heavenly Father knoweth that ye have need of all these things.

But seek ye first the kingdom of God, and his righteousness; and all these things shall be added unto you.

Take, therefore, no thought for the morrow; for the morrow shall take thought for the things of itself. Sufficient unto the day is the evil thereof.

ALMIGHTY GOD, we draw nigh to thee in faith and humility to offer our evening worship. How great the privilege to look up to thee and call thee Father! How blessed are they who have him for their friend who made heaven and earth, and orders all things therein! We pray that we may abide in thy favor; may be kept in thy family; may always find thee near. Having sought first the kingdom of God and his righteousness, may all other things be added unto us. Thou knowest what we have need of. May thy bounty supply our wants. May thine arm be stretched out to protect us. May thy Holy Spirit sustain and strengthen us. And when it seems good unto thy wisdom to visit us with trials and afflictions, may thy grace sanctify all our sorrows, and make them instrumental to our eternal benefit.

To thy grace and care we commend our friends and relations. We beseech thee to guard them from evil, and grant them all things convenient to them; and when they shall have finished their appointed course on earth, to bring them to thine everlasting kingdom.

Bless the old and the young. May children be blessed in their parents, and parents in their children. Bless those who are coming on, and those who are in the midst of their work, and those who are passing away. Be thou the God and the Guide of all.

Let us go to rest, this night, secure in thy gracious protection. Keep us from distrustful thoughts. May our minds have rest in thee. Let us rise in the morning prepared for the duties of the day. And when at last we are called to sleep the sleep of death, may we fear no evil, but rejoice in the sure hope of a brighter morning, through Jesus Christ our Saviour. Amen.

XXXV.

For the True Riches.

And he spake a parable to them, saying, The ground of a certain rich man brought forth plentifully:

And he thought within himself, saying, What shall I do, because I have no room where to bestow my fruits?

And he said, This will I do: I will pull down my barns, and build greater; and there will I bestow all my fruits and my goods.

And I will say to my soul, Soul, thou hast much goods laid up for many years; take thy ease, eat, drink, and be merry.

But God said to him, Thou fool, this night thy soul shall be required of thee: then whose shall those things be which thou hast provided?

So is he that layeth up treasure for himself, and is not rich toward God.

Eternal God, thou only Source of all good, we admire the wisdom and mercy which are displayed in thy ordinances, whereby it is provided that seasons of thoughtful reflection and needful rest should constantly follow hours of busy toil. The day is thine; the night also is thine; and in their regular succession may we ever acknowledge the love of Him who careth for us.

For what we have enjoyed in the day that is now ended, we offer the tribute of our hearts. For what we have left undone that we should have done, or have done that we ought not to have done, we implore pardon. Erase from our souls, O God, the impression of evil we may have thoughtlessly incurred. Print deeper there the mark of every truth which has moved us, of every virtue which has drawn forth our esteem and love. Let all the experience we meet with from day to day leave some profitable lessons for our future warning and instruction. We would not live in vain: we would not be cumberers of our Lord's ground. We desire to increase in knowledge and virtue continually. We would be wiser and better with every added day.

Great God, how solemn and momentous is the end for which thou givest us a day more of life! May we seriously ponder it. May we feel that we are living for a purpose whose importance eternity alone can fully show. Wilt thou, who didst give thy dearly-beloved Son for our salvation, fulfil in us the design of his divine mission. Help us with unfeigned faith to accept the gracious words which he brings, and to embrace the Gospel which he has sealed with his blood. May the love of Christ constrain us to devote ourselves unreservedly to his service. Let all hardness and impenitence be removed from our hearts. Let our whole natures be brought into harmony with thy perfections, and be transformed by the renewing influences of thy truth and grace into the likeness of Jesus Christ.

Almighty Father, we pray that the blessed example and the solemn instruction of thy dear Son may never pass from our minds. May his meekness, gentleness and purity, be ours. May we learn to bear and to do thy will, even as he did. In him may we find peace to our souls. Let no sin have dominion over us. Let all selfishness, and pride, and anger, and malice, be banished from our hearts. May we live to do good and be useful in the world. May we make timely Christian preparation for death. Suffer us not to wander in unbelief and guilt from the only way that leadeth to eternal life. Keep us from that love of this world which may make us forget the world that is to come. Save us from that bondage to uncertain riches through which we may lose the true riches that fade not away. In the midst of all thy bounties help us so to live that the summons may not find us unprepared or unwilling, if this night our soul should be required of us.

Father, through the darkness that now encompasses us wilt thou protect us from all evil. Safely conduct us along the pilgrimage of life. Fit us to die the death of the righteous, and finally grant us a part in the blessedness of heaven. Amen.

XXXVI.

For Renewed Diligence.

But ye, brethren, are not in darkness, that that day should overtake you as a thief.

Ye are all the children of light, and the children of the day: we are not of the night, nor of darkness.

Therefore let us not sleep, as do others; but let us watch and be sober.

For they that sleep, sleep in the night; and they that be drunken, are drunken in the night.

But let us who are of the day be sober, putting on the breastplate of faith and love; and for an helmet the hope of salvation:

For God hath not appointed us to wrath, but to obtain salvation by our Lord Jesus Christ,

Who died for us, that, whether we wake or sleep, we should live together with him.

Wherefore comfort yourselves together, and edify one an other, even as also ye do.

Our Father which art in heaven, the day is thine, and the night also is thine. Thou sendest the morning light to summon us to activity, and thou gatherest about us the shades of evening that we may sleep and rest. How manifold is thy goodness! We are thine, made, and preserved, and saved by thee, and thine we would be by choice and solemn consecration.

At the close of another day, laden with new experience of thy great goodness, we would renew our vows. May we feel the solemn call to revive and quicken our diligence. How many hopes and aspirations of our morning hours are lost in the cares, struggles or pleasures, of the day! O thou Searcher of our hearts, if we this day have done aught that is well pleasing to thee, we rejoice, and thank thee for opportunity and strength. And wilt thou look in mercy upon our failures and defects. Though so far from what we should be, may we neither lose sight of our high vocation, and become indifferent, nor sink through despondency to faithless despair.

Almighty God, encourage us from thy holy word. If weak, thy service will make us strong; if our feet stumble upon the dark mountains, the light of Christ will give us noonday; and if prodigals afar from thee feeding our meaner appetites, in penitence we may return home. We thank thee for the hope of forgiving mercy. May we not abuse that mercy. Awaken us to unceasing and earnest activity while our day of life lasts, and till the long night cometh. Help us to put on the whole armor of God, and to enter with renewed courage upon that service which is appointed to us, that we may obtain salvation through our Lord Jesus Christ.

Father of all the families upon earth, may thy blessing rest upon this our home. We come here from our more outward and public concerns, and here may we meet thee, and see ourselves as thou seest us. May our life and health be precious in thy sight. May love, harmony and peace, come as good angels into the midst of us.

O thou ever-present Guardian, be with us this night, defend us in its lonely watches, and let thy peace possess our souls. O hear and graciously keep us; for thine is the power, and to thee be rendered everlasting praise, through Jesus Christ our Lord. Amen.

XXXVII.

Lowly Service.

Then he cometh to Simon Peter: and Peter saith to him, Lord, dost thou wash my feet?

Jesus answered and said to him, What I do thou knowest not now; but thou shalt know hereafter.

Peter saith to him, Thou shalt never wash my feet. Jesus answered him, If I wash thee not, thou hast no part with me.

Simon Peter said to him, Lord, not my feet only, but also my hands and my head.

So after he had washed their feet, and had taken his garments, and was set down again, he said to them, Know ye what I have done to you?

Ye call me Master and Lord: and ye say well; for so I am.

If I then, your Lord and Master, have washed your feet; ye also ought to wash one another's feet.

For I have given you an example, that ye should do as I have done to you.

Verily, verily, I say to you, The servant is not greater than his lord; neither he that is sent greater than he that sent him.

If ye know these things, happy are ye if ye do them.

FATHER ALMIGHTY, who with more than a father's solicitude, with more than a mother's tenderness, dost cherish and watch over us, we draw near with our evening tribute of prayer and thanksgiving unto thee, who hearest prayer, and dost not refuse the offering of praise from humble and contrite hearts. Blessed be God, that once more we are gathered together for this holy duty, in circumstances so favorable and hopeful. May we all count up the mercies of our God, and find in them the motives to urge us forward in the duties of a holy life. May thy goodness lead us to repentance of our sins. May it animate us with a purer and warmer charity. May it give new vigor to faith, new force to virtuous resolution. May it draw our hearts continually heavenward.

Accept the toils and endeavors, the self-denials and the patient endurance, which we may have successfully attained to, by thy grace helping us, this day. Forgive our many imperfections and our many sins. Father, we would bow low before thee. Compared with thy perfect holiness, we feel ourselves unworthy to look up to thee, and to call ourselves thy children. If thou shalt grant us more time and opportunity for improvement, we pray that we may be enabled to make the best use of it, and may be ever growing in knowledge and virtue as we increase in years.

Great Father of mankind, may the same blessings which have made us a happy family be extended to all the families of men. Inspire us with the most earnest desire to be useful in every relation we sustain. May the spirit of Jesus, who came not to be ministered unto, but to minister, be in our hearts. In the footsteps of our divine Saviour may we delight to walk. Let our love to him ever prompt us to love all those whom God has placed within the reach of our kind offices. Willingly and joyfully may we render to them any service, counting none too lowly if it may contribute to the comfort of those with whom our lot is cast. Make us more prompt to show courtesy, affection, a yielding of our preferences, and a study of others' wishes, in our daily intercourse; so that our lives, if marked by the stewardship of no great trusts, may be filled full of useful and pleasing service, in the humble occurrences of every hour. Dispose us to pity and commiseration, to forbearance and forgiveness. Open our hearts wide to the claims of all our fellow-creatures upon our aid and care, our good-will and affection, and may our influence and example be a blessing throughout the sphere in which they may be felt. Knowing the duty and the precious worth of these things, may we inherit the benediction, Happy are ye if ye do them.

And now, O Father, may thy peace descend upon us. May thy merciful protection be over us; may we sleep undisturbed by any evil, under thy watchful eye; and when we awake may we rejoice that we are still with thee. Amen.

XXXVIII.

Cheerfulness in our Lot.

Two things have I required of thee; deny them not to me before I die:

Remove far from me vanity and lies; give me neither pov erty nor riches; feed me with food convenient for me;

Lest I be full, and deny thee, and say, Who is the Lord? or lest I be poor, and steal, and take the name of my God in vain.

He that loveth silver shall not be satisfied with silver, nor he that loveth abundance with increase: this is also vanity.

I know both how to be abased, and I know how to abound: everywhere and in all things, I am instructed both to be full and to be hungry, both to abound and to suffer need.

We are troubled on every side, yet not distressed; we are perplexed, but not in despair;

Persecuted, but not forsaken; cast down, but not destroyed;

As unknown, and yet well known; as dying, and behold, we live; as chastened, and not killed;

As sorrowful, yet always rejoicing; as poor, yet making many rich; as having nothing, and yet possessing all things.

FATHER of all Mercies, we thy children, sheltering ourselves under thy watchful eye and protecting care, would offer to thee our evening tribute of praise. Accept our thanks for the past day; for all it has brought of thy bounty; for all it has offered of thy grace; for all it has witnessed of kindly offices and sweet affections; for all which will live in our memories of its opportunities well improved, and its duties faithfully done.

Before closing our eyes in sleep, we would seek thy forgiveness of our sins, and implore of thee those spiritual graces which we feel that we need. May we bow before thee in the spirit of a cheerful acquiescence in the lot which thy providence hath assigned to us. Save us, O God, from ever being anxious, distrustful, or repining. Believing that thou art the ruler over the whole earth, and that all things are ordered by thine unerring wisdom, may we learn in whatsoever state we are therewith to be content. Thou knowest what is truly best for us; we would have no will but thine. If the lines fall to us in pleasant places, to thee be the praise. If sickness and sorrow overtake us, thou art our portion, and in thee will we put our trust. Fully assured, O Lord, of thy watchful providence, we would be cheerfully satisfied with our lot, and look on every untoward event of life with patience and serenity, assured that thou canst bring good out of seeming evil.

To thee, the Rock of our salvation, we will fly in every extremity of ill; for thou wilt never leave or forsake the children of thy care. As all things come of thee, may our conversation be without covetousness. Put far from us all envious dispositions, and murmuring thoughts. Thankful for past mercies, we would indulge no unseemly anxiety for the morrow, knowing that futurity is in thy hands. With present health and comfort, we would cast all other cares upon thee, who carest for us.

Grant, O God, that thy peace, which passeth all understanding, may continually possess our souls. May no corrupt and selfish desires interrupt the devout cheerfulness of our spirits. Let not sin have dominion over us, to lead us astray from the paths of godliness and contentment. Daily laying up for ourselves treasures in heaven, may we enjoy here that pure satisfaction which follows the diligent practice of righteousness, and be prepared to enter hereafter into life eternal. We implore these blessings of thy mercy through Jesus Christ our Lord, while for this night, and for our future lives, we commit ourselves to thy guardian care. Amen.

XXXIX.

Domestic Unity.

Behold, how good and how pleasant it is for brethren to dwell together in unity!

It is like the precious ointment upon the head, that ran down upon the beard, even Aaron's beard; that went down to the skirts of his garments;

As the dew of Hermon, and as the dew that descended upon the mountains of Zion: for there the Lord commanded the blessing, even life forevermore.

Behold, bless ye the Lord, all ye servants of the Lord, which by night stand in the house of the Lord.

Lift up your hands in the sanctuary, and bless the Lord.

The Lord, that made heaven and earth, bless thee out of Zion.

O God, the light of every heart that sees thee, the life of every soul that loves thee, we, thy children, pray that thou wouldst lighten our darkness, sustain our faintings, save us from the death of sin, and grant us life eternal. Enter, we beseech thee, into our hearts, speak peace unto this house, abide with us always, and command thy blessing to descend upon us as the dew upon the mountains of Zion.

Keep us continually, O God, in thy fear. May we be followers of that which is good, and disciples of thy Son Jesus Christ, obeying his precepts, and imitating his example. Let our bodies be in constant subjection to our souls, our senses to our reason, and our reason to thy divine and gracious instruction; that so, both outwardly and inwardly, we may be fully disposed to do thy will.

May we, thy children, know from our experience how good and how pleasant it is to dwell together in unity. May we be kind and faithful to each other, and to all with whom we are in any way connected. And may we be always sensible of our relationship to thee, our heavenly Father, and feel that whether sleeping or waking we are still with thee. Keep and defend us this night. Grant unto us quiet and restoring slumbers. Bring us to the light of another morning in safety, and when our days and nights on earth are numbered and finished, grant that we may behold each other in the light of eternal day, and be members together of thy family in heaven. And this we ask in the name of Jesus Christ, our blessed Lord and Redeemer. Amen.

XL.

Looking to the End.

The Lord is not slack concerning his promise, as some men count slackness; but is long suffering to us-ward, not willing that any should perish, but that all should come to repentance.

But the day of the Lord will come as a thief in the night; in the which the heavens shall pass away with a great noise, and the elements shall melt with fervent heat, the earth also, and the works that are therein, shall be burned up.

Seeing then that all these things shall be dissolved, what manner of persons ought ye to be in all holy conversation and godliness;

Looking for and hasting unto the coming of the day of God, wherein the heavens, being on fire, shall be dissolved, and the elements shall melt with fervent heat?

Nevertheless we, according to his promise, look for new heavens, and a new earth, wherein dwelleth righteousness.

Wherefore, beloved, seeing that ye look for such things, be diligent that ye may be found of him in peace, without spot, and blameless.

God of the evening, while the curtain of night falls around us, thy imperfect creatures, to thee the darkness and light are both alike. We would realize that thine eye never slumbers; that it is ever upon us, and upon us only for our good. Having experienced thy watchful and beneficent care through another day, we would in this quiet evening hour gratefully and devoutly acknowledge it.

We humbly confess our unworthiness. We pray that we may be forgiven; and by true repentance, by consistent and thorough faithfulness, by reforming what is wrong and perfecting what is right, may we commend ourselves to thee and our consciences, and show as we best can our sense of that unceasing and infinite goodness, which is new every morning, and renewed every evening, and every moment of our life.

O God, as we now yield ourselves to rest under the shadows of night, may we yet more repose under the shadow of the Almighty, of thine all-wise and most merciful protection. If thou shalt permit our eyes to open again on earthly scenes, may we awake with powers refreshed, and spirits invigorated, and resolute for the work of duty. Give thine angels charge over us this night, that our sleep may be rest and our waking peace.

And when that night cometh, that sooner or later comes to all, in which the heavens shall pass away, and the work of life can no more be done, may we be found prepared to awake in thy likeness, and to enter on the rest of thy people, in those heavenly mansions which the great and good Saviour has gone before to prepare for his faithful followers. Thus, though all these things of earth shall be dissolved, we would according to his promise look for new heavens and a new earth, wherein dwelleth righteousness. May not the shadows of time obscure the realities of eternity. But, grateful for thy long-suffering, remembering that the day of the Lord will at last come when we look not for it, may we be diligent that we be found of him in peace, without spot and blameless. And to thy holy name be the glory forever. Amen.

XLI.

Passing On.

Behold, I show you a mystery; We shall not all sleep, but we shall all be changed,

In a moment, in the twinkling of an eye, at the last trump (for the trumpet shall sound); and the dead shall be raised incorruptible, and we shall be changed.

For this corruptible must put on incorruption, and this mortal must put on immortality.

So when this corruptible shall have put on incorruption, and this mortal shall have put on immortality, then shall be brought to pass the saying that is written, Death is swallowed up in victory.

O death! where is thy sting? O grave! where is thy victory?

The sting of death is sin; and the strength of sin is the law.

But thanks be to God which giveth us the victory, through our Lord Jesus Christ.

Therefore, my beloved brethren, be ye steadfast, unmovable, always abounding in the work of the Lord, forasmuch as ye know that your labor is not in vain in the Lord.

OUR FATHER, who hast given us the light and life and enjoyments of another day, blessed be thy name for these and all the rich tokens of thy fatherly goodness, from the beginning to the present time. Let a fervent gratitude warm our hearts, that we may never forget or forsake thee, the fountain of all good, who hast never forgotten or forsaken us.

We give thee hearty thanks for the active duties,

the labors of love and usefulness, which thou hast ordained as the means of our earthly discipline and our preparation for the life to come. If we have failed this day in reverence to thee or obedience to thy most holy commandments, if we have thought or done evil to our fellow-men, we pray that we may be forgiven and restored to thy paternal love. If we have injured our own bodies or souls, and marred thy divine image within us, we beseech thee, the source of all health and all spiritual regeneration, to heal and to redeem us.

And now, since our days on earth have been lessened, lead us onward and upward more and more, in faith and affection, to the heavenly world. While all things here below are passing away, and we can look for no eternal home on earth, may we lay up our treasures and build our hopes in heaven, that when this mortal shall put on immortality death may be swallowed up in victory.

O God, thou again drawest around us the curtains of evening, and declarest thy glory in the starry skies. Keep us in peace and safety, great Guardian of our lives, during the hours of darkness and sleep, and may we be refreshed by quiet slumbers. Let it please thee to guard all our dear friends, wherever they may be, at home or abroad, on land or sea, and to bind our hearts to them in ever new ties of love and spiritual sympathy. Command thy divine blessing on the poor, the sick and the erring, that thy compassions and thy corrections may not fail in their several needs. Above all things, our heavenly Father, we pray for the coming of thy kingdom, and the doing of thy will on earth as it is done in heaven. May Jesus reign, from the rising to the setting of the sun, in all hearts and in all homes.

Graciously accept our evening tribute of prayer and praise in his holy and ever-blessed name who giveth us the victory over all danger, and over death itself; and unto thee, the King eternal, the Father almighty, be honor and glory, dominion and power, world without end. Amen.

XLII.

No Night There.

And I saw no temple in it: for the Lord God Almighty and the Lamb are the temple of it.

And the city had no need of the sun, neither of the moon, to shine in it: for the glory of God enlightened it, and the Lamb is the light of it.

And the nations of them who are saved shall walk in the light of it: and the kings of the earth bring their glory and honor into it.

And the gates of it shall not be shut by day: for there shall be no night there.

And they shall bring the glory and honor of the nations into it.

And there shall in no wise enter into it anything that defileth, neither whatever worketh abomination, or maketh a lie; but they who are written in the Lamb's book of life.

O Lord, be thou with us now that the evening is come, and darkness and silence and sleep await us. Thy beauty fades not away from us with the day. Thy stars are in the deep sky. The serene expanse is still full of thy greatness and thy benignity. The earth sleeps beneath thine overspreading watch. Nothing can be lost from thine eye. Thou shadest the earth and lightest the heavens. Father, we love thee. Holy, holy, holy, thou who leadest out the hosts of stars; the whole earth, by night and by day, dwells amidst the flow of thy glory.

As thus amidst the darkness of night thou showest the lights above us, so, O Lord, amidst the dimness which gathers over our short time of life, amidst its clouds and its shades, its infirmities, its bereavements and its sorrows, thou dost evermore unveil the celestial spheres, and their everlasting beauty and peace. May we lift up our eyes and see. May the faith in our hearts welcome and trust thy word, even when it seems far off in the distant heavens; may the hope, full of immortality, drink in forever the promises of thy love, and make us of good cheer; may the love flowing instantly from thee to us go up hourly through the deep mystery to thee, Fountain of good, pouring its charities on all whom thou hast made. So may we live here the heavenly life. So, while on earth, may we take in and give forth the higher presence; through the shadows which fall over us, may we make the substance a reality and a power; among men may we commune with thee, blessing our brethren. Living we are thine; to thee may we live forever.

Father, there is no death with thee. Open every eye to see thee; reveal to every soul the immortality which it bears within. The darkness hath passed; from thee shineth the true light. May the sons of men rejoice in the morning which hath turned night to day. May they behold the whole earth radiant with thy beams. May they go up into the mountain and hear thy voice. May they come down into the valley, building up their lives after the pattern which thou hast shown them. May they be transfigured to the likeness of thy dearest Son; so from the divine splendor may their faces shine, from its descending rays may their robes grow white. Through the powers of the eternal life, may all be strong to overcome the world, to remove evil, to win the crown of righteousness. As friend after friend departs, and we begin to walk on earth bereaved and alone, Father, be thou with thy lowly ones, and make all hearts glad with the open vision. As we enter into the shade and pass from mortal sight, may we see, not the gloom, but the glory, and rejoice in the day which has no night. Evermore in the depth of our hearts, breathing inspiration, and making all things divine, may we hear the celestial word, I am the resurrection and the life; he that believeth in me, though he were dead, yet shall he live; and whosoever liveth and believeth in me shall never die.

Blessed be thou, Word of the Eternal. Blessed be thou, who hast abolished death, and brought life and immortality to light. Blessed be thou, now and forever. Amen.

XLIII.

Help for the Needy.

O that men would praise the Lord for his goodness, and for his wonderful works to the children of men!

For he satisfieth the longing soul, and filleth the hungry soul with goodness.

Such as sit in darkness and in the shades of death, being bound in affliction and iron;

Because they rebelled against the words of God, and contemned the counsel of the Most High:

Therefore he brought down their heart with labor; they fell down, and there was none to help.

Then they cried to the Lord in their trouble, and he saved them out of their distresses.

He brought them out of darkness and the shades of death, and broke their bands asunder.

O that men would praise the Lord for his goodness, and for his wonderful works to the children of men!

OUR FATHER in heaven, thy children kneel before the throne of thy mercy, and humbly thank thee for all the blessings of this day, and for the privilege which we now enjoy of holding communion with thee, and praising thee for thy goodness and thy wonderful works to the children of men.

O God, if this day we have fallen into any sin; if we have weakly yielded to any temptation; if we have been angry without cause or beyond bounds; if we have been uncharitable, unjust, undutiful, or in any way unmindful of thee and thy laws, we beseech thee to forgive us in thy great mercy, and give us true repentance, that we may lie down this night in peace with the world, with ourselves, and with thee. And we pray thee, O Father, to watch over us this night, and protect us from all evil, and give to our eyes refreshing slumbers, so that we may rise in the morning with renewed power to serve thee. If we are to rise no more in this world, grant that we may wake in the next to life immortal, and the light of thy countenance forevermore.

We pray thee, also, to protect the whole sleeping world through the hours of darkness and helplessness. Be graciously with those, also, who by land or by sea must wake and watch. Soothe the pains of the sick; speak pardon and peace to sleepless consciences; guide the traveller on his way; preserve the mariner from the fury of the tempest, and direct him through the paths of the deep. Be a father to the fatherless; a deliverer to the oppressed; a friend to all who are under neglect or contempt, or in want, and especially to those who are persecuted for conscience and righteousness' sake. Be kind to all our friends and to all our enemies; to all who have prayed for us, and to all who have desired that we should pray for them. Mercifully, O God, Father Almighty, hear their prayers, and ours, which we offer in the name of our Lord Jesus Christ. Amen.

XLIV.

Saturday Evening.

Return to thy rest, O my soul; for the Lord hath dealt bountifully with thee.

For thou hast delivered my soul from death, my eyes from tears, and my feet from falling.

I will walk before the Lord in the land of the living.

What shall I render to the Lord for all his benefits toward me?

I will take the cup of salvation, and call upon the name of the Lord.

Accept, I beseech thee, the freewill offerings of my mouth, O Lord, and teach me thy judgments.

Thy hands have made me and fashioned me: give me under standing, that I may learn thy commandments.

Thy statutes have been my songs in the house of my pilgrimage.

I have remembered thy name, O Lord, in the night, and have kept thy law.

ALMIGHTY GOD and most merciful Father, in whose hands our times are, and whose are all our ways; on whom we are dependent for all the privi leges, blessings and comforts, of this life, and for all the means and instrumentalities of preparing us for a better.

We thank thee for thy kind and protecting care of us another day and another week; that thou hast kept us ever beneath thy watchful eye and protecting hand, and in great mercy hast brought us to the close of the day and of the week still surrounded with thy goodness, and still among the living to praise thee. Wilt thou forgive the sins of the day, of the week, and of our whole lives. May all thy mercies lead us to repentance, even to that repentance whose fruit is unto holiness, and whose end is everlasting life.

We commend ourselves to thy holy protection and keeping this night. May we lie down in the fear and love of God. May our sleep be quiet and refreshing to us. Spread over us the wing of an ever-guardian providence, and preserve us from every danger and from every alarm; and bring us to behold the light of another morning, even another of the days of the Son of man, in health and in peace. Prepare us, O God of the Sabbath, for the return of holy time. May we be in the spirit on the Lord's day. With the beams of the natural sun may the Sun of righteousness arise upon our souls with healing in his wings, and fill us with all joy and peace in believing. Give us such admiring views of thy creating power and wisdom, thy providential care and kindness, and thy redeeming love and grace, as shall fill our souls with the deepest reverence for thy character, the purest love of thy perfections, the liveliest hope in thy mercy, and the sublimest joy in thy more immediate worship and service. And at the close of the Sabbath day may we have the satisfaction of reflecting that we have devoted one day more to the service of our God and Redeemer; that we have made some advance in the Christian life, some better preparation for the joys and services of the kingdom and temple above.

We pray for those who are appointed to minister at thine altar, and to dispense the bread of life and the water of life to them who are ready to perish. May they be baptized anew with the spirit and power of the truth as it is in Jesus. And clad in the Christian armor may they go forth to their work with the fearlessness of men engaged in the service of God, and seeking the salvation of them that are lost. And wilt thou give them that best reward in this life, that purest of satisfactions, that greatest of joys to the teacher's heart, the satisfaction and the joy of seeing the people of their charge, under their ministration, crowding the gates of Zion, flocking to her solemn feasts, listening to divine instruction, and walking in thy truth.

We pray for our country and its rulers. May those who are appointed to rule over us prove themselves to be able men, such as fear God; men of truth, hating covetousness, seeking the good of their country and their race, and the glory of thy holy name. Under the protection of just and equal laws, and a wise and righteous administration, may the people lead quiet and peaceable lives in all godliness and honesty.

May the blessings which we ask for ourselves and our country be extended to the whole human family, until every nation, tongue and people, shall unite with the heavenly hosts in ascribing glory to God in the highest, because there is peace on earth, and good-will to men.

This our prayer we offer unto thee the Infinite Father, in the name and as the disciples of thy beloved Son, Jesus Christ. Amen.

XLV.

Sunday Evening.

The mercy of the Lord is from everlasting to everlasting upon them that fear him, and his righteousness to children's children;

To such as keep his covenant, and to those that remember his commandments to do them.

The Lord hath prepared his throne in the heavens; and his kingdom ruleth over all.

Bless the Lord, ye his angels, that excel in strength, that do his commandments, hearkening to the voice of his word.

Bless ye the Lord, all ye his hosts; ye ministers of his, that do his pleasure.

Bless the Lord, all his works in all places of his dominion: bless the Lord, O my soul.

Our Father who art in heaven. We thank thee that we have been visited with another day of sacred rest, rest for the body and rest for the soul. We thank thee for all the Christian privileges we have enjoyed; for all the spiritual refreshment and strength we have received; for every word of truth our ears have heard; for every penitent emotion our hearts have felt; for every good desire that has been awakened; for every worthy purpose that has been formed; for every holy aspiration that has been enkindled.

O God, give to all these Sabbath influences power to draw our souls upward, and to bring us nearer and nearer to thee in spirit and purpose, nearer and nearer to Christ in heart and life. O, that our souls might be so opened upward that the Father and the Son might come and make their abode with us; that we might be baptized afresh each day with the Holy Spirit, and with the fire of a sacred love for God and goodness. May we experience more and more of the renewing power of the Gospel. May the spirit of selfishness and sin be cast out of our hearts. May we become new creatures in Christ Jesus, filled and animated by a new love for God our heavenly Father, for man our earthly brother, and for whatsoever things are pure, honest, just, and lovely.

We pray for all mankind. Thou hast made of one blood all nations. We are all children of one Father; all dependent upon thy bounty and love. We pray that all may share in the blessings of the Gospel; that the truth and love and spirit of Christ may go forth with its redeeming power, until all hearts shall feel its benign and saving influence; until all hate, and retaliation, and war, and slavery, and intemperance, and every other form of evil and wrong, shall cease, and thy kingdom come on earth, and thy will be done in the hearts of thy children as it is done in heaven.

With this prayer upon our lips and in our hearts, we would seek the repose of another night. May we rest securely beneath the shadow of thy wings, and rise with the light of another morning refreshed and strengthened in body and in spirit for the duties of this week. We ask it as disciples of thy Son our Saviour. Amen.

XLVI.

Sunday Evening.

Abide in me, and I in you. As the branch cannot bear fruit of itself, except it abide in the vine; no more can ye, except ye abide in me.

I am the vine, ye are the branches; he that abideth in me, and I in him, the same bringeth forth much fruit; for without me ye can do nothing.

If a man abide not in me, he is cast forth as a branch, and is withered; and men gather them, and cast them into the fire, and they are burned.

If ye abide in me, and my words abide in you, ye shall ask what ye will, and it shall be done unto you.

Herein is my Father glorified, that ye bear much fruit; so shall ye be my disciples.

As the Father hath loved me, so have I loved you: continue ye in my love.

If ye keep my commandments, ye shall abide in my love; even as I have kept my Father's commandments, and abide in his love.

These things have I spoken unto you, that my joy might remain in you, and that your joy might be full.

MERCIFUL FATHER, whose we are, for thou dost give us life; whom we are bound to serve, for thou dost give us all our strength; to whom we should be always grateful, for thou dost bestow upon us all those blessings which make life desirable; we thank thee for the precious hours of this sacred day. By thy favor we have gone up to thy house together; we have united our hearts in prayer and praise with our friends and associates; we have listened to the words of thy servant, as he has spoken to us of our duty and thy will.

Our Father, help us to remember how highly thou hast blessed us, in giving us these holy and quiet hours of worship in thy house. How many of thy children do not yet know thee! How many of our fellow-men are in darkness, worshipping the works of their own hands! Help us to feel that thou dost require us to send to them these holy truths, these inspiring promises, which thou hast given to us.

Help us to feel that thou hast appointed us to the high and holy work of sending this divine light into heathen darkness; of pouring this water of life into the thirsty souls of thy suffering children. We pray that we may feel, more deeply than we ever yet have felt, our obligation to aid thy people in sending the Gospel of thy grace to those who are still destitute of its healing, saving power. May the joys of this day deepen in our hearts a sense of the true value of the Gospel, so that we shall be moved to more activity in every benevolent work.

We pray, our Father, that we may feel bound with stronger ties to our pastor, whose words have cheered and strengthened us this day. Let not the truths he has thus declared fall like good seed on stony places; but in the good ground of prepared minds, and tender consciences, and holy resolutions, may it bring forth good fruit to the glory of thy name. Help us all to coöperate in every good word and work, so that we may encourage his heart and strengthen his hands. May we receive him to our homes as a friend and brother, and may he be to all of us a son of consolation, and a minister of the grace of God.

O God, we pray for thy people in this place. May we all be united to Christ, even as the branch is united to the vine. Abiding in him, may we bring forth good fruits to the glory of thee the Father. Keep us from all delusions that would lead us away from our sure trust. Amid all the shows and strifes of the world, may we be determined to know only Christ and him crucified, as other foundation can no man lay.

And now, our Father, as the day is closing, we pray that its holy influences may go with us into the week; that we may be strengthened by them in the hour of temptation, and encouraged by them in the hour of difficulty, so that this week shall witness in us more purity of purpose, more holiness, generosity, kindness and forbearance, than we have ever before possessed.

As we retire to rest, we seek thy protection during the night. Keep us, our Father, and bring us to the light of another day, and to the active duties of another week, in strength and hope. Hear us, we pray thee, and bless us, as thou seest we need; and help us to render to thee the thanks which are due to thee, for thy great favors through Jesus Christ. Amen.

Occasional Prayers.

OCCASIONAL PRAYERS.

OCCASIONAL PRAYERS FOR A FAMILY.

I.

New Year.

Lord, thou hast been our dwelling-place in all generations.

Before the mountains were brought forth, or ever thou hadst formed the earth and the world, even from everlasting to everlasting, thou art God.

Thou turnest man to destruction; and sayest, Return, ye children of men.

For a thousand years in thy sight are but as yesterday when it is past, and as a watch in the night.

So teach us to number our days, that we may apply our hearts to wisdom.

Return, O Lord, how long? and repent thou concerning thy servants.

O satisfy us early with thy mercy; that we may rejoice and be glad all our days.

Make us glad according to the days in which thou hast afflicted us, and the years in which we have seen evil.

Let thy work appear to thy servants, and thy glory to their children.

And let the beauty of the Lord our God be upon us: and establish thou the work of our hands upon us; yea, the work of our hands establish thou it.

On the morning of another year, we bow ourselves before thee, O thou God of our lives, and seek thy blessing. In thy presence, which we now solemnly invoke, we consecrate ourselves renewedly to thy service. May the coming year prove a new year indeed, bringing new thoughts and better resolutions than we ever yet have formed. Happy, thrice happy will it be for us, if it lead us into a new and divine life. Should it bring us trials and sorrows, and take from us health and friends, still happy will it be if through thy grace we are enabled to use it well. Although it should strip us of our dearest earthly possessions, it will make us rich indeed if it give us wisdom and strength, and its memory will be precious forever. O, then with one mind and heart we would pause, and pray for light, and beseech thee to give us new convictions of the priceless worth of a godly and righteous life. Send down thy Spirit from the holy heavens to write upon our hearts, to record thy will upon those living tables in eternal characters.

We would no longer be in bondage to the world and its foolish and hurtful lusts. But we would have faith in God, and in the unutterable worth of our immortal souls. We would renounce the pleasures of sin and sense, and no more be led astray by the hollow promises and gaudy show of life. We know — in how many ways hast thou taught us!—we know that true peace can be found only in making thy will our supreme law, in submitting every desire to thee. But, O God, plain as the way of life is, we are prone to forsake it, and follow false guides, and take counsel of our own blinded minds, our own sinful thoughts. Vanity and passion, the desire of the eyes, and the pride of life, all these ensnare us and mislead our understandings, and cause us to neglect the things which it most solemnly concerns us to know and do. We do not *live*, but dream, walking in a vain show, ruled by the fear or the favor of the world; and we know not what a blessed thing it is, how divine the joy, to be one with thee, faithful servants of the living God, devoted friends and brethren of thy Son Jesus Christ.

Merciful Father, help thou our insensibility and unbelief. And now, as another year opens upon us, renew us in the whole temper of our minds. Regenerate our affections. Give us strength here and now to break away from every evil habit, and to set out with another spirit, to become new creatures, dead to the terrors and solicitations of the world, alive to God and to truth.

We may not live to see the beginning of another year. Long before the present year closes, we may be laid in the grave. O thou Disposer of life and of death, may we be found doing thy work, with our faces set heavenward and our whole souls bent upon living wisely and well. Let not this year be marked by broken vows, by a sinful surrender of our souls to the tyranny of wicked passions, by indolence and deadness of heart; but may it be forever memorable as a year rich in generous purposes and Christian deeds. And when we are called to stand at thy bar, may this year bear witness to virtuous resolutions carefully kept, to our growth in knowledge, in piety, and in love.

And may every coming year, every coming day, bear the same blessed testimony. By the divine power of a true spirit, may we convert all the changes of life, abundance and want, sickness and health, into opportunities of grace; and so may we be raised above the power of time, and breathe the air of an eternal world, even while we sojourn in this vale of shadows.

Almighty God, we would lay open our hearts before thee. Search thou us and show us ourselves, all the heights and depths of our own nature, the glory for which we are made, the perils to which we are exposed, the sins which we secretly nourish, and with lowly and earnest minds, with godly fear, may we toil day and night to obtain the end of our being, even the salvation of our souls. Let thy mighty power, which controls the courses of the universe, upholding worlds and systems of worlds, O, let it descend and inspire us, that, like the stars of the firmament, we may show forth the glory of God. Not unto us, not unto us, but unto thee, shall be rendered praises everlasting. Amen.

II.

A Day of Fasting.

Is not this the fast that I have chosen? to loose the bands of wickedness, to undo the heavy burdens, and to let the oppressed go free, and that ye break every yoke?

Is it not to deal thy bread to the hungry, and that thou shouldst bring the poor that are cast out to thy house? when thou seest the naked, that thou shouldst cover him; and that thou shouldst not hide thyself from thy own flesh?

Then shall thy light break forth as the morning, and thy health shall spring forth speedily: and thy righteousness shall go before thee; the glory of the Lord shall be thy rearward.

Then shalt thou call, and the Lord will answer; thou shalt cry, and he will say, Here I am. If thou shalt take away from the midst of thee the yoke, the putting forth of the finger, and speaking vanity;

And if thou shalt draw out thy soul to the hungry, and satisfy the afflicted soul; then shall thy light rise in obscurity, and thy darkness be as the noon-day:

And the Lord will guide thee continually, and satisfy thy soul in drouth, and make fat thy bones: and thou shalt be like a watered garden, and like a spring of water, whose waters fail not.

JUST and holy God, who lovest righteousness and hatest iniquity, to thee all hearts are open, all desires are known. Called this day to humiliation and prayer, do thou make it a sacred season to our souls, by impressing upon us every motive to sincere repentance and a holy life.

O Lord, our only hope is in thy mercy. With thee there is plenteous redemption; and having proclaimed thyself willing to forgive, we rely on divine compassion. We blush under the humiliating consciousness that thou hast been following us with thy loving-kindness, while we have been sinning against thee. Deep and abiding sorrow belongs to us. We would seek that forgiveness which thy word promises, and fly to that redemption of which Christ is the minister.

Righteous Father, we would examine ourselves as members of a family. If we have yielded to temptation, and the year past has seen us angry without cause and beyond bounds; if we have been uncharitable, unjust, undutiful, or unkind; if plenty has been abused by luxury, and liberty by licentiousness; if our ease and safety have only led to strife, envyings, and divisions; above all, if we have been indifferent to thy worship, restrained prayer, and forgotten the Saviour who died for us; if we have thus broken the ties which should bind us to one another and to thee, do thou, merciful God, convince us of our sins and folly, and lead us back to innocence, piety, and peace. May we no longer be hardened and blinded; but let it please thee to look in tender compassion on thy frail and forgetful children, who would now turn to thee with sorrowing and penitent hearts.

Universal Parent, we would recognize our near connection with the citizens of this nation; and as we now at thy footstool humbly and penitently confess our sins, we beseech thee mercifully to regard us all, prostrate before thee, and to hear the voice which will issue to-day from so many temples and closets, saying, Spare thy people, O Lord, and give not thy heritage to reproach. We mourn over the violations of piety and truth, of righteousness and law, of temperance and purity. We mourn over the existence of treachery, the displays of pride, the perpetration of cruelty, the guilt of rebellious lives. Especially we mourn over the neglect of the Bible, the Sabbath, and the sanctuary. These sins fill our faces with shame, and our hearts with dread. The land mourneth because of wickedness. O God, if we of this family have been partakers of any of these sins, may we this day humble ourselves lowly in the dust before thee in shame and self-reproach, and so repent that in future we shall be no more guilty of these offences. Cleanse us, thou pure and perfect Spirit, from every pollution, and restore us through him who died for us. Pour out upon thy people the spirit of prayer and humiliation, and show them the things which belong to their peace before this hour of reconciliation be past. O may they no longer abuse thy mercies, but keep this day such a fast as thou hast chosen; and, loosing every bond of wickedness, become a peculiar people zealous of good works.

Supreme Director of human affairs, while we lament the sins which cleave to us and to our country, and ask thee to spare those who penitently confess their faults, we would intercede for all sorts and conditions of men. Fountain of all power, bless those in authority; and may they who make and they who execute the laws be men of wisdom and justice, of industry and truth, of piety and peace. May they ever keep our land the happy abode of freedom and order, and may virtue and judgment run down as waters, and righteousness as a mighty stream. Endue with grace and clothe with godliness the ministers of religion. May they do honor to thy truth in their public services and private conduct. Faithful and fearless, may they show thy people their transgressions. We beseech thee to bless all seminaries of learning, instructors of youth, and patrons of education, and grant that all our means of mental, moral and religious advancement may be thankfully acknowledged and diligently improved. Prosper those who labor, and may lawful trade in all its branches receive thy blessing.

Compassionate Father, we again ask thy favor on the purposes of this day. May a spirit of seriousness and self-reflection pervade all classes, and the humiliation professed be felt in truth. God forbid that we should confess sins which we do not feel, or retain those we confess. Do thou give us such a deep persuasion of the evil of sin, that we shall wholly for sake it.

Author of nature, we ask thy smiles on the opening season. Order all things in much mercy for us, and whatever earthly good thou shalt deny us, deny us not thy heavenly grace. May the year be crowned with thy goodness, and we be permitted to rejoice before thee at its close, as the true disciples of Christ.

In the name of an ever-gracious Redeemer we offer our prayer, ascribing to thee all praise forever. Amen.

III.

A Day of Thanksgiving.

I will extol thee, my God, O King; and I will bless thy name for ever and ever.

Every day will I bless thee; and I will praise thy name for ever and ever.

Great is the Lord, and greatly to be praised; and his greatness is unsearchable.

One generation shall praise thy works to another, and shall declare thy mighty acts.

I will speak of the glorious honor of thy majesty, and of thy wondrous works.

And men shall speak of the might of thy terrible acts; and I will declare thy greatness.

They shall abundantly utter the memory of thy great goodness, and shall sing of thy righteousness.

The Lord is gracious, and full of compassion; slow to anger, and of great mercy.

The Lord is good to all; and his tender mercies are over all his works.

All thy works shall praise thee, O Lord; and thy saints shall bless thee.

They shall speak of the glory of thy kingdom, and talk of thy power;

To make known to the sons of men his mighty acts, and the glorious majesty of his kingdom.

Thy kingdom is an everlasting kingdom, and thy dominion endureth throughout all generations.

The Lord upholdeth all that fall, and raiseth up all those that be bowed down.

The eyes of all wait upon thee; and thou givest them their meat in due season.

Thou openest thine hand, and satisfiest the desire of every living thing.

The Lord is righteous in all his ways, and holy in all his works.

The Lord is nigh unto all them that call upon him, to all that call upon him in truth.

He will fulfil the desire of them that fear him: he also will hear their cry, and will save them.

My mouth shall speak the praise of the Lord, and let all flesh bless his holy name for ever and ever.

Bless the Lord, O our souls, and all that is within us bless his holy name. Bless the Lord, O our souls, and forget not all his benefits. Indulgent Father, in thee all goodness dwells, from thee all blessings flow. On this anniversary we come as a family around this altar, to pay our tribute of joyful thanks for the many blessings, public and private, temporal and spiritual, which thou hast given and continued to us in the year past.

Mornings and evenings have returned with the visitations of thy love, and the joy of thy salvation. Laden as we have been with thy bounties, may it be found that our hearts are filled with thy love, and our lips tuned for thy praise. We would adore that goodness which glows in the sun, refreshes in the breeze, distils in the fruitful dew, descends in the copious showers, smiles on us by day and watches over us by night, opens upon us in the joyous spring, and gladdens our hearts in the bounteous autumn. O Lord, if we speak of thy mercies, they are more than we can number.

Our guardian God, we thank thee for thy care of the members of this family, and for permitting so many to meet this day to rejoice together in health, prosperity, and friendship. Blessed be God for the ties which bind us to one another, and for that communion of hearts which gives a blessedness not of earth to our social enjoyments and family affections. We thank thee for thy gifts through the past season. We thank thee for the food that has nourished, for the raiment that has clothed, and for the health that has cheered us. We have sat under our own vines and in the shelter of our own dwellings, having none to molest or make us afraid. In whatever degree the strength of our memories, the clearness of our understandings, and the tranquillity of our passions, have been preserved, to thee be the praise. We thank thee for the good influences of parental education; for the salutary lessons received from pious ministers, and for all the benefits derived from reading, conversation, and experience. Especially we thank thee for the continuance of our religious favors, the spiritual manna, the bread that came down from heaven, the Gospel of Jesus, the words which minister everlasting peace. O God, thy goodness is above all praise. Thou art holy in all thy works.

We thank thee for our public blessings: that we enjoy liberty, safety, and plenty; that we do not groan under the miseries of tyranny, bloodshed, and ruin; that thou hast ever opened thy liberal hand, and given us our meat in due season. We bless thee for the comforts of good neighborhood, for the labors of the wise, the means of education, the privilege of public worship, the support of civil order, the administration of justice, for every encouragement to well-doing, every manifestation of useful truth, and for all the hopes of the Gospel of thy Son.

Bountiful Supporter of the world's great family, while we ask the continuance of thy blessings, we especially ask for wisdom to improve them aright. Let not our prosperity destroy us, and thy gifts become the means of nourishing pride and presumption, lust and intemperance, but do thou dispose us to a grateful and prudent use of thy bounties. Above all, we desire to value temporal things by their relation to eternity; and may we never think we prosper unless our souls prosper; or that we are rich unless we are rich towards thee; or that we are wise unless we are wise to salvation.

In the spirit of the Gospel, we would extend our good wishes to all beings capable of happiness. Bless, we pray thee, all our rulers, judges, and officers in authority. May our land be the abode of truth and freedom, of religion and peace. Let thy mercy de scend on thy whole church; purify it by thy Spirit, and preserve it from error. Strengthen its ministers, and touch their lips with the fire of thine altar. Prosper the means of education; enlighten the ignorant; convert the unbelieving; cheer the persecuted; relieve the distressed; speak peace to troubled consciences; strengthen the weak; confirm the strong; deliver the oppressed from him who spoileth him, and succor the needy who hath no helper. Open in every land an asylum for distress. Multiply the cheering fruits of hospitality and kindness; cause the tear of sympathy to console the afflicted; scatter the cloud that hangs over the mind of the upright; avert the tempest which is ready to break on the innocent, and erect in every heart an altar for thy praise.

Giver of every good, as we this day rejoice in the blessings of the harvest, we pray that we may make it a day of temperate feasting and religious gladness. Let not our abundance become a snare to us; but may we honor thee under all our enjoyments, and whether we ĕat or drink, or whatever we do, do all to the glory of thy holy name.

Praise ye the Lord. Praise thy God, O Zion! Let everything which has breath praise the Lord. Amen.

IV.

Christmas.

And there were in the same country shepherds abiding in the field, keeping watch over their flock by night.

And, lo, the angel of the Lord came upon them, and the glory of the Lord shone round about them; and they were sore afraid.

And the angel said unto them, Fear not: for, behold, I bring you good tidings of great joy, which shall be to all people.

For unto you is born this day, in the city of David, a Saviour, which is Christ the Lord.

And this shall be a sign unto you; Ye shall find the babe wrapped in swaddling-clothes, lying in a manger.

And suddenly there was with the angel a multitude of the heavenly host praising God, and saying,

Glory to God in the highest, and on earth peace, good-will toward men.

Blessed be the Lord God of Israel; for he hath visited and redeemed his people,

And hath raised up a horn of salvation for us, in the house of his servant David:

As he spake by the mouth of his holy prophets, who have been since the world began:

That he would grant to us, that we being delivered out of the hand of our enemies, might serve him without fear,

In holiness and righteousness before him all the days of our life.

And thou, child, shalt be called the prophet of the Highest, for thou shalt go before the face of the Lord to prepare his ways;

To give knowledge of salvation to his people, by the remission of their sins,

Through the tender mercy of our God; by which the day-spring from on high hath visited us,

To give light to them that sit in darkness and in the shades of death, to guide our feet into the way of peace.

GLORY be to thee in the highest heavens, O thou God of our salvation! Thou hast proclaimed peace on earth, and infinite good-will to men. Unto us has been born a Guide and Deliverer. Glad tidings from heaven he brought; holy is the truth which he uttered, immortal the hope he inspires. We hail the morning which commemorates his birth. We rejoice that we too may hear the song heard by the wondering shepherds. We thank thee that we may unite in the joyful commemoration which makes us one with millions of thy children in all parts of the world. We praise thee that we may take up the glad memories and the holy hopes of this day, and help bear them onward to millions who shall come after us. Glory to God in the highest that, through thy tender mercy, the day-spring from on high hath visited us, to give light to them that sit in darkness and in the shadow of death, to guide our feet into the way of peace. And while to thee, his Father and our Father, his God and our God, we bring these our grateful acknowledgments, we would offer our prayers that we may be more deeply impressed with a sense of that divine grace which commended thy love to us, in that while we were yet sinners Jesus Christ came not to condemn the world, but that the world through him might be saved.

We adore thy providence in the advent of this great messenger from heaven. We gratefully acknowledge thy hand in the special gifts with which he was endowed, and in the miraculous power which he exercised; and thank thee that by signs and wonders he was approved of thee as thine anointed, the Son of thy love, the chosen revealer of thy will. In thine own Spirit, given unto him without measure, the spirit of grace, of truth and of power, we joyfully see the testimony thou didst bear to his authority. Thanks be to thee that he came clothed, not in royal pomp, but in the ornaments of a lowly and single mind; and that as in him appeared a divine compassion and benignity, we behold in him thy glory, the glory as of the only-begotten Son of God, full of grace and truth.

We praise thee that thou hast thus revealed thyself in the flesh, and that the divinity which shines through all things hath appeared most brightly of all, in a living shape, in one made in all points as we are, who, though rich, for our sakes became poor, and took the form of a servant. Thus hast thou drawn near to us, and we are enabled to see the invisible, and hold communion with the uncreated and the everlasting. For all that thy beloved Son did and suffered, for his words of truth, for his triumph over the powers of darkness, for his serene and unfaltering faith and his unfailing love, for his readiness to taste of death for our sakes, for the mysterious and immeasurable impression he made on a guilty world by his sacrifice on the cross, for his glorious resurrection and ascension, and that he still lives at thy right hand, we would, on this day, bring thee the offerings of devout gladness and praise.

O, may a sense of thine abounding mercy be inscribed upon our inmost souls, by the influence of thy Holy Spirit. May our whole being be moulded by the truth as it was set forth in Jesus, and may we reflect, in some humble degree, the living glory which shone so steadily in him. Lead us to him in all lowliness of spirit, to trust in him as the redeemer of souls. Thus shall we best express our gratitude, when by the cleansing and renewal of our souls they shall, through thy grace, be transformed into his divine image. Like him may we conquer the world. For thy truth and grace may we hold ourselves ever ready to live and to die. Give unto us the spirit of self-sacrifice. May all that earth can bribe us with be as dross in comparison with the consciousness of fidelity to God. Save us from our sins. Save us from the corruptions of our hearts. Break our slumbers. Let the light of Christ search our souls and scatter our darkness. Never may we prove false to those interests for which he came into the world, and when in it gave his body to be broken, and his blood to be poured out on the cross.

O Thou who art working in and through all things to fulfil the purposes of infinite wisdom, give thy holy word new power among men. Let not the Lord Jesus lie buried and forgotten. Raise him up the conqueror of the world, and give him an everlasting empire in our hearts, and let every eye see him, and every tongue confess him to be Lord, to the glory of thee, the Father. Every year, as this joyful anniversary comes round, may it find the world more and more in harmony with the song of the angel choir. Draw Christians of different names together, and unite them by ties of mutual respect and love. May all nations, and kindreds, and tongues, and languages, be filled with his spirit, and be governed by his law. Let all superstition, and injustice, and slavery, and intemperance, and fraud, disappear before that religion which came down from heaven, bringing precious and divine gifts unto men. Soften all hearts. Quicken all consciences, that every form of evil may vanish, and that thy grace may abound, and thy saving truths be known to all hearts. And to thee shall be rendered everlasting praise. Amen.

V.

Close of the Year.

Lord, make me to know my end, and the measure of my days, what it is; that I may know how frail I am.

Behold, thou hast made my days as a handbreadth; and my age is as nothing before thee: verily every man at his best state is altogether vanity.

Surely every man walketh in a vain show: surely they are disquieted in vain: he heapeth up riches, and knoweth not who shall gather them.

And now, Lord, what wait I for? my hope is in thee.

Deliver me from all my trangressions: make me not the reproach of the foolish.

Hear my prayer, O Lord, and give ear to my cry; hold not thy peace at my tears: for I am a stranger with thee, and a sojourner, as all my fathers were.

O spare me, that I may recover strength, before I go hence, and be no more.

O Thou in whose sight a thousand years are but as a day, all things on earth are passing away, but thou remainest one and the same, and to thy years there is no end. Thy providence has brought us to the close of another year, and we would raise our thoughts above the flight of time to the eternity in which thou dwellest, and to those things which know no change, but from glory to glory.

The departing year in its course has carried hence the hopes and treasures of many hearts. Friends, with whom at its beginning we exchanged affectionate greetings, have disappeared, and their coming steps we shall hear no more. Many who welcomed the past year with hopes as confident as ours have entered the silent mansions of the dead, never to return. Merciful God, open all our hearts to hear the solemn voice that now addresses us. Thou alone knowest how near the last hour is that we spend beneath the sun. Soon the day shall come whose evening light our eyes shall never see. Bring home to us a sense of our mortality. And teach us so to number our days that we may apply our hearts with all diligence to the search after wisdom. Make the point of time at which we now stand a gate of heaven. Bless to our sanctification the solemn lessons of the past.

Well may we rejoice, O God, that we still live in the possession of this hour of prayer, this means of grace. We deplore, before thee, that the closing year bears hence so scanty a record of our spiritual growth, that it testifies to so many broken vows, to resolutions fervently formed one moment, and disregarded the next. Another leaf in the book of time is about to be turned down, and what is written there we cannot erase; and we mourn, merciful Father, that it has so much to fill us with shame. We are humbled under a sense of our manifold deficiencies, our repeated transgressions, our wilful devotion to the idols which our own passions have set up. Dispose us to thorough self-communion. May we prove our own hearts faithfully, and tear off all their disguises, and confess all our sins, with an overcoming desire to forsake them forever. Make us to feel that life is too solemn to be wasted in vain wishes and regrets. Save us from supposing that tears alone will wash away the guilt of sin. Let us not flatter ourselves with a barren sensibility. But may we consider well that no repentance is acceptable in thy sight which does not reform the whole life.

Breathe, O God, a divine life into our hearts, the life of faith, that we may obtain a lasting dominion over the evil that is in the world and in ourselves. Daily, hourly, may we watch and pray, lest we fall into temptation. Help us to form that habit of mind which reads in all the changes of life lessons of holy wisdom. The past and the future admonish us of the infinite value of the present. May every moment be used in the sight of God, and as fraught with momentous consequences, with our weal or our woe. O that it may be given us, in thy grace, to walk henceforth as becometh our great vocation, as the children of God and the friends of Jesus. So, when the hour of our departure comes, it shall find us ready, enriched with treasures of which death cannot rob us, filled with thy Spirit.

For thy favor to this household we render thee our united thanks; for the health and prosperity we have enjoyed, and for the trials we have been called to bear. Prepare us for the hour of separation, and for reünion in the abodes of the blest. Chasten the fond hopes of the young. Save them from that love of pleasure which would render them heedless to their true peace — the salvation of their souls. May they seek for good in doing good and being good. Do thou make the sacred sense of rectitude supreme in their hearts. Guide us all through the coming perils of life. To thee may we always turn with our whole souls, in every time of trouble, as to our best friend; and unto thee shall be the glory forever. Amen.

VI.

In a Time of Trial.

Wherefore, seeing we also are encompassed with so great a cloud of witnesses, let us lay aside every weight, and the sin which doth so easily beset us, and let us run with patience the race that is set before us,

Looking to Jesus the author and finisher of our faith; who for the joy that was set before him endured the cross, despising the shame, and is set down at the right hand of the throne of God.

For consider him that endured such contradiction of sinners against himself, lest ye be wearied and faint in your minds.

Ye have not resisted to blood, striving against sin.

And ye have forgotten the exhortation which speaketh to you as to children, My son, despise not thou the chastening of the Lord, nor faint when thou art rebuked by him:

For whom the Lord loveth he chasteneth, and scourgeth every son whom he receiveth.

If ye endure chastening, God dealeth with you as with sons

O Thou whose ear is ever open to the cry of thy children, hear us, we beseech thee, in this the time of our need. We devoutly thank thee for the innumerable mercies which have blessed every period of our past existence; may we be alike able to adore thee for the various instances of affliction with which thou hast seen fit to visit us.

Hitherto, O Father, thou hast given us strength equal to our day; thou hast overruled the sorrows and trials of our lives to the promotion of our best interests. Be thou yet our strength and our refuge. Upon thee would we cast ourselves, for time and for eternity. All our interests we would confide to thy keeping. One thing we would earnestly seek after,— that may we pursue all the days of our lives,— to feel, alike in joy and sorrow, in privation and abundance, in life and at the hour of death, that under thy government all is well.

O pardon us, we entreat thee, if our hearts have ever mistrusted thy wisdom or goodness. Pardon us, if in sorrow we have hesitated or been disinclined to come to thee. Forgive the frailties and misgivings of our nature. May our weakness be made perfect in thy strength. Give unto us thy Holy Spirit. Cast the mantle of thy love over us, that we may learn to trace thy hand and trust thy goodness in every event.

May the example of our Saviour be ever before our eyes; may his patience in trial, his resignation to thy will, his assurance of thy favor, be constantly the chief objects of our desire and pursuit. To us, as they did to him, may these dispositions impart strength to sustain and energy to conquer our trials; and may that same happy composure of spirit, by which the last and the severest scenes of his life were signalized, be enjoyed by us during every period, and especially in the trying moments of our pilgrimage.

Devoutly, O God our Father, do we thank thee for his sufferings as well as for his teachings; for his death as well as for his life; and because we have a High Priest that can be touched with the feeling of our infirmities, do we come boldly unto the throne of grace, that we may obtain mercy, and find grace to help us in the time of need. May we, in imitation of Jesus, learn patience by the things we suffer; may patience have with us its perfect work; and thus finally may we, through thy mercy in Christ, be permitted to enjoy that perfect salvation of which, by his obedience unto death, he became the author.

And now, O God, to that eternal weight of glory may we have our eyes steadily directed, so that our present afflictions may appear light, and, through him who loved us and gave himself for us, may purify our hearts, and preserve us unto the end. Hear us, O God our Father, in these our supplications; hear us for the sake of thy infinite mercy manifested by

Christ; and through him, our Mediator and Lord, do we ascribe unto thee, the Source of all mercy, and the God of all consolation, the glory due unto thy name. Amen.

VII.

For a Friend Dangerously Ill.

The Lord will strengthen him upon his bed of languishing; thou wilt make all his bed in his sickness.

Now a certain man was sick, named Lazarus, of Bethany, the town of Mary and her sister Martha.

(It was that Mary who anointed the Lord with ointment, and wiped his feet with her hair, whose brother Lazarus was sick.)

Therefore his sisters sent to him, saying, Lord, behold, he whom thou lovest is sick.

When Jesus heard that, he said, This sickness is not to death, but for the glory of God, that the Son of God may be glorified by it.

Father of Mercies, from thee cometh all hope. To thee our inmost souls lie open. Thou hearest the prayers that are springing there, beyond all power of utterance, for our suffering friend. Thou knowest how ardently we desire that this sickness may not be unto death; that thy blessing may descend upon the means used for the restoration of thy servant, and give success to the efforts of human skill. Spare, O Lord, we beseech thee, and grant that strength may be restored.

Turn our sorrow into joy. Give unto us the garment of praise for the spirit of heaviness. Let thy servant live and bless thy name.

But, O God, not our will, but thine, thy perfect will, be done. Be this the prayer of our hearts, as well as of our lips. Shed abroad within and all around us the peace of entire submission. May we all, and thy suffering servant especially, repose unwavering faith in thee. Being truly penitent for all offences, may a voice be heard from heaven whispering hope. Give the assurance of thine everlasting mercy. Encompass and sustain the spirit in the hour of darkness with thoughts of heaven. Enable us all to rise far above the clouds of this mortal state, to sit in heavenly places, with him who was made perfect through sufferings, and where thou art revealed working in all things to produce boundless and everlasting good. Let not the monitory voices of life and death fall upon heedless ears. May we gird on the armor of righteousness, and so be prepared to part with the near and the dear, and to follow them at thy bidding, supported by that faith in thy blessed Son which takes the sting from death, and despoils the grave of its victory.

Be with us, heavenly Father, in all temptations. May every fear be still, every murmur hushed, every heart exalted into holy communion with thee. To thee may we leave all issues, with peaceful trust. And whether our blessings remain or depart, let our faith in God abide; and by all events, whether joyous or sorrowful, may we grow in this saving grace, and to thee shall be the glory forever. Amen.

VIII.

Recovery from Sickness.

I love the Lord, because he hath heard my voice and my supplications.

Because he hath inclined his ear unto me, therefore will I call upon him as long as I live.

The sorrows of death compassed me, and the pains of the grave gat hold upon me: I found trouble and sorrow.

Then called I upon the name of the Lord: O Lord, I beseech thee, deliver my soul.

Gracious is the Lord, and righteous; yea, our God is merciful.

The Lord preserveth the simple: I was brought low, and he helped me.

Return unto thy rest, O my soul; for the Lord hath dealt bountifully with thee.

For thou hast delivered my soul from death, mine eyes from tears, and my feet from falling.

I will walk before the Lord in the land of the living.

Our hearts ascend in thankfulness to the Dispenser of all good. Thou hast redeemed thy servant from the grave. When brought very low, thou didst show thy healing grace, and give the hope of recovered strength. Thou hast lifted a burden from our hearts. We rejoice that a dear friend has been spared to us. We pray that the life which is prolonged through thy blessing may be consecrated to thee. May it be given with redoubled diligence to the work of duty, and show its lifelong gratitude by a more thoughtful walking in the way of thy will.

We pray for ourselves. May we lay up thy warnings in our hearts. In the hours of returning gladness let us not forget the days of darkness that are gone for a while, but which in thy own time are to come again. By listening thoughtfully to the past, may we be prepared for the future. Admonished of the uncertainty of life, may the ardor of our attachments be chastened. Let us not lay up our hearts' treasure on earth, where decay and death corrupt, but may we rejoice in the imperishable possessions of truth and virtue, and feel that they are garnered safe above all the changes and uncertainties of this world.

And now, O Father, as we enter upon a new season of hope and joy, we would consecrate ourselves anew to thy holy service. Draw us closer to thee. Do thou reign supreme over our affections. Be thou loved with all our strength, and give us the unfailing joy of minds filled with thy Spirit, and growing in holiness for ever and ever. Prepare us for that time when the infirmities of our mortal bodies shall be thy instruments to sever our ties to this world. Receive us then to that world where sickness and sorrow are not known, through Jesus Christ our Lord. Amen.

IX.

A Prayer from Parents on the Birth of a Child.

So God created man in his own image, in the image of God created he him.

Lo, children are an heritage of the Lord.

He maketh his servants to be the joyful parents of children.

He hath put a new song in our mouth, even praise to our God.

I will be the God of your children from one generation to another.

OUR FATHER in heaven, we now look up unto thee with especial gratitude, with joyful devotion. Thou hast not only joined us twain together in the tenderest relation, but thou hast permitted us now to become parents. Thou hast presented to our hands and bestowed on our hearts this most precious treasure, a child of our own. We thank thee fervently for the opening and sweet delight of parental affection.

But, O Being of beings, this is thine offspring, râther than ours. Thou art the framer of the body and the father of the spirit, and thou art now and thou ever wilt be the life of the life; and thou lovest the child more than we, even in the utmost, can love; for thy name is Love, and thou art infinite. Through us, thou but reachest forth this image of thyself into existence. Making us nearest in earthly relationship, thou hast made us also nearest in endearing attachment, that through our opportunity and care this child may be faithfully nurtured. Into our persons thine own gracious providence would descend, that the frail body may be preserved from harm, that the faculties may be trained for usefulness here, and that the immortal soul may be prepared for an ever-blessed hereafter.

We now earnestly pray that we may truly appreciate our sacred office, and feel our solemn responsibility. May we most deeply realize that upon us, more than upon any others, the welfare of this little one both for time and eternity will depend. But, O how weak we are of ourselves! Father Almighty and most merciful, we utterly rely upon thee; all our strength and success must come from thee. Dispose us therefore to frequent prayer, that in our ignorance, and sinfulness, and helplessness, thou mayest be near with thy Divine compassions. Assist us to guard this priceless trust from the temptations of the world; and may we be especially watchful against those tendencies within, which are ready to start forth into sin and lead to misery. May we be wise and diligent to repress every depraved appetite and passion, and early to fill the soul with love for God. O save us from the folly, from the great wickedness, of ever becoming ourselves the foremost and most dangerous tempters to evil. Suffer not that affection, which thou hast implanted in our bosoms to insure fidelity, to degenerate into debasing indulgence.

Rather may we turn the opening soul toward thee, that thine own Holy Spirit may flow in with purifying power. Especially may we set the face of this little child, from the earliest capacity, to look unto Jesus, and in due time bear to the Saviour's arms an offering which he will bless. Dispose us to fulfil all righteousness, and to lead our loved one into the way of perfect discipleship to the Divine Master. Thus bring a new-created spirit into the fullest communion with Christ, and to the reception of his salvation.

Now, O Father of Light, to these ends wilt thou open our understandings to thy word; dispose us to embrace all its holy truths. God of all grace, pour into our hearts thy regenerating and sanctifying Spirit. We would not cease to cry unto thee to make us perfect even as thou art perfect. Thus in self-distrust and humility, but in faith and hope, we consecrate ourselves to the sacred duties of parentage. To thy service, anew and more than ever, we now dedicate our home.

"Our Father which art in heaven, hallowed be thy name. Thy kingdom come. Thy will be done on earth as it is in heaven. Give us this day our daily bread. And forgive us our trespasses, as we forgive those who trespass against us. And lead us not into temptation, but deliver us from evil. For thine is the kingdom, and the power, and the glory, forever. Amen.

X.

Death of a Child.

And they brought young children to him, that he should touch them; and his disciples rebuked those that brought them.

But when Jesus saw it, he was much displeased, and said to them, Suffer little children to come to me, and forbid them not: for of such is the kingdom of God.

Verily I say to you, Whoever shall not receive the kingdom of God, as a little child, he shall not enter therein.

And he took them up in his arms, put his hands upon them, and blessed them.

Take heed that ye despise not one of these little ones: for I say to you, that in heaven their angels do always behold the face of my Father who is in heaven.

O God, who art thyself a Father, who knowest every feeling thou hast wrought into the parental heart, we appear before thee now bowed down with sorrow. The child that thou gavest us, the delight of our eyes, the joy of our hearts, thou hast taken away, and this infant blossom hath withered at early morn. O thou Comforter of the afflicted, be nigh unto us, and let faith and hope, the blessed token of thy presence, fill our hearts.

In faith would we follow this departed child in its ascending flight. The tie which bound it to us is broken, but it never can be separated from thee. We called it ours, but it was thine, and to thee it is united far more intimately than to us. It was sent hither with the will of him who doeth nothing in vain, and by the same wise will it is summoned hence. Help us to recognize it as the sacred property of God, as it were an angel alighting among us for a little while, upon a mission of love. May we rejoice, with a joy deep beyond utterance, at the thought of that goodness which lent us that precious treasure to gladden our hearts, although but for a brief space. A messenger from heaven has been here. May the heavenly tidings which it brought be graven on our inmost souls, not to be erased by the grief of the present hour, but deepened by the tears which we shed. Sanctify the memory of this dear child, and may it prove a fountain of blessed and saving thoughts. May that other world which thy Gospel hath unveiled rise before our faith in new brightness, as the home of the beloved. May we be drawn unto him who took children in his arms and said, Suffer them to come unto me, for of such is the kingdom of heaven. O may we henceforth be more in earnest in the great work of life. May we strive more diligently to prepare ourselves for communion and fellowship with the pure and the blessed in thine everlasting kingdom.

Almighty God, what shadows we are! What is our life? It is vapor, which appeareth for a little while, and then vanisheth away. We take a few steps in life. We suffer and we enjoy, and then we disappear from the face of the earth forever. But, blessed be God, we are not wholly dust. There is a spirit within us which can never taste death, and which, by all the changes of life, thou art calling, as by so many voices from heaven, to glory, honor, and immortality. Thou art speaking to us now by this event which hath filled our souls with sadness. Speak on, O Lord; for thy servants hear. Hearkening to the warning voice, let us not indulge in idle sorrow, but may we arise and gird up our loins, and resolve to use diligently every moment of our sojourn on earth, seeing that we know not what an hour may bring forth, and that now is the accepted time, now the gates of salvation stand open before us, and we may enter into life eternal.

O thou God of parents and children, since we may be so soon and suddenly separated, quicken us in the discharge of our duties one towards another. When we are called to part, save us then from the anguish of bitter remembrances, from the painful recollection of unkind words, and unfeeling neglects. Let the thought of the parting hour rise before us to check every evil disposition, to allay our rising anger, to quench all unhallowed heats. May every day bind us more and more closely together. And when we go, one after another, to the narrow house appointed for all the living, O, may immortal hopes sanctify our departure. Thou wilt watch over our slumbering dust, and not one of us shall be forgotten before thee. Thou wilt welcome us to a higher sphere; we shall behold the good and just that have gone before us, and our joy shall know no interruption, and no end. O, fulfil our holy desires. Inspire our hearts. Guard and guide us now and forever, and to thee shall be rendered everlasting praises. Amen.

XI.

Death of a Friend.

But I would not have you to be ignorant, brethren, concerning them who are asleep, that ye sorrow not, even as others who have no hope.

For if we believe that Jesus died and rose again, even so them also who sleep in Jesus will God bring with him.

For we know that if our earthly house of this tabernacle were dissolved, we have a building of God, an house not made with hands, eternal in the heavens.

Therefore they are before the throne of God, and serve him day and night in his temple: and he that sitteth on the throne will dwell among them.

They shall hunger no more, neither thirst any more; neither shall the sun light on them, nor any heat.

For the Lamb who is in the midst of the throne will feed them, and will lead them to living fountains of waters: and God will wipe away all tears from their eyes.

O THOU, our refuge in trouble, and the rock of our trust, thou art our only abiding stay; and although clouds and darkness are now round about thee, we doubt not thine infinite good-will. O Lord, hear us, and be very present in our hearts, and fill them with thy consolations.

It has pleased thee to enter our family circle by that most mysterious of all human events, death. One with whom a little while ago we exchanged sweet counsel hath vanished, and these familiar places will know the departed no more. Our hearts are filled with sorrow; and as the beloved image of our friend rises before us, we are ready, in the anguish of bereavement, to exclaim, "Would to God we had died for thee!"

And now, as all things around us wear looks of sadness, and life is wrapped in gloom, we would turn unto thee, O Father, with hearts wounded and desolate, but, blessed be God, not without hope. Put underneath us the everlasting arms of thy power, and lift us out of the shadow of this affliction. Lead us from this darkness into the light, full of glory, in which thou dwellest. Let not this sorrow prove too great for us, blinding our minds, and hardening our hearts. May we receive it as descending from heaven, bringing heavenly gifts. Dispose us to discern the working of thy hand; and while our dearest earthly joys are departing, come thou. in the fulness of thy love, and abide with us and in us forever, and may we have abundant cause to say, "It is good for us that we have been afflicted."

While in times past we have been prone to live forgetful of the grave, though always open before us;

while we have promised ourselves that to-morrow will be as to-day, and even more abundant, and that the mountain of our prosperity stands strong and cannot be moved, now, O Father, break up our insensibility to the nearest and most solemn realities, that we may no longer pursue shadows which fade away in our grasp. By the removal of the near and dear, may we be led to commune with ourselves and with thee; to see the vanity of life, and the momentous interests of eternity. Blessed be God, light hath streamed down upon us from above, through the opening into the heavens which received the ascending Lord and Saviour. O, help us to hear his voice in gentle accents of love say to each of us, Let not your hearts be troubled, neither let them be afraid. In my Father's house are many mansions. Whosoever liveth and believeth in me shall never die. Give us, gracious God, O give us unspeakable thanks for the comfort of these precious truths.

And now, heavenly Father, who hast purposes of good in all thy dealing with thy children, we pray that we may clearly see and deeply feel this present affliction to be sanctified to our eternal welfare. To this end may it be met and endured with profound submission to thy most holy will. May we take heed to that divine example which, in thy great goodness, has been granted in our Lord and Saviour, the Man of Sorrows. Help us to learn of him how to obtain strength from the heaviest burdens, and draw the waters of everlasting life from the lowest depths. May we see now how blessed it is to endure with meekness, to cherish an unfaltering faith in God, and to give ourselves up entirely to thee, saying, from our hearts, "Do with us and with ours as seemeth to thy perfect wisdom best. Thy will be done."

We thank thee, O Father, for the many kind friends still spared to us, and for the rich consolation of their sympathy. Bless all their offices of love; and as one after another goes from our circle to return no more, may we, whose day on earth is prolonged, be knit more and more closely together. Do thou form amongst us those ties which death cannot destroy. We would not mourn, O God, as without hope. All are in thy holy keeping, the living and the dead. The friends whom we love depart, but still thy providence is around them. The dust returns to the earth as it was, but the spirit ascends to God who gave it, to pursue, if attaining to the resurrection of the just, that higher life into which death is but a new birth. Let this faith spring up like a fountain to gladden our souls. Let it rise upon us like a light of heaven, and scatter every cloud.

Give us strength to return to the duties of life with increased diligence and with purer aims. May our walk henceforth be more thoughtful, now that the shadow of the grave lies upon our path. Of that mysterious change, through which one has now passed, and which, in thy time, awaits us also, may we cherish no appalling thoughts. May we regard it as a step in our immortal progress which will no longer seem gloomy and dark when the lights of eternity have fallen upon it. And when we are called to follow our departed friend, may we be found in the way of righteousness, and with a hope within that shall triumph over the grave. Lead us into that world where all tears are wiped from all eyes; and, joined to the glorious assembly of the just made perfect, may we look back upon the tribulations of this world as the instrument of thy choicest grace. And to thee shall be ascribed praise and glory everlasting. Amen.

OCCASIONAL PRAYERS FOR THE CLOSET.

I.

Self-Consecration to God.

O God, who seest in secret, and searchest the hearts of the children of men, behold me thy child as I bow before thee in this private and solemn act. Thou hast been my Guardian and Guide in all times past, giving me all that I have, and all that I hope for. Amid thy bounties and mercies have I lived, with one painful thought on my soul. O Lord, it is the thought that I am not thine; that I have not given myself to thee; that I have not purposely chosen and consciously taken thee for my master, and offered and consecrated my heart, will and strength, to thy service. Thou knowest how often I have thought to do this, and have said, I will make haste and delay not to pay unto the Lord my vows, and bind myself to him in an everlasting covenant, that shall not be broken. But thou knowest likewise, O merciful and compassionate God, how often the cares of the world, and the sin that is here on my heart, have prevented me, and I have not made my peace with God.

Gracious and blessed Father, me thy frail creature, me thy guilty child, wilt thou now behold and bless. And while I pour out before thee confessions of my past neglect, help me to prove the sincerity of my soul in this solemn hour. In a duty I have so long postponed, by an offer free and unreserved, I do now present myself unto thee, O God, avouching thee to be my God and my portion forever. Accept this consecration to thee. Take me, O God, thy creature and child, to do with me as seemeth to thee to be right. To thee I give myself, and bind myself by these solemn vows. Come by thy Holy Spirit, and take possession, and make my soul thy temple. Dwell in me from this time forth, moulding my will to thine, forming my affections after the pattern of thy dear Son; and hereafter may neither death nor life, nor things present nor things to come, be able to separate me from thy love.

And now, O God, let this solemn act be sealed and registered in heaven. Over all the sins of my heart, and the temptations of the world, may this be my triumphant song — I can do all things through him who strengtheneth me. And, thine here on earth, may I be found thine when thou shalt come with thy holy angels; may thy mark be on my forehead, and the spirit of thy son Jesus be in my heart, when the Lord shall receive them that are his. Amen.

II.

For the Gift of the Holy Spirit.

FATHER of Infinite Love, I thank thee for all thy wonderful and most merciful gifts, but above all for the gift of thine own Holy Spirit. Thou art willing to descend into the heart of man, and make that unworthy place thy constant dwelling. Thou art, this moment, offering even to me, thy sinning servant, this blessed privilege, this boundless good. I am very weak, and ignorant, and erring, and disobedient. But thou, O my God, art ever willing, and ever waiting, to strengthen, to enlighten, to guide, to pardon me. And the assurance of this divine condescension and deliverance I nave in my Saviour. It is by him, and and by him alone, who is my gracious Redeemer and ever-living Lord, that the Comforter cometh into the world.

Blessed be thy holy name, O thou who art his Father and my Father, that his promise is thus fulfilled, which he gave to his first disciples, when he declared that he would come to his own and abide with them forever. And even as that Eternal Word which was with thee in the beginning came forth into our corrupted and enfeebled race to restore it, was made flesh and dwelt among us, and suffers us to behold thy glory, full of grace and truth, in the face of Jesus Christ, so when he ascended up from the body into that glory which he had with thee before the foundation of the world, he breathed the Holy Spirit into his church, and gave himself to be thus the perpetual light and life of his followers. I would praise thee for his advent and humiliation, for his wondrous union with humanity, for his ascension to thy right hand, and now especially for his undying presence and power, in this Spirit which he hath given. O my Heavenly Father and Friend, may I be personally a partaker in this unspeakable grace. Make me a true follower of thy Son's steps, and a real member in his spiritual Body, that I may share in the immediate influences of his love. Unite my heart to his pure and tender heart. Suffer me to lean my head in his bosom, to cling to his hand, to kneel humbly at his feet. Bring me into a more vital and inward fellowship with him, whom to know and to trust is everlasting blessedness.

And to that end, I entreat thee to take away from me all dispositions that obstruct the entrance of the Spirit into my breast. Subdue my pride; curb my ambition; soften my hard self-will; put out the unholy fires of lust; set me free from inordinate attachments to any of the gains, or pleasures, or pursuits, or honors, of this world. But open my soul to welcome, without hindrance, the coming of my Master. May he find my heart a room prepared and clean for its celestial guest. May I be as one of those that watch, daily and hourly, for their Lord. Help me to overcome the evil that is within me and round about me on every side; to hold fast simplicity and sincerity; to conquer my spiritual enemies; to banish those hateful passions, and to forsake those dangerous practices, which must drive thy sweet influence away, separate me from the society of Jesus, and offend thee who hatest all iniquity. Save me, I beseech thee, from the guilt of quenching thy Holy Spirit.

And while I ask that thou wilt pour these quickening and purifying streams into my breast, I pray also that the fruits of the Spirit may appear in all parts of my life. Being born again of thy grace, may I show forth the power of that regeneration in the beauty of holiness, in a right and truthful conversation, in the meekness of wisdom, in a brave and upright conscience, in honest dealings, in charity, in gentleness, in temperance, in purity, in long-suffering, in forgiveness, in reverence and piety. Sanctifying me within, wilt thou regulate all my outward conduct and relations, my individual habits and my intercourse with others, by the same Spirit. And when thou hast thus recreated me in my Saviour's likeness, and renewed within me a righteous soul, and permitted me to serve thee through all my days on earth, grant, I humbly pray, that I may come into the great company of those that are redeemed and forgiven, and that I may join that heavenly host in ascribing all glory and thanksgiving unto the Father, and the Son, and the Holy Spirit. Amen.

III.

For Newness of Life.

ALMIGHTY CREATOR, Father of Jesus Christ my Lord! Thou didst breathe into me the breath of my natural life. Inspire me now, I beseech thee, with the life that is spiritual and immortal. Thou didst frame this body, so fearfully and wonderfully made. Hallow it by an indwelling soul devoted to thy will. Let its frailty, its disorders, its perishableness, make me only the more diligent and faithful in consecrating all its powers to thy service. The faculties of my mind were planted and attempered by thy wondrous skill. Subdue them to thy perfect authority, and let them rejoice to bow at thy righteous control. The affections and sympathies of my heart were all wakened by thine unsleeping love. May they rise first of all to thee, and find their noblest exercise in the adoration of thy wisdom and mercy, so that all my mortal friendships shall be made stronger and purer, by being mingled with the higher love which binds my heart to heaven.

But O, thou Searcher of hearts, thou knowest that I am stained within and without by the defilements of sin. I am not clean; I am not just; I am not good. The bright heavens over my head are impure in thy sight; how much more this offending breast! The world has too much power over me. I am too much the victim of its delusions, and the slave of its passions. Grant me deliverance by thy Holy Spirit. I am too apt to conform to its wicked customs, to be overborne by its proud fashions, to be led astray by its base examples. O, break this vile bondage, and bring me into the liberty of the sons of God. I am too self-seeking in my business, too harsh in my speech, too uncharitable in my judgments, too impatient in my temper, too fond of ease and indulgence, too devoted to the way that seems pleasant in my own eyes. Scatter these deceptions and snares. Show me my peril and guilt. Rouse me to repentance, and then, merciful Father, pardon me, and restore me unto thyself.

But thou seest, my God, that the root of all my outward transgressions is an unsubmissive and unreconciled heart. Bend my stubborn will, therefore, and break down every feeling that rebels at thy law. The sin is in the depths of my heart. I feel that my disease is in the inmost dispositions and hidden state of my soul. Reach after it there, I pray thee, and purge it thence. No superficial sorrow or fitful effort can drive it away. Nothing can save me but a renewal of my inmost being, through the inworking of thy grace. Give me that hearty and thorough repentance which is unto life, and needeth not to be repented of. Pour into the springs of thought and feeling within me a quickening and converting energy. Hold up before me, in thy word and providence, that law of awful purity which is a terror to the conscience, and which is the condemnation of my life. Alarm my indifference. Urge my sluggishness. Hasten my steps in the return from the far country to my Father's house. Reveal to me the promise and the peace that dwell forever in that blessed home, and so lead me, from under the stern and fearful discipline of a law which maketh nothing perfect, into the liberty of grace; from the obedience of a servant to the free and filial trust of a child; from the dread of penalties and the seeking of rewards, to a better hope and the love that casteth out all fear. Make me a true disciple of the cross.

Lord God Almighty, with thee all things are possible. I implore this infinite good, this glorious salvation by thy Son. Work it out within me, I beseech thee, in thine own way, and by such instruments as thou wilt; by pain or joy, by suffering or comfort, by sickness or health, by peace or by grief. Only so chasten me that I may be wholly thine. So renew me that I shall say and feel, in all things, "Thy will be done." And so refashion my sinning soul, that I shall be a new creature in Christ Jesus, and by the power of his redemption. And thine shall be all the glory, through him who is the Mediator of the new covenant. Amen.

IV.

Prayer when Oppressed by Difficulties in Theology.

INFINITE and Eternal Being, whose nature and whose ways no finite mind can comprehend, thou seest how my frail reason is burdened, how my thoughts are oppressed, how my words are silenced, in meditating on thy decrees and dispensations, on the prevalence of evil, and on the prospects of human kind. O my Lord, these mysteries are too awful and too painful for me. Help me, I pray thee, to repose on the belief of thy divine perfection, who art supremely just and holy, merciful and good, and with whom all things are possible. Let me never forget or doubt that God is love: and great as may be the difficulty of reconciling the state and history of our race with that glorious and delightful truth, O give me strength to hold fast the invaluable declaration and supreme manifestation of it, and to believe that it shall at last be developed in all its cloudless and overcoming splendor.

Teach me ever to believe with the heart that fact which is the marvellous and crowning demonstration of thy essential love; that God so loved the world that he spared not his own Son, but delivered him up for us all; that he is the propitiation for our sins, and not for ours only, but also for the sins of the whole world; that Jesus was made lower than the angels in order that he, by the grace of God, should taste death for every man; that he gave himself a ransom for all; that as the Lamb of God he taketh away the sin of the world; and let me not entangle myself in strifes of words and perplexities of speculation, which would restrict the largeness of this grace. Merciful Father, never may I forget that we know but parts of thy ways; that man's mind and man's systems are limited and dark, and that human hearts are deceitful and erring. O give me to believe that there is something beyond and above their view and mine, in the glory, efficiency and vastness, of thy great salvation. Let me cease from man, whose breath is in his nostrils, for wherein is he to be accounted of!

Save me and mine, I beseech thee, good Lord, from all fundamental and ruinous error, from all haughty and presumptuous reasonings, but specially from distrustful and despairing thoughts of thee, of thy glorious administration, and thy holy purposes. O grant me strength to believe that it is for wise and gracious reasons thou permittest me to be variously tried, perturbed and tempted, and peculiarly so at times, by pondering the high and surprising mysteries of thy procedure and decrees. O Lord, be pleased to extricate me from all trials, as they shall successively or together occur; and at present particularly from this arduous trial of faith. Give me, I entreat, that calm and happy confidence in thee which may keep me at ease for fulfilling duty, allowing me to prosecute with renewed strength those endeavors which thy providence and grace alone can encourage and empower me to pursue. I ask all through the all-prevailing mediation of my Saviour Jesus Christ. Amen.

V.

Prayer for Patience under Trials and Fears.

O Thou who still leadest me in thy own dark, mysterious way, thou beholdest the doubts and discouragements which oppress my mind and weigh upon my spirit, and seest that I have no vigor and resolution to bear up against them. Yet, Lord, thou art able to bear me through. Help me, most merciful Father, to commit my way unto thee.

Thanks be to thee that thou hast ever taught me that it is not in man that walketh to direct his steps. O bring the blind by a way that he knoweth not; lead him in paths which he hath not known. These things do unto him, and forsake him not. Heavenly Father, new cares succeed the former; and thus will it be until I put off this tabernacle, and the pilgrimage of mortality is ended. O teach and strengthen me to meet them all with a more steadfast and submissive mind. Give me grace to remember that the period hastens on when these toils and conflicts shall be all forever past; that thou meanwhile knowest my frame, and art acquainted with all my infirmities; and while I feel that I can have no shadow of merit on which to ground a single hope, O, let hope arise and augment in thy free, boundless mercy, through thy beloved Son; the delightful hope that, when the pains of time have ceased, that glorious Saviour will receive even me, who have been so unbelieving and so unworthy, with those most dear to me, into the rest which remaineth; where we shall know perfectly how to serve him, and shall experience no inability, no incompetence, no reluctance, to attempt and fulfil what we know.

And now, O God, make me docile under the discipline of thy providence; and if I walk in darkness and have no light, give me grace still to trust in the name of Jehovah, and stay myself upon my God. Thou knowest, O Discerner of the heart, how little ability I now have to act, how little capacity to pray, how many and great anxieties oppress me, and how liable I am by an unwatchful state of mind to render myself even less fit for contending with them; but yet, O gracious God and Father of our Lord Jesus Christ, thou canst still hold me up, thou canst bear me through. How often in past times hast thou said to the waves of trouble, Hitherto shall ye rise, but no further! How often have I had to say, Hitherto the

Lord hath helped me. Suffer me not to despond, but enable me patiently to wait and hopefully to confide, through my Saviour and Redeemer. Amen.

VI.

The Prayer to be said in the Beginning of a Sickness.

O ALMIGHTY GOD, merciful and gracious, who in thy justice didst send sorrow and tears, sickness and death, into the world as a punishment for man's sins, and hast comprehended all under sin, and this sad covenant of sufferings, not to destroy us, but that thou mightest have mercy upon all, making thy justice to minister to mercy, short afflictions to an eternal weight of glory; as thou hast turned my sins into sickness, so turn my sickness to the advantages of holiness and religion, of mercy and pardon, of faith and hope, of grace and glory. Thou hast now called me to the fellowship of sufferings. Lord, by the instrument of religion let my present condition be so sanctified that my sufferings may be united to the sufferings of my Lord, that so thou mayest pity me and assist me. Relieve my sorrow, and support my spirit; direct my thoughts, and sanctify the accidents of my sickness, and that the punishment of my sin may be the school of virtue, in which, since thou hast now entered me, Lord, make me a holy proficient, that I may behave myself as a son under discipline, humbly and obediently, evenly and penitently, that I may come by this means nearer unto thee; that if I shall go forth of this sickness by the gate of life and health, I may return to the world with great strength of spirit, to run a new race of a stricter holiness and a more severe religion: or if I pass from hence with the outlet of death, I may enter into the bosom of my Lord, and may feel the present joys of a certain hope of that sea of pleasures in which all thy saints and servants shall be comprehended to eternal ages. Grant this through Jesus Christ our dearest Lord and Saviour. Amen.

VII.

Prayer After a Night of Pain.

How many days and nights of bodily ease, most merciful God and Father, hast thou, in my past life, graciously vouchsafed to me! And now that it hath been thy will to permit or to ordain the interruption of that ease in the hours when I desired rest, I beseech thee to save me from murmuring thoughts and discontented feelings. Save me from the unbelieving suspicion that these sensations come by fate or chance; that thou regardest not the lot of thy frail creatures, or that such trials are too small for thy notice, and unfit to be a subject of prayer. Guard me by thy heavenly grace, O Lord, from repining, as though a hard and strange thing happened unto me when I am thus visited, even were thy discipline far more severe and lasting.

O let me not forget that thus thy servants have been called to suffer in all ages; that thus, and inexpressibly more, my Redeemer suffered, and that I ought humbly to expect, and then patiently receive, such a portion of like suffering as thy providence and grace may determine; which will probably, in remaining years or days, be a larger and heavier share than hitherto. Often have I read and heard and thought of those who on earth endured great tribulation, but are departed to the realm where there shall be no more pain. I have admired their acquiescence, and thy grace thus manifested in them; but now, when it toucheth me, how little am I prepared to meet the same infliction, to trust fully in the same Deliverer, and to anticipate the same repose!

O grant me fortitude, heavenly Father; and above all, since affliction too often has but increased my proneness to sinful thoughts, and wishes, and imaginations, open my eyes, I beseech thee, and awaken my heart to this peril; show me that all my hope of peace, and of escaping from deep unhappiness, must depend on being freed, through thy grace, from unholy tempers of mind. Convince me more profoundly that to be spiritually-minded is life and peace, and strengthen me more effectually to shun the misery of the carnal mind which is death. And now, if it be thy holy will, O God, mercifully remove this pain. Indulge me, gracious Lord, with quiet rest; and help me, notwithstanding present sensations, to do somewhat, though it be but little, this day in some department of my duties. Assist me also to think believingly on that blessed state into which no pain, or unrest, or weariness, can enter. O give me and mine a part in that glorious, perfect immunity from sins and griefs, through him who suffered for our sakes. Amen.

VIII.

Prayer after the Death of a Dear Christian Relative.

O MY God and Father, who only hast immortality, who hast originated and bestowed all the ties of kindred in this our mortal state, thou hast been pleased to take from me a near and dear and faithful friend. Help me, I pray, to bless thee that I have had the great benefit of that friend's affection, counsel, and Christian kindness. Let me praise thee also for the assured hope that one so dear, so valuable to me, lived by faith, and then fell asleep in Jesus. Make me willing to resign this friend and helper unto thee. Teach me to have no distrust of thy parental care and pity towards them that fear thee, when I review the sufferings through which the departed past. While I feel that the follower of Christ was thus painfully made conformable unto his death, do thou, gracious Lord, strengthen me firmly to believe that the same power and mercy shall gloriously conform my dear friend to the likeness of his resurrection.

And now, forgetting the things which are behind, may I henceforth press more strenuously along the mark for the prize of the high calling of God in Christ Jesus. Cause that all lessons derivable from the example and sentiments, from the faith, humility and patience in sufferings, of the departed, may be durable and fruitful in my heart; and may this and every instance of a truly Christian departure from our transitory life make us newly and profoundly grateful for thy holy Gospel, the only hope of offending, helpless, dying creatures.

O grant, most merciful Father, through Christ Jesus, that the most salutary thoughts which have been excited in this season of affliction may be so fixed, or so rëawakened, as to bring forth riper, happier fruits of earnest piety than have been yet produced; and do thou prepare me and all for the bodily pains of advancing life, for the heavier pangs of mortal sickness, and for the great conflict of death. Finally, so fill me with certain hope and undoubted love towards thee, as to give inward assurance of a life immortal, through Jesus Christ. Amen.

IX.

A Prayer before a Journey.

O ALMIGHTY GOD, who fillest all things with thy presence, and art a God afar off as well as near at hand; who didst send thy angel to bless Jacob in his journey, and didst lead the children of Israel through the Red Sea, making it a wall on the right hand and on the left; be pleased to let thy angel go out before me and guide me in my journey, preserving me from sudden and sad accidents, from falls and errors. And prosper my journey to thy glory, and to all my innocent purposes; and preserve me from all sin, that I may return in peace and holiness, with thy favor and thy blessing, and may serve thee in thankfulness and obedience all the days of my pilgrimage; and at last bring me to thy heavenly country, there to dwell in thy house, and to sing praises to thee forever. I implore this through him who is the Shepherd of the flock, the Bishop of all souls, and who, whether we be at home or abroad, in life and in death, will keep all who are committed to him. Amen.

X.

For Temperance.

O ALMIGHTY GOD and gracious Father of men and angels, who openest thy hand and fillest all things with plenty, and hast provided for thy servant sufficient to satisfy all my needs; teach me to use thy creatures soberly and temperately, that I may not with excess of meat or drink make the temptations of mine enemy to prevail upon me, or my spirit unapt for the performance of my duty, or my body healthless, or my affections sensual and unholy. O my God, never suffer that the blessings which thou givest me may either minister to sin or sickness, but to health, and holiness, and thanksgiving; that in the strength of thy provisions I may cheerfully, and actively, and diligently, serve thee; and so feast at thy table here that I may be accounted worthy to be admitted to the eternal supper of the Lamb; and to thee, through the Son and Holy Spirit, shall be glory forever. Amen.

XI.

For a Contented Spirit, and the Grace of Moderation and Patience.

O Almighty God, Father and Lord of all creatures, who hast disposed all things and all chances so as may best glorify thy wisdom, and serve the end of thy justice, and magnify thy mercy, by secret and indiscernible ways bringing good out of evil; I most humbly beseech thee to give me wisdom from above, that I may adore thee, and admire thy ways and footsteps, which are in the great deep, and not to be searched out. Teach me to submit to thy providence in all things; to be content in all changes of person and condition; to be temperate in prosperity, and to read my duty in the line of thy mercy; and, in adversity, to be meek, patient and resigned; and to look through the cloud, that I may wait for the consolation of the Lord, and the day of redemption; in the mean time doing my duty with an unwearied diligence, and an undisturbed resolution, having no fondness for the vanities or possessions of this world; but laying up my hopes in heaven and the reward of holy living, and being strengthened with thy Spirit in the inner man, through Jesus Christ our Lord. Amen.

XII.

For the Grace of Obedience: to be said by all Persons under Command.

O Eternal God, great Ruler of men and angels, who hast constituted all things in a wonderful manner, making creatures subject to man, and one man to another, and all to thee, the last link of this admirable chain being fastened to the foot of thy throne; teach me to obey all those whom thou hast set over me, reverencing their persons, submitting to all their lawful commands, cheerfully undergoing those burdens which the public wisdom and necessity shall impose upon me; at no hand murmuring against government, lest the spirit of pride and mutiny, of murmur and disorder, enter into me, and consign me to the portion of the disobedient and rebellious, of the despisers of dominion, and revilers of dignity. Grant this, O holy God, for his sake who for his obedience to the Father hath obtained the glorification of eternal ages, our Lord and Saviour Jesus Christ. Amen.

XIII.

A Prayer to be said by Parents for their Children.

O ALMIGHTY and most merciful Father, who hast promised children as a reward to the righteous, and hast given them to me as a testimony of thy mercy, and an engagement of my duty; be pleased to be a father unto them, and give them healthful bodies, understanding souls, and sanctified spirits, that they may be thy servants and children all their days. Let a great mercy and providence lead them through the dangers and temptations and ignorances of their youth, that they may never run into folly, and the evils of an unbridled appetite. So order the events of their lives, that, by good education, careful tutors, holy example, innocent company, prudent counsel, and thy restraining grace, their duty to thee may be secured in the midst of a crooked and untoward generation; and if it seem good in thy eyes, let me be enabled to provide conveniently for the support of their persons, that they may not be destitute and miserable in my death; or, if thou shalt call me off from this world by an early summons, let their portion be, thy care, mercy, providence, over their bodies and souls; and may they never live vicious lives, nor die violent or untimely deaths; but let them glorify thee here with a free obedience, and the duties of a whole life; that, when they have served thee in their generations, and have profited the Christian commonwealth, they may be co-heirs with Jesus in the glories of thy eternal kingdom, through our Lord Jesus Christ. Amen.

XIV.

A Prayer to be said on the Feast of Christmas.

O HOLY and almighty God, Father of mercies, Father of our Lord Jesus Christ, the Son of thy love and eternal mercies, I adore and praise and glorify thy infinite and unspeakable love and wisdom, who hast sent thy Son from the bosom of felicities to take upon him our nature, and our misery, and our trials; and hast made the Son of God to become the son of man, that we might become the sons of God and partakers of the divine nature: since thou hast so exalted human nature, be pleased also to sanctify my person, that, by a conformity to the humility and laws and sufferings of my dearest Saviour, I may be united to his spirit, and be made all one with the most holy Jesus. Amen.

XV.

A Prayer of Preparation for the Holy Sacrament.

O MOST gracious and eternal God, the helper of the helpless, the comforter of the comfortless, the hope of the afflicted, the bread of the hungry, the drink of the thirsty, and the Saviour of all them that wait upon thee; I bless and glorify thy name, and adore thy goodness, and delight in thy love, that thou hast once more given me the opportunity of receiving the greatest favor which I can receive in this world, even the body and blood of my dearest Saviour. O take from me all love for sin or vanity; let not my affections dwell below, but soar upwards to the element of love, to the seat of God, to the regions of glory, and the inheritance of Jesus: that I may hunger and thirst for the bread of life, and the wine of elect souls, and may know no loves but the love of God and the most merciful Jesus.

Grant therefore, O God, that he who is my Saviour, whose body is my food, whose righteousness is my robe, who is the priest and the sacrifice, the master of the feast and the feast itself, the physician of my soul, the light of mine eyes, the purifier of my stains; that he may enter into my heart and cast out from thence all impurities, all the remains of the old man; and grant I may partake of this holy sacrament with much reverence, and holy relish, and great effect, receiving hence the communication of the holy body and blood, for the establishment of an unreprovable faith, of an unfeigned love, for the fulness of wisdom, for the healing my soul, for the blessing and preservation of my body, for the taking out the sting of temporal death, and for the assurance of a holy resurrection, for the ejection of all evil from within me, and the fulfilling all thy righteous commandments, and to procure for me a mercy and a fair reception at the day of judgment, through thy mercies, O holy and ever-blessed God. Amen.

XVI.

Prayer before the Sacrament of the Lord's Supper.

THIS day, O our Creator, Preserver and Redeemer, thou invitest me to review here in an especial manner all thy benefits. Let me be grateful that thou didst hallow one day of seven, in memory of the great work of creation; and that now, each Christian Lord's day, while it celebrates this first of miracles, commemorates that other expression of thy love, the resurrection of the Saviour of the world. Thanks be to thee that on this Lord's day we, and multitudes of those who name his name and trust in his salvation, may keep the feast which shows forth the Lord's death until he come.

Let me adore thee, O my God, for that sacred and mysterious offering which procures our pardon; for the solemn burial, which, with all its attendant circumstances, proved the reality of the Lord's death; and for that glorious resurrection and ascension which sealed the acceptance and efficacy of the one great sacrifice. Incline and quicken and strengthen me this day to remember and review these great events believingly, devoutly, and joyfully. O let the sorrows of life around me, and the sure prospect of infirmity and dissolution before me, and the deep sense of manifold sin within me, endear exceedingly and above all price the assurances of a Saviour's love, and work, and purpose. O grant to me, and those who shall commune with me, and all throughout the world who shall engage in this sacred ordinance, rightly to discern the Lord's body; his sufferings, his grace, his life-giving power. By a living and effectual faith may we become one body in him; with him to die to sin, and with him to rise into joint and endless blessedness.

Lord, grant us those desires, resolves and hopes, those aspirations and heavenly aids, during and after this ordinance, which will make it truly an inestimable privilege, truly a means of eternal blessings through Jesus Christ my Lord. Amen.

XVII.

Prayer to be used by a Sunday-School Teacher before engaging in Religious Instruction.

O Thou who seest my whole heart, and knowest all my unfaithfulness, how can I hope, except by thy special blessing and surpassing mercy, to be an instrument of spiritual good, while I am myself so low in spiritual attainments, so worldly, so indifferent, so weak in faith, and so unworthy in thy sight. Yet, O my God, thou canst cause the earthen vessel, the broken vessel, the too often dishonored vessel, to receive and convey the balm and medicine of thy heavenly truth, to the praise and glory of thy own name. O deign to bless my feeble endeavors and ministrations this day. Let the prayers which shall be poured out be uttered in a believing, contrite, grateful, earnest spirit. Let the words of comment and enforcement which may be offered be words of truth and soberness, conducing to the edification of Christians, and the conviction and renovation of those who as yet believe not.

O Thou that hast all hearts in thy almighty hand, be pleased so to move and guide my failing mind and heart, and those of others, that we may derive from these means of grace wisdom, and strength, and new devotedness. Fix in my soul, and in every soul present, more forcibly than ever, the practical and prevailing persuasion, that to depend on thy help is indispensable; that to be spiritually-minded is life and peace; that to serve thee in simplicity and godly sincerity, through Jesus Christ, is the way of true freedom and exaltation, of true content and joy; that nothing in the tents or palaces of wickedness or earthly pleasure can compare with the happiness of walking in the light, as thou art in the light. O let the blood of Christ purify us from all iniquity; and do thou take away every evil thought and imagination of the heart, confirming each right and self-denying aim and resolve within us, that we may live and die unto the Lord, and be meet for his undefiled home and rest.

Heavenly Father, make all the services of the day, and of the remaining Lord's days which thou mayest grant us upon earth, effectual for these great ends to us and ours, and to all in every place whom we love or ought to love; and bring us all together in the one temple of thy eternal grace and glory, through Jesus Christ our Lord and Saviour. Amen.

COLLECTS.

I.

Our Leader and Defender.

ASSIST us mercifully, O Lord, in these our supplications and prayers, and dispose the way of thy servants toward the attainment of everlasting salvation; that among all the changes and chances of this mortal life, they may ever be defended by thy most gracious and ready help, through Jesus Christ our Lord. Amen.

II.

Guidance from God.

O GOD, the protector of all who trust in thee, without whom nothing is strong, nothing is holy, increase and multiply upon us thy mercy, that, thou being our ruler and guide, we may so pass through things temporal that we finally lose not, the things eternal. Grant this, O heavenly Father, through Jesus Christ our Lord. Amen.

III.

The Divine Keeping.

Almighty God, who seest that we have no power of ourselves to help ourselves, keep us both outwardly in our bodies and inwardly in our souls, that we may be defended from all adversities which may happen to the body, and from all evil thoughts which may assault and hurt the soul, through Jesus Christ our Lord. Amen.

IV.

Continual Help.

Assist us, O Lord, in all our doings, with thy most gracious favor, and further us with thy continual help; that in all our works begun, continued and ended in thee, we may glorify thy holy name, and finally by thy mercy obtain everlasting life, through Jesus Christ our Lord. Amen.

V.

For Direction and Preservation.

O almighty Lord and everlasting God, vouchsafe, we beseech thee, to direct, sanctify and govern both our hearts and bodies, in the ways of thy laws, and in the works of thy commandments, that through thy most mighty protection, both here and ever, we may be preserved in body and soul, through our Lord and Saviour Jesus Christ. Amen.

VI.

The Cross.

ALMIGHTY GOD, we beseech thee graciously to behold this thy family, for which our Lord Jesus Christ was contented to be betrayed, and given up into the hands of wicked men, and to suffer death upon the cross. And this we beg in the name of our Mediator, through whom we ascribe unto thee all honor and glory, now and ever. Amen.

VII.

The Example.

ALMIGHTY GOD, who hast given thine only Son to be unto us both a sacrifice for sin and also an example of godly life, give us grace that we may always most thankfully receive this inestimable benefit, and daily endeavor ourselves to follow the blessed steps of his most holy life, through the same Jesus Christ our Lord. Amen.

VIII.

Confession.

ALMIGHTY and most merciful Father, who knowest our weakness, and art acquainted with every action of our lives, and every secret of our hearts, we acknowledge in thy presence our imperfections and sins, and fervently pray that thou wouldst be gracious unto us, and forgive us, and help us to forsake all that is evil and cleave to all that is good, and to make thee and thy approbation the objects of our supreme regard; so that we fail not at last to attain that eternal happiness which thou hast promised to thy faithful servants, through thine infinite mercy in Jesus Christ our Lord. Amen.

IX.

For Pardon.

ALMIGHTY and everlasting God, who hatest nothing which thou hast made, and dost forgive the sins of all those who are penitent, create and make in us new and contrite hearts, that we, worthily lamenting our sins, and acknowledging our wretchedness, may obtain of thee, the God of all mercy, perfect remission and forgiveness, through Jesus Christ our Lord. Amen

X.

God Working Within.

ALMIGHTY GOD, unto whom all hearts are open, all desires known, and from whom no secrets are hid, cleanse the thoughts of our hearts by the inspiration of thy Holy Spirit, that we may perfectly love thee, and worthily magnify thy holy name, through Christ our Lord. Amen.

XI.

For the Holy Spirit.

O GOD, who art ever more ready to hear than we are to pray, and who hast promised the assistance of thy Holy Spirit to those who truly seek it, we humbly beseech thee to fulfil thy gracious promise to us thy servants, and grant us that light and help without which we know nothing and can do nothing. O, guide us by thy counsel, defend us by thy might, purify us by thy Spirit, and keep us in thy fear and love continually; and thine shall be the honor, and the glory, and the praise, through Jesus Christ our Lord. Amen.

XII.

Keeping the Heart.

O ALMIGHTY GOD, who alone canst order the unruly wills and affections of sinful men, grant unto thy people that they may love the thing which thou commandest, and desire that which thou dost promise, that so, among the sundry and manifold changes of the world, our hearts may surely there be fixed, where true joys are to be found, through Jesus Christ our Lord. Amen.

XIII.

Freedom from Error.

ALMIGHTY GOD, who showest to those who are in error the light of thy truth, to the intent that they may return into the way of righteousness, grant unto all those who are admitted into the fellowship of Christ's religion that they may avoid those things that are contrary to their profession, and follow all such things as are agreeable to the same, through Jesus Christ our Lord. Amen.

XIV.

In Temptation.

Almighty and most merciful God, it is our earnest desire and humble prayer that thou wouldst enable us to resist and overcome temptation. May neither the allurements of vicious pleasure, nor the difficulties of a virtuous course, deter us from the practice of our duty. To whatever trials our integrity may be exposed, may we have strength to preserve it uncorrupted; that, having endured temptation, we may receive the crown of eternal life, which thou hast promised to the righteous by Jesus Christ our Lord. Amen.

XV.

Amid Perils.

O God, who knowest us to be set in the midst of so many and great dangers, that, by reason of the frailty of our nature, we cannot always stand upright, grant to us such strength and protection as may support us in all dangers, and carry us through all temptations, through Jesus Christ our Lord. Amen.

XVI.

Submission in Trial.

O MOST gracious and merciful Father, we desire to resign ourselves and all our interests to thy disposal, in the humble hope that thy mercy will never forsake us, and that thou wilt cause all things to work together for our good. We would submit patiently to thy will under all our afflictions; and we humbly pray that we may so pass through the changes of this world as finally to be prepared for the enjoyment of perfect and eternal happiness in the world to come, through Jesus Christ our Lord. Amen.

XVII.

Social Duties.

O THOU God and Father of our Lord Jesus Christ, give us grace, we humbly beseech thee, to act in every relation and condition of life as thy children, disciples of thy Son, and members of the general family of mankind. May we love one another with pure hearts fervently, and heartily unite our endeavors to promote each other's happiness; that in this life we may experience how good and how pleasant it is for brethren to dwell together in unity; and that we may be prepared for an eternal abode in the regions of endless peace and joy, through thine infinite mercy, declared unto us by Jesus Christ our Lord. Amen.

XVIII.

Holy Examples.

O ALMIGHTY GOD, who hast knit together thine elect in one communion and fellowship, in the mystical body of thy Son Jesus Christ our Lord; grant us grace so to follow thy blessed saints in all virtuous and godly living, that we may come to those unspeakable joys which thou hast prepared for those who unfeignedly love thee, through Jesus Christ our Lord. Amen.

XIX.

Thy Kingdom Come.

ALMIGHTY and most merciful God, who wouldst have all men to be saved, and come to the knowledge of thy truth; regard in mercy, we beseech thee, those parts of the earth where the Gospel is not known, and bring them to the knowledge, obedience and love, of the religion of thy dear Son. We also pray for the whole Christian world; that all who profess the faith of the Gospel may hold it in unity of spirit, in the bond of peace, and in holiness of life. We entreat thee more particularly to assist us to govern our hearts by the blessed law of charity, that, together with all our fellow-Christians, we may continually become here on earth more worthy of the glorious society in heaven, where charity never faileth; which we beg in the name of Jesus Christ, the head of all things to the church, through whom we ascribe to thee blessing and praise, for ever and ever. Amen.

XX.

Numbering our Days.

LORD of life and death, of all ages and all worlds, give us to know the value of our fleeting years. While we have time, let us improve it as we ought; let us not forsake thee in life, nor fall from thee in death; and O, keep us, we entreat thee, from that second death, which must come upon the heedless and impenitent. Save us, and bring us to dwell with thee, where weakness, danger and death, shall find no room. Grant this, O Lord, for thine infinite mercy's sake, through Jesus Christ our Lord. Amen.

XXI.

Before Reading the Bible.

BLESSED LORD, who hast caused all holy scriptures to be written for our learning, grant that we may in such wise hear them, read, mark, learn, and inwardly digest them, that, by patience and comfort of thy holy word, we may embrace and ever hold fast the blessed hope of everlasting life which thou hast given us in our Saviour Jesus Christ. Amen.

XXII.

After Reading the Bible.

O God, who in times past didst speak to the fathers by the prophets, and in these last days to us by thy Son; we thank thee for the volume of thy holy word; for the plain and ample directions it contains; for the sublime instructions it affords; for the consolations and hopes it presents to the penitent, the afflicted, and the dying; for the immortal life it reveals to man; for the eternal glory and happiness it promises to those who love and strive to obey thee. May we be enabled, by the light and assistance which it gives to our ignorance and frailty, to order our steps aright, to keep thy laws and ordinances blameless, and steadily to pursue that path of virtue and true holiness which leads to everlasting life. And this we humbly beg in the name of our Saviour Jesus Christ. Amen.

XXIII.

Before Public Worship.

Lord of all power and might, who art the author and giver of all good things, graft in our hearts the love of thy name, increase in us true religion, nourish us with all goodness, and of thy great mercy keep us in the same, through Jesus Christ our Lord. Amen.

XXIV.

After Public Worship.

ALMIGHTY GOD, we humbly thank thee for the privileges of religious worship and instruction which we have at this time enjoyed. Forgive whatever thou hast seen amiss in us, and whatever may have been said contrary to the truth and to thy holy word. Accept the sincerity of our devotions, and cause the good seed of thy word to spring up and bear a hundred-fold in our hearts and lives. Teach us to love thee more and serve thee better day by day; and when our days on earth are ended, may we be received to thine eternal joy, through Jesus Christ our Lord. Amen.

XXV.

Christmas.

ALMIGHTY GOD, who hast given us thine only-begotten Son to take our nature upon him, and as at this time to be born of a virgin; grant that we, being regenerate, and made thy children by adoption and grace, may daily be renewed by thy Spirit. And this we beg in the name of Jesus Christ, through whom we ascribe unto thee all honor and glory now and ever. Amen.

XXVI.

New Year.

O God, the unfailing source of light and mercy, who hast brought us to the beginning of this year, and art sparing us to love thee, and to keep thy commandments; give us, we beseech thee, a solemn sense of the importance of time, and of diligence in improving the talents thou hast placed in our hands; and enable us so faithfully to discharge our duty in this life, that when we shall appear before thee at thy great tribunal we may be found worthy of that eternal kingdom which thou hast promised by Jesus Christ our Lord. Amen.

LITANIES.

I.

O God, our heavenly Father, who by thy Son hast redeemed the world, and by thy Holy Spirit dost govern, direct, and sanctify the hearts of thy faithful servants, have mercy upon us, thy children.

Have mercy upon us, O Lord.

Remember not, Lord, our offences, neither take thou vengeance of our sins; spare us, good Lord, spare thy people, we beseech thee, whom thou hast redeemed by the most precious blood of thy Son.

Spare us, good Lord.

From all evil and mischief; from sin; from the assaults of temptation; from all blindness of heart; from pride, vain-glory, and hypocrisy; from envy, hatred, and malice, and all uncharitableness; deliver thy children, good Lord.

Good Lord, deliver us.

From lightning and tempest; from plague, pestilence, and famine; from battle and murder, and from death unprepared for,

Good Lord, deliver us.

From all sedition, and rebellion; from all false docrine, contention, and division; from hardness of heart, and contempt of thy word and commandment,

Good Lord, deliver us.

In all time of our tribulation; in all time of our prosperity; in the hour of death, and in the day of judgment,

Good Lord, deliver us.

We humbly beseech thee to hear us, O Lord God, and that it may please thee to rule and govern the holy Christian church in the right way, and to illuminate all ministers of the Gospel with true knowledge and understanding of thy word, and that both by their preaching and living they may set it forth and show it accordingly; and that it may please thee to endue all our rulers and magistrates with grace, wisdom and understanding, that they may execute justice and maintain truth; and that it may please thee to bless all schools and seminaries of learning; all instructors of youth, and all means of true knowledge, virtue, and piety;

We beseech thee to hear us, good Lord.

That it may please thee to bless and keep all thy people, and give to all nations unity, peace, and concord;

We beseech thee to hear us, good Lord

That it may please thee to give us a heart to love and fear thee, to hear meekly thy word, to receive it with pure affection, to bring forth the fruits of the

Spirit, and diligently to live after thy commandments;

We beseech thee to hear us, good Lord

That it may please thee to bring into the way of truth all such as have erred and are deceived; to strengthen such as do stand; to comfort and help the weak-hearted; to raise up those who fall; and finally to give us victory over all temptations;

We beseech thee to hear us, good Lord.

That it may please thee to succor, help and com fort, all who are in danger, necessity, and tribulation; to preserve all who travel by land or by water, all sick persons and young children; to show thy pity upon all prisoners and captives; to defend and provide for the fatherless children and widows, and all who are desolate and oppressed;

We beseech thee to hear us, good Lord.

That it may please thee to have mercy upon all men; and to forgive our enemies, persecutors and slanderers, and to turn their hearts;

We beseech thee to hear us, good Lord.

That it may please thee to give and preserve to our use the kindly fruits of the earth, so that in due time we may enjoy them;

We beseech thee to hear us, good Lord.

That it may please thee to give us true repentance, to forgive us all our sins, negligences and ignorances, and to endue us with the grace of thy Holy Spirit, to amend our lives according to thy holy word;

We beseech thee to hear us, good Lord.
O Lord, grant us thy peace.
Lord, have mercy upon us.
O Lord, deal not with us after our sins;
Neither reward us after our iniquities.

II.

O God, whose nature is ever to have mercy and forgive, receive our humble petitions; and though we be tied and bound with the chain of our sins, yet let the pitifulness of thy great mercy loose us.

Graciously hear and forgive us, O Lord.

Save us, we beseech thee, from wandering thoughts, low desires, and vain imaginations, and from the waste of our time and the neglect of thy warnings; save us from idle words and corrupt communications, from an impatient and irreverent spirit, from hatred and wrath, from all selfishness, uncharitableness, and deadly sin.

Save us, we beseech thee, O Lord.

Almighty Father, who hast given thine only Son to die for our sins, and to rise again for our justification; grant us to put away the leaven of malice and wickedness, that we may always serve thee in pureness of living and truth, and finally pass the grave and gate of death to our joyful resurrection.

Grant this, we beseech thee, O Lord.

Grant unto us to be poor in spirit, that ours may

be the kingdom of heaven; give unto us godly sorrow and mourning, that we may be comforted; meekness, that we may inherit the earth; hunger and thirst after righteousness, that we may be filled; grant unto us to be merciful, that we may obtain mercy; to be pure in heart, that we may see God; to be peace-makers, that we may be called the children of God; and to be patient in all trouble, that our reward may be great in heaven.

Grant this, we beseech thee, O Lord.

Lord of all power and might, who art the author and giver of all good things, graft in our hearts the love of thy name, increase in us true religion, nourish us with all goodness, and of thy great mercy keep us in the same, through Jesus Christ our Lord.

O Lord, keep and defend us forever.

O God, by whose Spirit the whole body of the church is governed and sanctified; receive our supplications and prayers which we offer before thee for all estates of men in thy holy church, that every member of the same in his vocation and ministry may truly and faithfully serve thee. Give wisdom also to our rulers and magistrates, that they may always incline to thy will, and walk in thy way; and grant thy blessing to all schools and teachers, that knowledge, virtue and piety, may increase and be established among us.

Graciously hear us, O Lord God.

Show thy mercy, O Lord, to all men; be a friend to the poor and friendless, and a father to fatherless children; be a guide and defence to all travellers by land and by water; enlighten the ignorant; comfort the afflicted; bless our friends and benefactors, and bless our enemies; and fill the whole world with thy truth, mercy, and love.

Graciously hear us, O Lord God.

Kindly preserve us, O God, from temporal danger and bodily pain; may we temperately enjoy the fruits of the earth in their season; supply our wants according to thy wisdom, and grant that we may so pass through things temporal that we finally lose not the things eternal.

Graciously hear us, O Lord God.

Favorably with mercy hear our prayers.

O gracious Father, have mercy upon us.

O Lord, let thy mercy be shown upon us;

As we do put trust in thee.

O God, heavenly Father, from whom all good things do come, we thank thee for life and all its blessings, for religion and all its consolations, hopes and joys; we thank thee for the life and doctrine, the death, resurrection and ascension, of thy Son Jesus Christ; for Christian faith and Christian fellowship. Grant us thy grace, that we may be truly grateful; that we may constantly serve thee on earth, and at last may be found meet to be partakers with the saints in light, through the great Mediator and Redeemer, Jesus Christ. Amen.

III.

O Thou of whom and through whom and to whom are all things, help us with one mind and one mouth to glorify thee, even the Father of our Lord Jesus Christ.

O Thou, who art the God of patience and consolation, grant us to be like-minded one toward another according to Christ Jesus.

O Thou, who art the God of hope, fill us with all joy and peace in believing, that we may abound in hope, through the power of the Holy Ghost.

May we be full of goodness, filled with all knowledge, able also to admonish one another.

May those that are strong bear the infirmities of the weak.

May we follow after the things which make for peace, and things wherewith one may edify another.

Save us, we beseech thee, O heavenly Father, from being conformed to this world, from thinking of ourselves more highly than we ought to think, from being wise in our own conceits, from being overcome of evil, and enable us to overcome evil with good.

Hear us, good Lord.

If we have, at any time, held the truth in unrighteousness; if when we have known God we have not glorified him as God, nor been thankful; if we have changed thy truth into a lie, and worshipped the creature more than the Creator;

Forgive us, we beseech thee, O our Father.

If we have not liked to retain thee in our thoughts; if we have despised thy goodness, forbearance and long-suffering; if our heart has been impenitent and hard; if we have dishonored thee by breaking thy law;

Forgive us, we beseech thee, O our Father.

If the good which we would we do not, and the evil which we would not, that we do; if to will is present with us, but how to perform that which we will we find not; if, when we would do good, evil is present with us; if we find a law in our members warring against the law of our mind, and bringing us into captivity to the law of sin in our members;

Help us, we beseech thee, O our Father.

Being justified by faith, may we have peace with thee, through our Lord Jesus Christ, and rejoice in the hope of the glory of God.

Shed thy love in our hearts by the Holy Ghost.

May the law of the Spirit of life in Christ Jesus make us free from the law of sin and death, and make us walk, not after the flesh, but after the Spirit; may we not receive the spirit of bondage again to fear, but the spirit of adoption, whereby we call thee Father;

Being led by thy Spirit, may we become thy children.

May nothing separate us from the love of Christ; neither tribulation, nor distress, nor persecution, nor famine, nor nakedness, nor peril, nor the sword;

In all these, may we be more than conquerors through him who has loved us.

May neither death nor life, nor angels, nor powers, nor things present, nor things to come, nor height, nor depth, nor any creature, separate us from the love of God which is in Christ Jesus.

May nothing separate us from thy love.

May we confess with our mouth the Lord Jesus, and believe in our heart that God has raised him from the dead;

May we believe with our heart unto righteousness, and confess with our mouth unto salvation.

We beseech thee, heavenly Father, that we may be enabled to present our bodies a living sacrifice, holy and acceptable to thee, being transformed by the renewing of our mind.

Whether we live, may we live unto the Lord; and whether we die, may we die unto the Lord.

May our love be without dissimulation; may we abhor that which is evil, cleave to that which is good; be kindly affectioned one toward another; not slothful in business, fervent in spirit; rejoicing in hope, patient in tribulation, continuing instant in prayer; distributing to the necessities of our brethren, given to hospitality.

May we rejoice with those that rejoice, and weep with those that weep.

May we render unto all their dues.

May we love our neighbor as ourselves.

May we cast off the works of darkness, and put on the armor of light.

Awaken us, O Lord, from our sleep.

Now unto him that has power to establish us according to the Gospel, and the preaching of Jesus Christ;

To God only wise, be glory through Jesus Christ, forever. Amen.

IV.

O Thou, who didst command the light to shine out of darkness, and hast shined in our hearts, to give the light of the knowledge of the glory of God in the face of Jesus Christ, establish us in Christ and anoint us.

Seal us thine, O Lord, and give us the earnest of thy Spirit in our hearts.

O God, the Father of our Lord Jesus Christ, the Father of mercies, and the God of all comfort, who comforteth us in all our tribulation, give us grace and peace.

Confirm us unto the end, that we may be blameless in the day of the Lord Jesus.

O Thou, who wilt bring to light the things of darkness, and make manifest the counsels of the hearts, and whose Spirit searcheth all things, help us to renounce the hidden things of dishonesty, and to speak as in the sight of God.

Take away, Lord, the veil from our hearts, and let the light of the glorious Gospel of Christ, the image of God, shine upon us.

May we not walk in craftiness, nor handle the word of God deceitfully; may we judge ourselves, and not be judged; may we keep under our body and bring it into subjection; may we watch, quit us like men, and be strong; and having the spirit of faith, may we believe, and therefore speak.

Grant, O Lord, that we faint not; but though our outward man perish, may our inward man be renewed day by day.

May our light afflictions, which are but for a mo ment, work out for us a far more exceeding and eternal weight of glory; while we look, not at the things seen and temporal, but at the things not seen, but eternal.

Reveal to us, O Lord, by thy Spirit, what eye hath not seen, nor ear heard, nor the heart of man conceived.

May we be enriched by thee with all utterance, and with all knowledge; may we be perfectly joined together in the same mind and in the same judgment;

may we be perfect, may we be of good comfort, may we live in peace;

May the God of love and peace be with us.

Help us to stand fast in the liberty wherewith Christ has made us free, and not be entangled again with any yoke of bondage; knowing that the kingdom of God is not meat nor drink, but righteousness, peace, and joy in the Holy Spirit.

May we be zealously affected always for that which is good.

Help us to show the fruits of the Spirit; love, joy, peace, long-suffering, gentleness, goodness, faith, meekness, and temperance.

If we live in the Spirit, may we also walk in the Spirit.

As we have opportunity, help us to do good to all men, and especially to those who are of the household of faith; to bear one another's burdens, and so fulfil the law of Christ; to crucify the flesh, with its affections and lusts; to sow to the Spirit, and of the Spirit to reap life everlasting; and not to be weary in well-doing, believing that we shall in due season reap, if we faint not.

V.

O Thou, who art the one God and Father of all; who art above all, and through all, and in us all; who hast adopted us as children in Jesus Christ, thy Son.

in whom we have redemption, even the forgiveness of our sins; quicken us, we beseech thee, who have been dead in trespasses and sins.

O Thou, who art rich in mercy, for the sake of thy great love wherewith thou hast loved us, make us alive in Christ.

O God, our Father, the Father of glory, we pray thee to give us the spirit of wisdom and revelation in the knowledge of thyself, that we may know the hope of thy calling, and the riches of thine inheritance, and the greatness of thy power, which thou hast wrought in Christ, when thou didst raise him from the dead, and make him sit at thine own right hand in heavenly places.

We pray thee to raise us up also, and make us sit in heavenly places with him.

O Thou, the Father of our Lord Jesus Christ, grant us to be strengthened with might by thy Spirit inwardly; that Christ may dwell in our hearts by faith; that, being rooted and grounded in love, we may be able to understand the breadth, and length, and depth, and height, of the love of Christ, and be filled with all the fulness of God.

Help us, heavenly Father, to come in the unity of the faith, and the knowledge of the Son of God, to the stature of a perfect man, to the measure of the fulness of Christ.

Help us to walk with all lowliness and meekness, with long-suffering, forbearing one another in love;

endeavoring to keep the unity of the spirit in the bond of peace; to put away all bitterness, and wrath, and anger, and evil-speaking, with all malice.

May we be kind to one another, tender-hearted, forgiving one another, even as God, in Christ, hath forgiven us.

May we be followers of thee, as dear children, and walk in love, as Christ has loved us; redeeming the time; having the fruit of the Spirit in all goodness and righteousness and truth; speaking to ourselves in psalms and hymns and spiritual songs, singing and making melody in our hearts unto the Lord.

May we give thanks, always, for all things, unto God our Father, in the name of the Lord Jesus.

Help us to be strong in thee and in the power of thy might; to put on thy whole armor, that we may be able to stand in the evil day; girt about with truth, having on the breastplate of righteousness, our feet shod with the Gospel of peace, taking the shield of faith, the helmet of salvation, and the sword of the Spirit.

Help us to pray always, with all prayer and supplication, in the Spirit, and watch thereunto with all supplication and perseverance.

May peace be to all the brethren, and love, with faith, from God our Father, and the Lord Jesus Christ.

Grace be with all them that love our Lord Jesus Christ in sincerith. Amen.

VI.

O God, our heavenly Father, who hast loved us, and hast given us everlasting consolation and good hope through grace, we beseech thee to comfort our hearts, and to establish us in every good word and work.

Hear us, O God, and direct our hearts into thy love, and into the patient waiting of Christ.

O God, our Saviour, who wilt have all men to be saved, and to come to the knowledge of the truth; and hast manifested thyself to us, by the appearing of Jesus Christ, who hath abolished death and brought life and immortality to light through the Gospel, we beseech thee to hear us.

Give to us, O God, the spirit, not of fear, but of power, and of love, and of a sound mind.

O Thou, who art the blessed and only potentate; the King of kings and Lord of lords; who only hast immortality; dwelling in the light which no man can approach unto; whom no man hath seen nor can see; to thee be honor and power everlasting.

We give thee thanks, O our Father, who hast made us meet to be partakers of the inheritance of the saints in light.

Thou hast delivered us from the power of darkness, and hast translated us into the kingdom of thy dear Son, in whom we have redemption, even the forgiveness of our sins.

May we therefore fight the good fight of faith, and lay hold on eternal life, following after righteousness, godliness, faith, love, patience, and meekness.

We pray thee to forgive us, O God, if we have set our affections upon things below, instead of things above; if, professing to know thee, we have denied thee by our works; if through the love of money we have fallen into temptation and a snare; if we have indulged those passions which war against the soul; or if we have done anything through strife or vainglory.

Forgive us, we beseech thee, these and all our sins.

May we work out our salvation with fear and trembling, not counting ourselves to have attained; may we forget the things which are behind, and reach forth unto those which are before; approving the things which are excellent, being sincere and without offence, filled with the fruits of righteousness, and doing all things without murmuring or disputing.

Grant that our conversation be as becometh the Gospel of Christ, and may the peace of God rule in our hearts.

May we watch and be sober; may we put on charity, which is the perfect bond; may we comfort one another, and edify one another; not returning evil for evil, but following ever that which is good; may we rejoice evermore, pray without ceasing, and in everything give thanks; may we prove all things, hold fast that which is good, and abstain from all appearance of evil.

O God of peace, we pray thee to sanctify us wholly.

O God, if thou hast not appointed us unto wrath, but to obtain salvation by our Lord Jesus Christ, preserve our spirit, soul and body, blameless unto his coming; and the grace of our Lord Jesus Christ be with us all, for ever and ever. Amen.

VII.

O God, the Father of lights, with whom is no variableness nor shadow of turning; from whom cometh down every good and perfect gift; we ask of thee wisdom, who givest to all men liberally.

We would ask, O God, in faith, nothing wavering; believing that, if we draw nigh to thee, thou wilt draw nigh to us.

O Almighty God, who canst not be tempted with evil, neither canst tempt any man; we confess that we are drawn away by our own lusts and enticed; but we beseech thee, O our Father, who art very pitiful and of tender mercy, who dost resist the proud, but givest grace to the humble, to hear the prayer of faith and raise us up.

If we have committed sins, may they be forgiven

us; if we have known to do good and done it not, if we have been hearers of the word, and not doers also, deceiving our own selves; forgive us, O God, and save us.

May we not have the faith of Jesus Christ with respect of persons; may we not despise the poor; may we not have faith without works, but show our faith by our works; and, laying aside all that is impure, receive with meekness the ingrafted word, which is able to save our souls.

Help us to look into the perfect law of liberty, and continue therein, and so to receive the crown of life which the Lord has promised to them that love him.

Give us, Lord, the wisdom from above, which is first pure, then peaceable, gentle and easy to be entreated, full of mercy and good fruits, without partiality and without hypocrisy.

O Thou, who art light, and in whom is no darkness at all, may we walk in the light, and have fellowship with thee.

O Thou, who art love; may we dwell in love, and so dwell in thee; may our love be made perfect, and be free from all fear; may we be born of God, and overcome the world; may we keep thy commandments, and love thy children.

O God, grant that we love thee, not in word and tongue, but in deed and truth, and hereby know that we are of the truth, and assure our hearts before thee.

May we not love the world, nor the things which are in the world; may we remember that the world passes away, with all that is in it; and that if we love the world, the love of the Father is not in us.

Grant these our prayers, heavenly Father, we beseech thee, for thine infinite mercies' sake, in Jesus Christ. Amen.

VIII.

Blessed be the God and Father of our Lord Jesus Christ, who according to his abundant mercy hath begotten us again unto a lively hope by the resurrection of Jesus Christ;

To an inheritance incorruptible, undefiled, and that fadeth not away, reserved in heaven for us.

O God our Father, who hast redeemed us by the precious blood of Christ, and taught us to be holy as thou art holy; and who, without respect of persons, judgeth every man's work;

Help us, we pray thee, to pass the time of our sojourning here in fear.

O God, the Father of Jesus Christ, whom, though not having seen, we love; in whom, though now we see him not, believing, we rejoice; who was foreördained before the foundation of the world, but was manifest in these last times; make us, like him, holy in all manner of conversation.

Purify our souls in obeying the truth, through the Spirit, unto unfeigned love of the brethren; and may we love one another with pure hearts fervently.

O Thou, whose eyes are over the righteous, and whose ears are open to their prayers, but whose face is against them that do evil, make us all of one mind, having compassion one of another, loving as brethren, not rendering evil for evil, nor railing for railing, but contrariwise, blessing.

Adorn us with the hidden man of the heart, with that which is not corruptible, with the ornament of a meek and quiet spirit.

Add to our faith, virtue; and to virtue, knowledge; and to knowledge, temperance; and to temperance, patience; and to patience, godliness; and to godliness, brotherly kindness; and to brotherly kindness, charity.

May we all become a holy priesthood, to offer up spiritual sacrifices, acceptable to God, and to show forth the praises of him who hath called us out of darkness into his marvellous light.

May we follow him who has suffered for us, leaving us an example, that we should follow in his steps, and being dead to sin should live to righteousness; when reviled, may we not revile again, but by well-doing put to silence the ignorance of foolish men; may we refrain our tongue from evil, and our lips that they speak no guile; may we sanctify the Lord God in our hearts, so that all may be ashamed who falsely accuse our good conversation in Christ.

Grant, O Lord, that, if it be thy will, we may suffer for well-doing, rather than for evil-doing.

May the time past of our lives suffice us to have disobeyed thee; for the time to come may we be sober and watch unto prayer; may we have fervent charity among ourselves; that God may in all things be glorified through Jesus Christ, to whom be praise and dominion for ever and ever.

May the God of all grace, who hath called us to his eternal glory by Christ Jesus, after that we have suffered for a while make us perfect, establish, strengthen, and settle us; and to him be glory and dominion forever. Amen.

www.ingramcontent.com/pod-product-compliance
Lightning Source LLC
LaVergne TN
LVHW010200110826
845151LV00002B/563

* 9 7 8 1 4 2 5 5 3 6 4 5 9 *